The publisher and the University of California Press Foundation gratefully acknowledge the generous support of the Joan Palevsky Endowment Fund in Literature in Translation.

The Consuming Fire

The Consuming Fire

*The Complete Priestly Source, from
Creation to the Promised Land*

———

Liane M. Feldman

UNIVERSITY OF CALIFORNIA PRESS

University of California Press
Oakland, California

© 2023 by Liane Feldman

Cataloging-in-Publication Data is on file at the Library of Congress.

ISBN 978-0-520-38365-4 (pbk. : alk. paper)
ISBN 978-0-520-38366-1 (ebook)

Manufactured in the United States of America

32 31 30 29 28 27 26 25 24 23
10 9 8 7 6 5 4 3 2 1

For Ari

CONTENTS

ILLUSTRATIONS

ACKNOWLEDGMENTS

The idea for this project was born out of regular requests from friends and colleagues for "the verses for the P story of . . ." After a few years of pulling together notes and sending them along in response to such requests, it dawned on me that it might make sense to put together an edition of this text to make the work that lived in various files, programs, and Post-it notes more widely available. My first expression of gratitude is to those friends and colleagues, too numerous to mention by name, who continually showed an interest in this quirky, intriguing, and at times utterly opaque text, both for their own research and for their classrooms. Your genuine interest and excitement to share this text with your students inspired me to create this edition and translation.

The research that stands behind this project began in 2012 when I was an MA student, writing a final paper for a composition of the Pentateuch course on the identification of independent priestly and nonpriestly strands in Numbers 32. That paper was later my first published article. In the decade that has followed since writing that course paper, I have worked on this larger project of laying out a new source critical analysis of the biblical "P" source in fits and starts, but at almost no point was it something I worked on alone. I owe much gratitude to a number of scholars, colleagues, and friends who listened to me think through ideas, challenged some of the more outlandish ones, and consistently showed an interest and investment in helping me to get this right—or as right as one can when reconstructing a hypothetical source document.

I have benefitted immensely from the wisdom and generosity of Joel Baden, for whom I wrote that course paper in 2012, and with whom I continue to debate source critical issues to this day. He has been an unwavering supporter of this project from its inception and has spent countless hours talking through source critical divisions of particularly challenging passages and reading drafts along the way. Our discussions never failed to sharpen my thinking and challenge my assumptions, and for that I remain grateful.

This book benefitted from regular discussions with many other colleagues over the years, on big issues such as source identification to translational approach to smaller ones such as how to render a specific turn of phrase or the discussion of a certain literary feature of the text. The conversations were so numerous over such a lengthy period of time that I hesitate to list the colleagues for fear of leaving someone out, but I will nonetheless try: Catherine Bonesho, David Carr, Simeon Chavel, Jessie DeGrado, Daniel Fleming, Simcha Gross, Charles Huff, Eric Jarrard, Madadh Richey, Julia Rhyder, Baruch Schwartz, and Jeffrey Stackert. I would like to thank Samuel Boyd, and Thomas Bolin for reading early drafts of this manuscript and offering insightful feedback.

Candida Moss not only read and commented on multiple early drafts of this translation, but she also spent hours talking through issues of translation, organization, and presentation of the materials in this book. Her perspective was invaluable at every stage of this project, and I am grateful for the many, many insights she generously offered along the way. The introduction to this book benefitted immensely from the keen critical and editorial eye of Annette Yoshiko Reed. I would also like to thank my student, Abigail Beech, for the work she did in editing this manuscript just prior to its submission. Her keen eye and attention to detail saved me from numerous embarrassing errors. I am also grateful for the assistance of Abigail Beech and Christine Jensen with reviewing the final proofs of this book. (Though all mistakes, of course, remain my own.)

I am also grateful to the anonymous readers of this manuscript for their enthusiasm for this project, and for their helpful suggestions. This book could not possibly have come into being without the incredible support of my editor, Eric Schmidt, who believed in this project from our first conversation and guided it (and me!) through every stage from proposal to production, nearly all of it in the midst of the COVID-19 pandemic.

Finally, I must thank my husband Ari, who spent more time than anyone listening to me talk about "P" and think through various ideas that appear in these pages or are hinted at in the notes. Every page of this edition benefitted immensely from his constant support, patience, clear thinking, and intelligence. He has a way of seeing right to the heart of any issue and of bringing a fresh perspective to it. More than once I found myself working out a particularly tricky translation with him at the dinner table, and more than once he sat, listened, and then offered up the perfect English idiom. For this, and for so many other reasons, this book is dedicated to him.

TRANSLATOR'S NOTE

WHY CREATE THIS TRANSLATION?

The primary reason I wanted to create this edition and translation of the biblical priestly narrative was because I felt strongly that this story needed to be presented as a work of literature in its own right. For many biblical scholars, the work of pentateuchal criticism is the work of deciphering and disentangling the various layers of text and identifying their possible authors. We tend to focus on the small details or shorter segments of stories with an eye always toward questions related to dividing the text into its various sources. It is much rarer to consider the entirety of a source—even one so well agreed upon as the priestly source—as a coherent piece of literature.

This is all the more the case when we include the ritual and legal materials in the books of Exodus, Leviticus, and Numbers as a part of the priestly narrative. There is no existing edition of the biblical priestly narrative that contains its ritual and legal elements; these tend to be excerpted, marked as secondary, or otherwise ignored. The biblical priestly narrative should be understood as an independent literary work, and it deserves to be read as such. Polychrome bibles, while helpful when it comes to identifying sources, still hamper one's ability to read one source from beginning to end, apart from other sources. In presenting the biblical priestly narrative alone, I am making a strong claim that this—or something near to this—is how it once existed in antiquity and that this is how it deserves to be read: as a literary whole.

It is also my hope that when the biblical priestly narrative is read on its own, it becomes more apparent how centrally important the ritual and legal materials are to the development of the plot and the overall literary profile of this text. The biblical priestly narrative, as I have presented it here, challenges modern ideas of what counts as "literary" in the ancient world. Too often we create categories of "literary" and "nonliterary" in relation to our contemporary aesthetic ideals. It is important to remember that these are not the aesthetic ideals of the mid-first millennium BCE in ancient Israel. Just because sacrificial instructions do not appeal to us as literature does not mean that they were not considered literary in the ancient world. Multiple authors and editors created the biblical priestly narrative over the course of multiple centuries, each one working to craft a story, perhaps a history, of their religion. In a way, the creation of this edition is an invitation to look at this text from a new perspective, and with a wider sense of what counts as "literary" in the ancient world.

The creation of this edition began more than a decade ago with the careful identification of the pentateuchal priestly source from the perspective of the neodocumentary hypothesis. It continued with years of analysis of the relationship between the traditionally "narrative" elements of the text and its ritual and legal materials, a project that culminated in my first book, *The Story of Sacrifice*. What I realized in writing that book is that so much of it relied on the shared knowledge among biblical scholars about what constitutes "P"—what I've been calling the priestly narrative.

Among specialists, we have a shared understanding of what is or what is not priestly, and that understanding has shifted somewhat from the source critical divisions that were done in the early twentieth century and that are the basis of current polychrome editions of the Pentateuch. The problem is that while scholars who work in this subfield might have a clear sense of what belongs to this source, scholars in other subfields, students, and nonacademic readers might not. They are reliant on older, outdated scholarship. I wanted to create this edition in part to externalize knowledge that currently exists in the minds (and across hundreds of publications) of pentateuchal scholars. That is not to say that all pentateuchal scholars will agree with the entirety of how I have presented the priestly source; not all pentateuchal scholars agree with the neodocumentary hypothesis, after all. But the vast majority of what is presented here will be familiar to those who have been working on this material, and it is my hope that by publishing it in this form it will now become accessible to a broader audience as well.

Presenting this text to a broader audience necessarily meant creating a new translation of it. One of the paradoxes of this project is that the biblical priestly narrative is simultaneously one of the most translated texts in the world and at the same time a text that has rarely, if ever, been translated. As a part of the Pentateuch, which itself is a part of the Hebrew Bible/Old Testament, the texts that belong to the priestly narrative have been translated countless times into hundreds of languages over the last 2,500 years. However, the priestly narrative is also a text that has rarely been read on its own, separated from the nonpriestly texts in the Pentateuch. There have been a handful of polychrome bibles,[1] and in one case the priestly narrative is said to be presented in its entirety, but most of the ritual and legal materials are absent.[2] All these texts either use a preexisting translation or translate the Pentateuch as a whole.

To the best of my knowledge, there has been no attempt to translate the biblical priestly narrative as an independent document. Such an undertaking is critically important for the study of this source. The literary style of the priestly narrative is distinct, and identifying literary artistry within the narrative depends in many cases on the accurate representation of that style in a translation. When a translator's focus is on the Pentateuch as a whole, this fact can be easily lost or overlooked. Similarly, there are a significant number of terms that have idiosyncratic or unique meanings within the priestly narrative, and these terms are nearly always mistranslated in translations of the compiled Pentateuch. For example, most translations of the Pentateuch render the Hebrew *hatta't* as "sin offering." Translating the term as sin offering has led interpreters to concoct various explanations for how childbirth can cause a woman to sin, since she must offer a *hatta't*

[1] J. Estlin and G. Harford-Battersby Carpenter, *The Hexateuch, According to the Revised Version*, vol. 2 (London: Longmans, Green, 1900); Richard E. Friedman, *The Bible with Sources Revealed: A New View into the Five Books of Moses* (New York: HarperOne, 2005).

[2] Antony F. Campbell and Mark A. O'Brien, *Sources of the Pentateuch: Texts, Introductions, Annotations* (Minneapolis: Fortress Press, 1993).

afterward. In reality, childbirth generates a form of impurity that ritually contaminates the sanctuary, a concept that is in no way linked to sin. The function of the *hatta't* is to remove that impurity and decontaminate the sanctuary: hence, decontamination offering is a more accurate translation of this term. The new translation I offer here is one that is meant to reflect, insofar as it is possible, the literary profile and distinct theological perspective of the biblical priestly narrative.

This edition and this translation have been created with two distinct audiences in mind, and as is the case with any such project, negotiating between those two audiences may leave both slightly dissatisfied. The main focus of this edition is to present the biblical priestly narrative in its own right. I have taken a neodocumentary approach to identifying this source, and as such there will undoubtedly be pentateuchal scholars who disagree with aspects of this edition. To that audience, I would like to say this is meant to be a starting point for further discussion about the priestly source. I have deliberately avoided discussing stratification within this text, precisely because this is such a heavily debated issue, and my hope is that by presenting a maximalist version of the priestly source, the door remains open for debate about its own compositional history. When translating this text and writing notes, my main focus was a nonspecialist audience. The notes themselves are meant to highlight specific moments of literary importance, patterns, themes, and very occasionally moments of redactional activity. Nonspecialists may find that some of the methodological discussions in the introduction or the few footnotes on redactional issues might be overly technical; I recognize that and have tried to keep such moments to a minimum. The translation itself is meant to be clear and accessible to those who have little or no background with biblical literature, while still being identifiably priestly for those familiar with this text in the Hebrew. My default orientation in this edition and translation is always toward accessibility for the nonspecialist.

MY APPROACH TO THIS TRANSLATION

When I began this translation, my intention was first and foremost to bring the biblical priestly narrative to life for its readers. It had been obscured by its combination with nonpriestly materials, and it had been stylistically and literarily further obscured by the harmonizing demands of translations of the compiled Pentateuch. My aim has been to treat the translation of this text as if it were any other piece of ancient literature.

When it comes to Bible translation, this is sometimes easier said than done. Translating stories that are culturally familiar, that are central to multiple religious communities, and that at times contain words and phrases that evoke strong feelings and memories presents its own kind of challenge. There has been a kind of freedom, though, in translating a text that from start to finish has not yet been translated on its own. Most people have never read the biblical priestly narrative. They have read the Bible, or the Torah, or perhaps even Leviticus, but this priestly narrative is something new. It is this pairing of something new and something ancient that has guided my translation approach in this volume.

The biblical priestly narrative may be recovered from what we now know as the Bible, but it is not itself the Bible; nor was it likely ever intended to be. One of the guiding principles of this translation is the avoidance of what might be termed "Bible-ese"—a specific kind of language that is rooted in centuries of biblical translation. Bible-ese often uses vocabulary that appears only in the context of the Bible, words like firmament, tabernacle, holocaust, or bloodguilt, or phrases such as "with a high hand" or "hardened his heart." Phrases like these represent idiomatic uses of biblical Hebrew that at one point were translated quite literally into English. Those literal translations have persevered throughout the years and created a kind of biblical English. In this translation, I have tried to avoid biblical English and instead chosen to render idiomatic Hebrew phrases into idiomatic modern American English. Similarly, I have eschewed the use of terms that tend not to be a part of regular English usage. Many translations of Leviticus, particularly older ones, will translate the *olah* offering as the "holocaust" offering. Semantically speaking, this is perfectly accurate; it designates something that is entirely consumed. Culturally speaking, this is not a use of the term holocaust that one would encounter in modern American English, and in fact using such a term could (and probably does) evoke thoughts of the Holocaust during World War II, which breaks the fictive universe of the story. A different kind of issue arises from something like "bloodguilt." This term appears throughout the biblical priestly narrative and is quintessentially biblical English.

The meaning is relatively clear: it designates the guilt of someone who is responsible for bloodshed. As it happens, there is a colloquial American English phrase that means the same thing: "the blood is on his hands," and so I have translated the term this way, rather than as "bloodguilt." I could offer dozens more examples of choices like these, but these two examples offer a sense of how I have approached this issue and the translational choices I've made in this volume.

Readers will not encounter biblical English; rather, it is my intention that they will encounter this story in a version of English more familiar to them. This does not mean, however, that my goal in this translation is to make the biblical priestly narrative sound like a modern American story. It is anything but that. The ideas and institutions in this story are worlds apart from our contemporary context. Animal sacrifice is the cornerstone of religious practice and God is understood in thoroughly anthropomorphic terms as an entity who has a physical body like that of human beings (only much larger) and who requires food and rest. Human beings generate various impurities, both intentionally and unintentionally. Tent-shrines are constructed in the middle of a desert, and people subsist on the miraculous appearance of a flaky breadlike substance that appears with the dew each morning for forty years. This is not a story that shares modern cultural, theological, or historical frameworks. In many ways the ideas that the biblical priestly narrative presents are deeply, deeply foreign for modern readers. One of the reasons I have chosen to translate in colloquial American English is so that these unfamiliar, idiosyncratic, and, in some cases, utterly baffling ideas come through as clearly as possible. The biblical priestly narrative as a story is one that will be challenging and strange for many modern readers. The process of translation by definition will inevitably obscure some of the original story; not everything from one language can be perfectly represented in another, especially in cases of intentional ambiguity in the start text—something relatively common in the priestly narrative. My aim in this translation is, as far as possible, to allow the idiosyncratic nature of the priestly narrative to exist in the story itself, and not in challenges presented by the language in which it is told.

A good example of this approach to presenting the unique vision of the priestly narrative in accessible modern American English is the case of the tabernacle. The central institution of this story, perhaps even its main character in some ways, is referred to in the Hebrew as the *mishkan* or the *ohel mo'ed*. Understanding what this structure is and how it is imagined to work is absolutely fundamental for understanding the priestly narrative as a whole. Traditionally, *mishkan* has been translated as "tabernacle" and *ohel mo'ed* has been translated as "Tent of Meeting." The latter is not a terrible translation, though is a bit static and archaic and, as such, I have opted for the shorter "Meeting Tent." The word "tabernacle," however, is the height of biblical English. Where do we see this word used other than in Bible translations, church names, and perhaps in reference to the name of a famous Mormon choir? Even then, do we really know what a "tabernacle" is, other than that thing that is described in a lot of detail in the second half of Exodus? My suspicion is that the word tabernacle does not evoke a particularly strong image in people's minds, and if it does it is likely not quite the image that the priestly narrative is attempting to convey.

Tabernacle is, of course, an accurate translation; it comes from the Latin term for tent or hut. The trouble is, even this translation does not quite convey what the priestly narrative means by the term. Sure, it is a tent (hence its also being called a Meeting Tent) but it is something much more than that. We can look to the Hebrew word itself to demonstrate this. Hebrew words are typically made up of three-consonant roots that are supplemented in various ways to turn them into verbs, adjectives, and nouns. The root of the word *mishkan* is *sh-k-n*, which means to live or dwell. The "m" on the front of it turns it into a particular type of noun that often designates the place of something. The literal meaning of *mishkan*, then, is the place of dwelling, or, as I'm calling it, the Dwelling Place. Specifically, it is Yahweh's Dwelling Place. By using this translation of *mishkan*, my goal is to evoke the concrete image of a divine home that is designed to be inhabited rather than an abstract temple-like space used for ritual purposes. The Dwelling Place is, quite literally, meant to be Yahweh's home in this story. It is designed so that he can live on earth among the Israelites. It has furniture, utensils, curtains, lights, and even incense to ensure it smells good. It is easy for modern readers to forget or gloss over this central point of the story precisely because it is so foreign to common ways of thinking about divine beings today. By using the term "Dwelling Place," I want to draw attention to this seemingly strange idea and to reinforce the image that is so clearly present in the Hebrew.

At the same time, there are limits to translation and I want to take a moment here to acknowledge this. There are some Hebrew terms in the priestly narrative about the meaning of which we simply cannot be exactly sure; it is therefore nearly impossible to translate them into English. These are nearly all objects that exist within the Dwelling Place or are a part of its maintenance. I should be clear that these are not *hapax legomena*, words that only occur once in the Hebrew Bible. These words appear again and again, and in some cases their roots are well known even if we cannot precisely pinpoint what the object being described is. One of the most significant examples of this comes in the story of Moses on Mount Sinai. When he descends from the mountain, he brings with him something called the *edut*. Later in the story, this *edut* is placed inside the ark that is itself placed in the inner sanctuary of the Dwelling Place. The story tells us that Yahweh lives in this inner sanctuary and that he sits over this ark. In a few places, the ark is even referred to as the ark of the *edut*. The Hebrew root behind this word means something like "witness" or "testimony," and that is almost certainly what the function of this object is. There are many such objects in the priestly narrative that are placed in the inner sanctuary that commemorate significant events in the history of the Israelite people and are meant to serve as a kind of reminder of those events. A portion of manna is preserved, for example, as well as Aaron's flowering staff that was used to demonstrate that Yahweh chose him as the leader of the people. The *edut* certainly serves a similar function, memorializing the event on Sinai.

What, exactly, the *edut* is, however, remains unclear. Traditionally, it has been conflated with the tablets that Moses brings down from Sinai in the nonpriestly story in the Pentateuch, but there is no evidence whatsoever in the priestly narrative that this should be understood as tablets. There are no laws given on Sinai in this story, and thus nothing to inscribe on tablets. We might be able to argue that the *edut* contains the *tabnit*, the plan, for the Dwelling Place, but this remains incredibly speculative. The approach I have taken in this case is to acknowledge the limits of translation. I am not willing to speculate about what specific object is being envisioned here, and so I do not want to, and in fact cannot, translate the term. In the case of the *edut* and others like it, I have chosen to simply transliterate the Hebrew word and provide a short note explaining what we do know about its possible referents.

As important as it is to me to portray the world of the priestly narrative as vividly in English as it is in the Hebrew, it is equally important that I do not misrepresent what we can know about the objects in that world. In some cases, we simply do not know what was being envisioned. As frustrating as that can be, I believe that we have to be honest about those limits to our knowledge, and so the approach I have taken here is one that is reflective of an awareness of those limits.

NAMES AND THE POLITICS OF TRANSLATION

The priestly narrative occupies a strange place between biblical and nonbiblical literature. The Bible as an entity postdates the composition of the biblical priestly narrative by at least seven hundred years. Yet it is the canonical Bible (and the creation of the Torah more specifically) that we have to thank for the preservation of this text. The vast majority of translations of the Bible have been done with religious communities in mind. In some cases, these are Jewish communities, but in most cases, these are Christian communities. The process of translating a text with a religious community in mind necessarily conditions some of the choices a translator makes. In this volume, I am consciously and adamantly not translating with a specific religious community or audience in mind. The way language works is that when people encounter an idea, they must integrate it into whatever ideas and beliefs they already possess. This is called apperception. All language is apperceived through preexisting political discourses. What I mean by this is that regardless of what I intend, those reading this translation will read it from the perspective of their own cultural, political, and religious contexts. Indeed, as the translator, I have done the same in creating this volume in the first place. This is important because I want to make it clear that I believe there is no such thing as a politically or religiously neutral translation; it cannot exist.

Language (such as this translation) that is apperceived through a preexisting political or religious framework will inherently privilege some identities or communities over others. Perhaps it is time to offer an example. One of the issues that presented me with the most difficulty in translating this text seems, on the surface, minor and unimportant: names. How do I treat names in this story? There are essentially two extremes and a spectrum in between. On the one side, I could normalize all the names into modern English—Moses, Aaron, Abraham. On the other side, I could simply transliterate the names into roman characters, preserving the way they sound in the Hebrew—Moshe, Aharon, Avraham. Some of these names would be recognizable to non-Hebrew speakers (Avraham), others less so (Moshe). But this is not only about recognizability. As I have been stating from the outset, my primary goal with this translation is to make the language familiar and the story accessible. Moshe, Yitzhak, Ya'akov, Yosef. These names might not be familiar to English-speaking audiences; these audiences may not recognize them as Moses, Isaac, Jacob, and Joseph. They would, on the other hand, be immediately recognizable to Hebrew speakers or those who are part of Jewish communities. The appeal of maintaining the Hebrew-sounding names is that they are often a part of some kind of wordplay or alliteration in the story. But is preserving that literary aspect worth privileging Hebrew-speaking or Jewish communities over others? By transliterating the names, I would create two circles of readers—those who are "in" on it and those who are not. The issue of how to treat names seems like a minor one, but it goes right to the heart of the challenge of translation itself. There is no perfect or correct choice in this case. No matter what I decided, it would not—could not—be politically or religiously neutral.

The decision I made about how to handle the issue of names in this translation is less important than the processes and power structures inherent in the process of translation that this question raises in the first place. That being said, it is worth briefly discussing the choices I made in this volume. I have chosen a kind of hybrid approach in this translation. For recurring characters, I have normalized names into their typical English forms—Abraham, Moses, Isaac, Joseph, for example. I have done the same with most familiar locations—Jerusalem, for example. If there is a significant wordplay for a given name in the Hebrew, I have added a note describing that for readers. For characters or places that appear infrequently, typically in genealogies or lists of land allotments, I have chosen to transliterate the names to more accurately reflect how they sound in the Hebrew. This departs from the practice in many modern Bible translations—Yafet instead of Japhet, for example, because there is no *j* in biblical Hebrew. One of the main reasons I have chosen to do this is because the genealogical and land lists at times make use of alliteration, assonance, or rhyming to hold certain segments together and I wanted to preserve that literary quality.

Finally, and perhaps most controversially, I should discuss my treatment of the divine name in this volume. The use of the proper divine name, sometimes referred to as the "tetragrammaton" because it is made up of four letters in biblical Hebrew, can be controversial. In religious circles, particularly in Jewish contexts, this divine name is not used, written, and certainly not pronounced. This is a tradition that can be traced back to at least the Hellenistic period with the Greek translation of the Pentateuch, which renders the tetragrammaton as κύριος, "lord," and likely reflects a tradition of reading the tetragrammaton as "adonai" (literally: my lord). Most modern translations take one of two approaches to translating the divine name. Most commonly, it is translated in small capital letters as LORD. Alternatively, in some more academic-leaning translations it appears as YHWH, representing the four consonants of the tetragrammaton. In this translation, I have deliberately avoided both these approaches. One of the major plot points of the biblical priestly narrative is the revelation of the divine name to Moses and then to the Israelites as a whole prior to their departure from Egypt. Earlier in the story, the divine character is consistently referred to as "Elohim" in the Hebrew, which translates to "God" in English. Once God reveals his name to Moses and the Israelites, that name—Yahweh—is used for the remainder of the story. Because most translations have some specific religious audience in mind, most translators will not write out the divine name in this way. My aim with this translation is to be different. I do not want to present this text as part of a "Bible" even as it is admittedly "biblical." When we read other stories from the ancient Middle East or Mediterranean, the names of gods are routinely spelled out—Marduk, Ba'al, Zeus. The main reason that this is not the case with biblical stories is because of preexisting religious beliefs and traditions. This translation is deliberately presenting the priestly narrative as a piece of ancient literature akin to the Ugaritic *Ba'al* epic, the Mesopotamian *Enuma Elish*, or Hesiod's *Theogony*. To that end, and because it is a significant element of the development of the priestly narrative, I have chosen to treat the

divine character in this story the same way that we routinely treat
divine characters in these other myths: by using his full name. I recognize that this might make some readers uncomfortable, but it is my
hope that it also allows those readers to encounter what might seem
like a familiar story in a fundamentally new way.

Introduction

What Is the Biblical Priestly Narrative?

The biblical priestly narrative is, first and foremost, a hypothetical document. To explain what I mean by this, and why this edition is not simply one scholar's imagination run wild, I first offer a very brief introduction. I survey some of its central points of agreement in the field of biblical studies about the composition of the first five books of the Hebrew Bible (Genesis, Exodus, Leviticus, Numbers, and Deuteronomy), commonly called the Torah or Pentateuch. Then I explain the specific methodological approach that stands in the background of this project.

Around the seventeenth century, scholars began to question, and ultimately reject, the idea that the Torah was written by Moses.[1] But if Moses did not write it, then who did? And more pointedly, how many people wrote it? Unfortunately, there is not a single answer to either question. Debates about the literary history and authorship of these five books began with Baruch Spinoza and continue to this day.

There are, however, a few broad conclusions that nearly all biblical scholars have come to agree on. Many of these conclusions can be

---

[1] The term "Torah" is often used in Jewish contexts to refer to the first five books of the Hebrew Bible. It typically signifies a coherent and religiously authoritative text. In academic discourse, it is more common to use the term "Pentateuch" to refer to these same first five books. In this introduction, I will primarily make use of the term "Pentateuch," and use the term "Torah" only when I am referring to the reception of this text in a Jewish context (either early or modern).

summed up in the statement that the Pentateuch is a composite text. Its division into five books was not original, but it is nevertheless made up of multiple parts with different authors. The Five Books of Moses are not five books, and they are also not by Moses.

The works that we now know as Genesis, Exodus, Leviticus, Numbers, and Deuteronomy are not an original part of this text; they are a result of choices made by scribes centuries after the texts that make up the Pentateuch were written. No one ever set out to write "Genesis." Instead, the book we now know as Genesis is the result of Persian and Hellenistic-era Jewish scribes being faced with technological limitations. In the latter half of the first millennium BCE, texts composed in Hebrew were written on scrolls made either of animal skins (parchment) or plant materials (papyrus). Today, all five books are commonly copied onto a single large scroll, which can be found in every synagogue.[2] But in antiquity, these scrolls could not be infinitely long; at some point they would tear. According to the scholar Menahem Haran, an estimate for the maximum length of a scroll at the time is roughly equivalent to the book of Chronicles, which spans more or less 1650 verses (in modern editions) or around 48 pages in modern print Bibles.[3] The Pentateuch, by comparison, covers about 146 pages or 5,845 verses—about three and a half times the size of Chronicles.

Since the Pentateuch was too long for a single scroll, ancient scribes chose to break it into five sections at relatively logical points in the story. Genesis narrates the creation of the world through the Israelites' descent into Egypt; Exodus covers the Israelites in Egypt through the revelation at Sinai; Leviticus describes the creation of a mobile tent-shrine and home for the Israelite god, Yahweh; Numbers tells of the Israelites' departure from Mount Sinai and their wanderings in the wilderness; and Deuteronomy is Moses's final speech to the Israelites on the day of his death while they stand at the edge of the Promised Land. Today, we are accustomed to thinking of "books" as what authors

[2] The first-known Torah scrolls date to the late antique period. For a more robust discussion of the history of the Torah scroll, see David Stern, *The Jewish Bible: A Material History* (Seattle: University of Washington Press, 2017), 11–62.

[3] To see a full discussion of this, see Menahem Haran, "Book-Size and the Device of Catch-Lines in the Biblical Canon," *Journal of Jewish Studies* 36 (1985): 5–8.

write. In this case, what we encounter now as the five "books" of the Pentateuch are the result of scribes reaching the limits of what a scroll could contain. Rather than completely filling one scroll and moving to the next, these scribes chose to make thematic divisions that resulted in five scrolls of unequal lengths.

But why would these scribes be faced with this problem at all? If the Pentateuch was too long for a single scroll, wouldn't an author have separated their own work into such sections when faced with this same limitation? This leads to one point that scholars largely agree on: the Pentateuch as we have it today was not composed in this form. One of the main contributions of pentateuchal scholarship over the last two centuries has been in showing that within the Pentateuch, there are multiple versions of stories that contradict each other in some way. This has led to the conclusion that the Pentateuch was made up of several smaller strands of texts that were each written by different authors. These strands were later combined into what we know today as the Pentateuch by a series of editors over an extended period of time.

This is what we mean when we say that the Pentateuch is a composite text: it is made up of multiple different compositions written by multiple authors. Each of these compositions would have been short enough to fit on a single scroll.[4] How many different compositions were there? How many different authors were responsible for the contents of what is now the Pentateuch? These remain open questions, investigated and debated by scholars in the field of pentateuchal studies. There is precious little agreement among scholars about these issues, with two notable exceptions. As Reinhard Kratz puts it, "we can distinguish and isolate two distinct literary strata within the Pentateuch: the book of Deuteronomy . . . and the so-called Priestly Writing (P)."[5] Most of the disagreement has been on the identification of authors and units within the nonpriestly, non-Deuteronomic strands.

[4] Menahem Haran, "Book-Scrolls at the Beginning of the Second Temple Period: The Transition from Papyrus to Skins," *Hebrew Union College Annual* 54 (1983).

[5] Reinhard G. Kratz, "The Pentateuch in Current Research: Consensus and Debate," in *The Pentateuch: International Perspectives on Current Research*, ed. Thomas B. Dozeman, Konrad Schmid, and Baruch J. Schwartz (Tübingen: Mohr Siebeck, 2011), 34.

The present book is focused on the priestly source; I will not enter into debates about other sources. For our purposes, what is important is that the existence of a distinct priestly source is broadly recognized by scholars. The vast majority of texts assigned to this source are widely agreed on. This is what makes an edition like this one possible: the source may be hypothetical, but there is a broad scholarly consensus about its content and concerns.

I will discuss these in greater detail below. For now, there are a few elements of the priestly source that are worth highlighting. First and foremost, the reason this source is given the name "priestly" is because one of its central concerns is with the communal practice of religion, which in this story (and in ancient Israel and Judah more generally) means a temple-based sacrificial cult. This source contains the most extensive and detailed descriptions of ritual practices, sacrifice, and purity laws in the entirety of the Hebrew Bible. No other text comes close to the level of detail provided in the priestly stratum until a tractate of the Mishnah (i.e., tractate Kedoshim) in the first centuries of the common era. This focus on temple ritual and the role of the priests in mediating those rituals has been taken as this source's defining characteristic. As we will see below, this conventional name can be a bit misleading.

Another significant characteristic of the priestly source is that it was not composed by a single author (or even a single school of authors). The priestly source, as scholars identify it today, is itself a composite text that has been edited and supplemented over the course of several centuries. At least two different editorial schools have been identified by scholars, the most significant of which is known as the "Holiness School."[6] This Holiness School is thought to be responsible for the second half of Leviticus (chapters 17–26) and many other smaller sections throughout Genesis, Exodus, and Numbers. A later set of priestly authors and editors has been identified in some of the texts in the book of Numbers, especially in the festival calendar in Numbers 28–29. What makes the layers in the priestly source different from the multiple layers in the Pentateuch as a whole is that they seem to have been added only to the priestly source itself, and not to the

[6] For the most complete discussion of the existence of a "Holiness School," see Israel Knohl, *The Sanctuary of Silence: The Priestly Torah and the Holiness School* (Winona Lake, IN: Eisenbrauns, 2007).

Pentateuch as a whole.[7] It is important to recognize this characteristic of the priestly source from the outset. This is a work composed by many hands over the course of many centuries. What enables it to cohere as a single identifiably "priestly" story is that all these authors and editors largely bought into and built on both the broad worldview and the specific plot points established in a first edition of the priestly source.

Finally, it is worth underscoring this final point: one of the reasons that the priestly source is largely recognized is because of its very distinct perspective and story. Many parts of the priestly source stand in direct contradiction with other nonpriestly texts found in the Pentateuch. Perhaps the most significant example of this is the priestly Meeting Tent, which is described to Moses on Mount Sinai and which will serve as Yahweh's Dwelling Place among the Israelites. According to the priestly source, this tent is very large and quite ornate, including skillfully embroidered curtains, gold and silver-plated furniture, and many different rooms. Crucially, this Meeting Tent is said to sit at the center of the Israelite community, with the people setting up camp all around it. There is another Meeting Tent described in a nonpriestly literary strand of the Pentateuch, though, and that one is quite different. That Meeting Tent is smaller, lacks any detailed description at all, is fit only for a single person (Moses), and sits at some distance from where the community lives. Contradictions like these serve as signals for scholars of the composite character of the Pentateuch and demonstrate that there is more than one perspective represented in it.

The work of identifying the different sources or layers in the Pentateuch is the work of recovering these different perspectives and different

[7] There are of course exceptions to this. A number of scholars understand the priestly stratum to be the latest source, written after all the others and meant to be a kind of redactional layer to hold the entirety of the Pentateuch together. Those scholars who argue this typically claim that the authors responsible for this were a part of one of these later priestly schools. One example of this is the work of Erhard Blum, whose most exhaustive treatment of this is found in *Studien zur Komposition des Pentateuch*, Beiheft zur Zeitschrift für die alttestamentliche Wissenschaft (Berlin: Walter de Gruyter, 1990), 221–360. For a summary of this approach in English, see Erhard Blum, "Issues and Problems in the Contemporary Debate Regarding the Priestly Writings," in *The Strata of the Priestly Writings: Contemporary Debate and Future Directions*, ed. Sarah Shectman and Joel S. Baden (Zürich: Theologischer Verlag, 2009), 31–44.

versions of the origins of the Israelites. Disentangling the priestly source from the other materials in the Pentateuch allows for the emergence of a version of a story that might seem familiar at first glance but actually presents a very different version of the story. But why is it important to present the priestly narrative on its own? What is at stake here? There are a few different ways to answer these questions. First, presenting the priestly narrative as an independent text challenges readers to engage with the entirety of the priestly perspective, one that does not marginalize ritual and law. In this way, this presentation of the priestly narrative counters the idea that it is an impoverished narrative. Rather, it is marked by its own concerns that cannot be reduced to a simplistic comparison with what other sources do or do not say.

This text also provides us with an opportunity to think more deeply about ancient scribes, practices of writing, and the reception of penta-teuchal texts in early Jewish communities. Before the advent of the printing press and publication as we know it today, writing was often a more collective endeavor. The biblical priestly narrative is no exception; there is not a single "author" of this story. It was written by many hands over the course of multiple centuries. To reduce this text to the work of a single "author" would be to ignore the complexity of its composition and the continued resonance in the community of the ideological perspective it promotes. Indeed, it is worth underscoring that this text promotes an ideology that is distinct from that of the Pentateuch or the Hebrew Bible as a whole. The predominant voice of the Hebrew Bible is a Deuteronomistic one, one that focuses on the failure of the Israelites to keep God's commandments and the punishments they face for those failures.[8] The biblical priestly narrative presents a fundamentally different perspective, one that is wholly optimistic about Israel's desire and ability to fulfill God's commands. Being confronted with this different perspective should push us to rethink the history of the Pentateuch and its reception in early Jewish communities. Since the formation of the Pentateuch in the fifth through fourth

---

[8] "Deuteronomistic" refers to the ideologies expressed in the Deuteronomistic History, which spans the books of Deuteronomy, Joshua, Judges, Samuel, and Kings. "Deuteronomic," on the other hand, refers only to the book of Deuteronomy. The two are related, but broadly speaking, Deuteronomistic theology builds on and extends Deuteronomic theology.

centuries BCE, scholars have often assumed that the redacted form of the Pentateuch is the primary text for early Jewish communities going forward. While the redacted form certainly represents one path, it is possible that another path forward might be identified in a continuation of the worldview and writing practices established in the biblical priestly narrative.

METHODOLOGY FOR IDENTIFYING THE PRIESTLY NARRATIVE

P in Genesis through Deuteronomy: A Neodocumentarian Approach

There are a number of different approaches that scholars take when it comes to identifying different sources or strata in the Pentateuch.[9] Many of these approaches are mutually exclusive and are based on very different models of how and when the various parts of the Pentateuch were composed. But, as noted above, where these different approaches overlap is in their general agreement about the existence of identifiable priestly and Deuteronomic sources. This means that the majority of the disagreement among pentateuchal scholars, from a methodological standpoint, is focused on the analysis of the nonpriestly, non-Deuteronomic materials in the Pentateuch. This also means that it becomes possible to sidestep some (though not all) of these debates in this book, because this book is an edition and translation of the priestly source. In this section, I will first address some of the major debates that continue about the nature of the priestly source, before then introducing the methodological approach I have taken in this edition and translation to identify the pentateuchal priestly materials. Finally, I will address one particular phenomenon that emerged in the combination of priestly and nonpriestly materials in

[9] This section is meant to provide an explanation of my methodological approach to creating this edition of the biblical priestly narrative. While it is meant to be clear and relatively easy to follow, it is undoubtedly the most technical section of this introduction. It is entirely possible to read this book without the materials discussed in this section. For those readers who may be interested in the motivation for creating this translation, but who find discussion of methodology too technical or tedious, I would suggest looking to the "Why Create This Translation" section of the translator's note for an abbreviated version of the main takeaways here.

the Pentateuch: the relocation of scenes from the priestly story to other places in the pentateuchal narrative.

One of the most significant debates about the priestly source revolves around whether it should be understood as an independent literary source or as a redactional layer that has been added to the existing nonpriestly materials to bring them together into a single story. A slight majority of scholars currently understand the priestly source as an independent source. But a not insignificant minority advance the idea that this source was created as a final redactional layer to bring together the majority of what we now know as the Pentateuch,[10] or they suggest that the priestly source stands somewhere between a source and a redaction because it contains characteristics of both.[11] My own approach to this text understands the priestly source as an independent literary text, but it is worth answering some of the objections to this position to explain why I hold this position.

The prevailing reason that scholars have questioned the independence of the priestly source is because when they compare the priestly story to the nonpriestly ones, the priestly source appears impoverished.[12] In short, it looks to them like a sparse and uninspired story in comparison with other parallels in the Pentateuch. There are two underlying assumptions that lead to this type of conclusion. The first is that all the ritual and legal materials in the priestly source are a very late supplement and should not be considered "part of the story."[13] The second is

[10] David M. Carr, *The Formation of the Hebrew Bible: A New Reconstruction* (Oxford: Oxford University Press, 2011), 292–97; Joel S. Baden, *The Composition of the Pentateuch: Renewing the Documentary Hypothesis,* Anchor Yale Bible Reference Library (New Haven, CT: Yale University Press, 2012), 177–88; Konrad Schmid, *The Old Testament: A Literary History,* trans. Linda Maloney (Minneapolis: Fortress Press, 2012), 147; Diana V. Edelman et al., eds., *Opening the Books of Moses* (London: Routledge, 2014), 46–47.

[11] Blum, "Issues and Problems," 31–44.

[12] Julius Wellhausen, *Die Composition des Hexateuchs und der historischen Bücher des alten Testaments* (Berlin: G. Reimer, 1899), 332; Frank Moore, *Cross, Canaanite Myth and Hebrew Epic: Essays in the History of the Religion of Israel* (Cambridge, MA: Harvard University Press, 1973), 294–95.

[13] Martin Noth, *A History of Pentateuchal Traditions,* trans. Bernhard W. Anderson (Atlanta: Scholars Press, 1981), 9; Suzanne Boorer, *The Vision of the Priestly Narrative: Its Genre and Hermeneutics of Time* (Atlanta: Society of Biblical Literature Press, 2016), 68–69.

that the priestly story should follow roughly the same plot and include the same characters and events as the nonpriestly and Deuteronomic stories. When the priestly story is lacking an episode that is present in a nonpriestly story, the assumption is that the priestly source could afford to omit it: if it wasn't independent, but was instead a combination of all the extant material, it could rely on the nonpriestly telling.[14]

Both of these assumptions share a particular perspective on what counts as "literature" and what a biblical narrative should look like. The second assumption, that the priestly source should narrate the same events as the nonpriestly texts, betrays the continued influence of the compiled form of the Pentateuch and the idea that there is one "right" version of Israelites' origin story. In this case, the distinctive perspective between sources, or between authors, are flattened to a degree. Authors are denied the possibility of choosing their own plot points, and instead are expected to conform to the "traditional" story. What we now think of as the "traditional" story, however, is later than the priestly source; it exists only in the form of the Pentateuch as we know it today.

There is ample evidence from biblical and ancient Jewish literature that authors can (and did) choose to tell the same story in very different ways, often for specific rhetorical or ideological purposes. One of the most readily apparent examples of this is the story of David in the book of Samuel compared with the story of David in the book of Chronicles. The story of David in the book of Chronicles is "missing" many of the stories found in the book of Samuel. Notably, those missing stories all portray David in a less than flattering light. But if one reads the story of David in Chronicles on its own, it coheres as a self-standing, independent narrative. It is only in comparing it to the story in Samuel that something appears to be "missing." The thing is that there is nothing missing in Chronicles; the author(s) simply chose to tell their version of the story of David, a version that unequivocally

[14] Erhard Blum, *Die Komposition der Vätergeschichte*, Wissenschaftliche Monographien zum Alten und Neuen Testament (Neukirchen-Vluyn: Neukirchener Verlag, 1984), 427; John Van Seters, *Abraham in History and Tradition* (New Haven, CT: Yale University Press, 1975), 285; Cross, *Canaanite Myth*, 294, 305.This is discussed in more detail in Baden, *Composition*, 180–81.

presents the king as good and just. It is a different story. The same can be said for the pentateuchal materials. The only reason to compare the priestly source and the nonpriestly source is if we first assume that they must tell the same story with the same goals. Why must this be the case? It is not only possible, but even likely, that different authors would have different perspectives or different agendas. This is, in part, the impetus for them to compose their own versions of a story about the origins of the Israelites.

The other assumption is the idea that ritual and legal materials must be a very late addition, and not an integral part of the narrative itself. This assumption was popularized in the early twentieth century by Martin Noth and has been widely followed ever since.[15] There are two related elements underlying this argument that should be brought to light. In the nineteenth century, scholars like Julius Wellhausen claimed that "authentic" Israelite religion is best preserved in the narrative stories of individuals directly interacting with their god. They thus assumed that laws and rituals were introduced only later, as a kind of degradation of religious practice because they impose something between the worshipper and their god. The second element is related: law and ritual are not literary—that is, they are not good literature. Both of these arguments come from very particular nineteenth-century sensibilities about religion and literature, respectively. In the case of the former, one can recognize a distinctively Protestant Christian ethos that emphasizes direct access to and relationship with one's god as allegedly more "authentic" than a "ritualized" form of religion such as Judaism or Catholicism.[16] In the case of the latter, the ideal of the literary in biblical studies is often identical with either the Romantic or Victorian ideals of literature. Early conversations about biblical poetry revolved around the concept of the sublime,[17] and treatments of biblical narrative laud its providential themes, sparse

[15] Noth, *Pentateuchal Traditions*, 8.

[16] For a discussion of the influence of political and religious ideologies in penta-teuchal criticism, see Jeffrey Stackert, *A Prophet Like Moses: Prophecy, Law, and Israelite Religion* (Oxford: Oxford University Press, 2014), 200–208.

[17] Robert Lowth, *Lectures on the Sacred Poetry of the Hebrews* (London: Thomas Tegg, 1839), 147–56.

and indirect characterization, and hidden artistry.[18] The literary is that which is concerned with what is beyond the natural realm while also being wholly immersed in it. Detailed laws, most of which appear to have no natural basis, and complex rituals invented to mediate access the supernatural sit somewhere outside what is considered literary.

More recent research has shown that literature in the ancient world is far more diverse than has often been recognized. Laws, rituals, genealogies, lists of borders, wilderness itineraries—all of these have a role to play in literary texts.[19] Indeed, they are literature. The heart of the biblical priestly narrative is a long series of ritual instructions and laws, all of which are presented as speeches from one character (Yahweh) to another (usually Moses). These ritual instructions and laws offer an incredible amount of detail addressing the *how* of sacrifice. When read on their own, there seems to be little explicit discussion of the *why*. But that is precisely because these ritual instructions and laws were never meant to be read on their own. They are framed as part of a broader story about the origins of ancient Israel and its cult. While the ritual instructions and laws offer the *how*, the *why* is the story as a whole. When we read the ritual and narrative materials together, a broader story emerges about the type of relationship Yahweh intends to have with the Israelites and how they will work together to make that possible.

To read the ritual instructions apart from their narrative context is to fundamentally misunderstand these texts. When scholars have done this, and many have, the goal has often been to reconstruct historical religious practice. Because these texts offer the most detailed account of the *how* of sacrifice, it is tempting to think that we can use them as a kind of window onto ancient temple worship. But it is not so

[18] Robert Alter, *The Art of Biblical Narrative* (New York: Basic Books, 2011), 25–54; Yairah Amit, *Reading Biblical Narratives: Literary Criticism and the Hebrew Bible* (Minneapolis: Fortress Press, 2001), 69–92; Erich Auerbach, "Odysseus' Scar," in *Mimesis: The Representation of Reality in Western Literature* (Princeton, NJ: Princeton University Press, 2003), 3–23.

[19] For example, an excellent analysis of the literary role of itinerary lists can be found in Angela R. Roskop, *The Wilderness Itineraries: Genre, Geography, and the Growth of Torah* (Winona Lake, IN: Eisenbrauns, 2011).

simple. These texts may reflect some level of historical accuracy, but it is nearly impossible to say which parts or how accurate they may be. We have little to no archaeological evidence from the First Temple period to compare with these texts, and what evidence we do have sometimes directly contradicts them.[20] In addition to this, these ritual instructions lack sufficient specificity to be followed. While they may seem incredibly detailed to a modern reader (and they are), steps are missing, contingencies ignored, and processes assumed. They cannot be a kind of "priestly manual" in their current form. These ritual instructions and laws are something else.

When read carefully, the ritual instructions and laws of the priestly source are replete with wordplays, puns, artistic repetitions, and literary devices. They also serve as a means to constructing the story world and animating the characters within it while defining boundaries, exploring relationships, and navigating the fundamental reorganization of society. These ritual instructions and laws form the backbone of the biblical priestly narrative. Within them one can find characterization, description, and drama. To read the priestly narrative without its ritual and legal materials is, quite simply, not to read the priestly narrative. A priestly narrative without these materials could be described as impoverished. But a priestly narrative that includes its ritual and legal materials is anything but. It is a rich and complex story about the foundation of the cult and Yahweh's navigation of his relationship with Israel. It tells a story wholly different from either the nonpriestly pentateuchal texts or the canonical Pentateuch. If we set aside the assumption that the priestly source must conform to the plot of the nonpriestly texts, and allow for the possibility that the priestly ritual and legal materials are an integral part of the narrative itself, then there is no compelling reason to suggest that the priestly source must be a redactional layer. Instead, it becomes not only possible, but necessary, to read it as an independent literary source. The approach that I take in this edition and translation to identify an independent priestly source most closely resembles the approach known as the neodocumentary hypothesis.

[20] For a discussion of the evidence available for historical religious practice and how that squares with its literary representation in the Pentateuch, see Liane M. Feldman, "The Idea and Study of Sacrifice in Ancient Israel," *Religion Compass* 14 (2020): 1–14.

The neodocumentary hypothesis emerged in the late twentieth century as a revision of the approach advanced most famously by Wellhausen in the late nineteenth and early twentieth century. Put simply, this approach hypothesizes that there are four distinct and independent strands in the Pentateuch, two nonpriestly (J and E), one priestly (P), and one Deuteronomic (D). At some point after each of these sources was independently composed, one or more editors combined the sources into a single text very similar to what we know as the Pentateuch today. The neodocumentary hypothesis emphasizes the distinction between literary and historical questions of these texts and positions itself as a "literary solution to a literary problem."[21] The problem is that, when read carefully, the Pentateuch as it stands contains numerous contradictions, narrative discontinuities, doublets, and sometimes triplets of single events. Taking the plot as its starting point, the neodocumentary hypothesis argues that one can separate these four strands by identifying contradictions and discontinuities in plot. For example, in the story of the flood once we are told that the flood lasts forty days (Gen 7:12) and later that it lasted 150 days (Gen 7:24). Or in the story of the plagues, Moses turns every bit of water in Egypt into blood (Exod 7:19). But later in the story, we're told that Moses turns only the Nile to blood (Exod 7:20) and that the Egyptians were able to find fresh water away from the Nile (Exod 7:24). If Moses turned every bit of water in Egypt to blood, this should not have been possible. These are both places where neodocumentarians would suggest the presence of two parallel stories. This approach differs from earlier versions of the hypothesis in that it does not give much weight to specific linguistic features or word choices. It is not determinative if one story uses "Elohim," for example, and another "Yahweh." It may be the case that different stories use different names for God, but this information emerges only secondarily after a plot-based analysis has been carried out first.

The edition and translation here follow a neodocumentary approach to the identification of the biblical priestly source. The priestly source identified in this edition will largely overlap with priestly sources identified with other methodological approaches; such is the distinctiveness of this story and this source. That being said, there will undoubtedly be

[21] Baden, *Composition*, 32, 249.

some differences between a neodocumentarian priestly source and a priestly source derived from another model of pentateuchal composition. One of the more significant differences will be that of layers within the priestly source itself. As I mentioned briefly above, the priestly source is itself a composite text, written by many different authors over the course of several centuries. A strict neodocumentarian approach aims to identify the sources as they existed immediately prior to their combination into a single Pentateuch.[22] It does not deny the fact that each of these sources might have a prehistory of their own and might be composite texts themselves, but it is not fundamentally concerned with identifying the layers within each source.

The approach that I have taken in this edition and translation is to include the most maximal version of the priestly source. I have included priestly texts that are identifiably later additions to an earlier story, but that I think have been added to an independent priestly source, prior to its combination with nonpriestly and Deuteronomic sources.

I have chosen not to mark or differentiate between layers of the priestly source in this edition for a couple of reasons. First and most important: it would distract from reading this story. The final version of the priestly source is itself a coherent story. Each time authors chose to supplement this priestly story, earlier versions of the story were lost.[23]

The priestly source that can be identified from the Pentateuch is what we are able to access, and this is a multilayer composite text. Second, there remains a significant amount of disagreement among scholars as to which texts are primary, and which are later additions within the priestly source. Delineating layers in this edition and translation would make the methodological divide between pentateuchal

[22] Ibid., 32.

[23] This sets aside, of course, the possibility that earlier versions of the priestly story continued to circulate among other scribal circles or even among the same scribal circles. Because no material evidence of this has yet been discovered, we cannot know for sure if this is the case. It is worth noting that texts rarely existed in a single copy and that even when supplemented, edited, and changed, earlier copies could and did continue to exist and circulate. A good example of this phenomenon is the books of Samuel, Esther, or Job, all of which exist in several different ancient versions. Because we do not have such manuscript evidence for the priestly source, we can imagine that something similar occurred, but in practice the only version of the priestly source that survived is the one that can be identified within the compiled Pentateuch.

scholars studying this text even broader. As it stands, my hope is that scholars can use this text as a starting point for arguments about (1) which texts we include in the biblical priestly source, and (2) stratification within that source. At the same time, I hope that this book will help to introduce the student and general reader to scholarly perspectives on the Pentateuch and what these perspectives can offer for our understanding of the world of the ancient Israelites.

THE LITERARY CONTEXT OF
THE PRIESTLY NARRATIVE
The Priestly Narrative: An Overview

In this section, I will offer a general summary of the biblical priestly narrative. In some ways, this story might sound familiar for those who have read the Bible or the Pentateuch before. While some readers might be tempted to skim through this summary assuming they know the contours of the story, it is worth taking a little more time here. This story is not the same as the compiled version; there are some fairly significant differences. I will very briefly highlight a few of these differences in the summary itself, and then spend more time comparing the biblical priestly narrative with the stories found in nonpriestly strands of the Pentateuch.

The biblical priestly narrative tells the story of the foundation of Israelite religious practice and, more specifically, its sacrificial cult. In many ways the main character of this story is neither human nor divine but is rather a structure referred to in the story as a *mishkan*, which I have translated here as Dwelling Place. This structure is designed to be a physical place for the Israelite god Yahweh to live on earth, quite literally in the middle of the Israelite encampment.[24] But perhaps it's best to back up a bit and trace the arc of this story from its beginning, because if there's one thing that this story makes clear, it's that adaptability to changing conditions is vitally important.

This story starts, fittingly enough, in the beginning with the creation of the heavens, the earth, and everything in them over the course of six days. Creation in this story is not ex nihilo; some undifferentiated substance exists and seems to be covered by waters. God's creation is, in essence, an act of separation and classification, which sets the stage

---

[24] See figure 1 for an illustration of the Israelite camp.

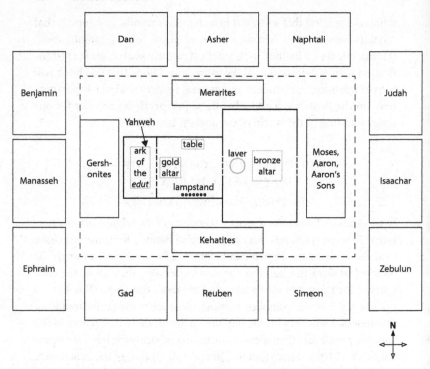

FIGURE 1. The arrangement of the priestly camp (according to Numbers 2–3).

for much of the rest of the story. As one of the final acts of creation, God simultaneously creates male and female human beings (notably not named Adam and Eve and not in a Garden of Eden). God tells these human beings that they should be vegetarians. This vegetarian ideal is quickly set aside, and the people and animals are found killing each other in relatively short order. God sees this and develops a plan to destroy the entirety of creation in order to start again. He allows only one family to survive because their patriarch, Noah, "walked with God." God then opens the windows in the sky and allows the flood-gates in the deep to burst open and waters cover the earth for 150 days (not forty), destroying everything except Noah, his family, and two of each type of animal that Noah has loaded onto an ark. When the flood ends, God establishes a covenant with Noah in which he promises never to destroy the earth by flood again. He also now permits the human consumption of animals for food, while prohibiting the human consumption of the animals' blood.

The story continues with the introduction of the figure of Abram (later Abraham) and his wife Sarai (later Sarah). Abraham, his son Isaac, his grandson Jacob (later renamed Israel), and his great-grandson Joseph occupy a relatively small part of the priestly story. While the stories of the patriarchs loom large in the compiled version of the Pentateuch,[25] in the priestly narrative, these characters receive scant attention and ultimately serve as a kind of bridge between two major sections of this story: creation and slavery in Egypt. When the story picks up in Egypt, the Israelites are found crying out to God for relief from the harsh labor they are enduring. God hears their cries and appoints a figure to lead them out of Egypt and to freedom: Moses. God introduces himself to Moses, and in the process reveals that his name is actually Yahweh. Yahweh tells Moses what he needs to do, and despite some objections on the part of Moses, he eventually agrees. What follows are a series of eight demonstrations of Yahweh's power to the Egyptians followed by a dramatic ninth: the death of all firstborn creatures (human and animal) across Egypt. (These events are often referred to as "plagues" but in the priestly narrative they are not presented in quite that way. They are meant to show the Egyptians the power of the Israelite God. It is also worth noting that in the priestly narrative there are only nine of these, and not the expected ten.) The deaths of the firstborn occur only after the Israelites are warned to mark their doors with blood and stay inside all night, which they do; therefore, their firstborn are spared. When morning arrives, the Israelites pack up and defiantly leave Egypt without asking Pharaoh's permission. When Pharaoh realizes this, he pursues them, but Yahweh tricks Pharaoh and his army and the latter end up drowned in the sea while the Israelites pass through safely on dry land.

Time in the priestly narrative is counted from this event. The departure from Egypt becomes the first day of the first month of the

[25] Throughout this introduction and edition, I am using the phrase "compiled Pentateuch" to refer to a version of the pentateuchal text that was created in the fifth through fourth centuries BCE by a series of editors compiling (or combining) the priestly, Deuteronomic, and nonpriestly stories into a single text.

first year. Three months later, the Israelites arrive at Mount Sinai and Yahweh gives Moses a series of detailed instructions—more of a blueprint—for building him a kind of mobile sanctuary tent, a Dwelling Place. Notably, these detailed instructions are not laws, and there is nothing resembling the Ten Commandments in them. Moses passes these instructions on to the Israelites, and they enthusiastically respond with an abundance of gifts of precious metals and expensive fabrics for this structure. They then spend the next nine months building. Finally, on the first day of the first month of the second year, Moses finishes assembling the Dwelling Place and the people begin an eight-day process of ordaining five men to serve as priests for this sanctuary and of inaugurating Yahweh's sanctuary.

The story of these eight days takes up more than half the entire priestly narrative. In the course of telling of this ordination and inauguration, Yahweh introduces the concept of sacrifice, explaining in great detail how and when it should be done, and by whom. Up to this point in the priestly narrative, not a single sacrifice has been offered. It is only now that Yahweh is present in the midst of his people that sacrifice can commence. These eight days are also the part of the story that many people tend to skip over—they are filled with detailed descriptions of sacrifice and extensive laws about purity. But, as noted above, this is the heart of the priestly narrative! In many ways, these eight days (which are narrated in Exodus 40 through Numbers 8) provide the answer to the question of what the priestly narrative is all about—the creation of a physical place and a way of life that enables Yahweh to live among the Israelites. After the debacle that precipitated the flood and the subsequent destruction of nearly all creation, Yahweh realized that he needed to keep a closer watch on his creation. Choosing to live among them was his means of doing that in this story, and this part of the story explains how this is possible.

On the twentieth day of the second month of the second year, the Israelites, organized into twelve tribes according to the twelve sons of Jacob, pack up and leave Mount Sinai. They make their way to the edge of the Promised Land and Moses sends a group of men into the land to gather intelligence and bring back their impressions. When they return, all but two of the men complain and tell Moses that there is no way they can conquer this land, even though Yahweh has promised they will. This makes Yahweh angry, of course, and in response he inflicts a twofold punishment: the spies who naysaid the land will die immediately and the rest of the Israelite community will be condemned to wandering in the wilderness for forty years until the entire then-adult generation dies out. What follows this is a cycle of complaints, rebellions and divine responses over the course of these years of wandering in the wilderness. Near the end of these forty years, the Israelites arrive at Mount Hor and Moses, Aaron (then the high priest), and his son Eleazar ascend the mountain. Yahweh commands Moses to take Aaron's special high priestly clothing off and to give it to Eleazar, thus making him the new high priest. Aaron then dies, marking the end of a generation. In the aftermath of Aaron's death, one of the Israelite leaders is found bringing a Midianite woman back to his tent, which sets off Yahweh's anger and a subsequent plague among the people. Eleazar's son Phineas sees this and kills the man and woman, thus stopping the plague. Yahweh still seeks vengeance. In response to this infraction, he commands the Israelites to attack the Midianites, which they do.

Finally, from the steppes of Moab, the Israelites begin their final preparations before their entry into the promised land of Canaan. While there, two of the twelve tribes realize that the land around them is quite good and they ask to stay behind and settle this land rather than a part of Canaan. Moses agrees, but only on the condition that they help the rest of the Israelites conquer the land of Canaan first. The two tribes agree to this stipulation, and in the meantime, they build up a number of cities in the area so that they can leave their wives, children, and livestock behind in safety while they go to war. Following this, a few other issues around land inheritance are worked out among the community, including allowing the daughters of a man who died without a son to inherit his portion. When these details of inheritance are worked out, Yahweh tells Moses that he will not enter the land with the rest of the Israelites. At Yahweh's command, he ascends the mountain, sees the whole land of Canaan, and then dies.

This is where the priestly narrative ends, at least in the version that we can recover from the Pentateuch—with the death of Moses and the Israelites poised to enter Canaan. In this edition, I have also included an appendix of possible priestly materials in the book of Joshua. My reasons for this are explained in more detail below. But by way of summary here, in the possible priestly materials in Joshua, the Israelites enter the land of Canaan on the tenth day of the first month, presumably of the forty-second year, though this is not specified. Because of the timing, they celebrate the festival of Passover on the fourteenth of that month, and then proceed immediately afterwards to conquer Jericho. After Jericho, they conquer Ai, and then continue to move throughout the land of Canaan, conquering each city in succession while killing their inhabitants, just as Yahweh had commanded. After the entire land has been conquered, Yahweh tells Joshua that it is time to apportion the land by lots, which he does. The story ends with the Israelite tribes each in their allotted portions of land living in safety, and with all of Yahweh's commands having been fulfilled.

Including Possible Priestly Texts in Joshua

One of the more idiosyncratic elements of this edition and translation is the inclusion of an appendix of possible priestly materials from the book of Joshua. In nearly all modern models of thinking about a priestly source, the book of Joshua is not included. In part, this is because it stands outside of the five books of the Pentateuch. Scholars occasionally talk about a "Hexateuch" that includes the Pentateuch plus Joshua, but this is becoming less common, and rightly so. One of the important distinctions between the Pentateuch and the book of Joshua is the way these books were edited. When it comes to the Pentateuch, neodocumentarians have shown that we can identify four independent sources that have been combined into one story, largely without adding, deleting, rearranging, or significantly changing any of the four independent stories. This model falls apart when it comes to the book of Joshua. One cannot identify four distinct strands in the same way, as there are clearly contradictions, narrative inconsistencies, and even doublets in the book. It is clear that Joshua, like the Pentateuch, is a composite text, but it is also clear that the way in which its component parts were edited together is quite different. In short, when it comes to the book of Joshua, scholars (including neodocumentarians, though they often do not talk about Joshua) imagine a much more active role for the editors. These editors will combine preexisting materials but sometimes they will rewrite them or revise them to better fit their distinct ideological perspective. Sometimes these revisions are easy to identify—a verse or two added in the middle of a story that brings in a plot point from another text (like the reference to Rahab in Josh 6:22–23)—and other times they are harder to pin down because they are more thorough revisions or rewritings of a text. In short, one of the major issues facing any scholar who wants to identify "priestly" materials in the book of Joshua is that what is "priestly" in Joshua may not look quite like the pentateuchal priestly texts. They may contain what scholars have called a "Deuteronomistic" framing, named after the school of scribes many scholars think was responsible for creating the book of Joshua.

So why did I choose to include possible priestly materials from Joshua in this edition? The short answer to this question is because the priestly narrative almost certainly did not end with the death of Moses at the edge of the Promised Land.[26] From its very beginning, one of the major motifs in the priestly narrative is that of command and fulfillment. Without fail, if Yahweh issues a command, it is fulfilled. Sometimes that fulfillment is delayed by days, weeks, or even years, but it is invariably fulfilled. It is possible to make a chart of each command and its corresponding fulfillment (and I have!).

This is not some minor point; it goes right to the heart of what this story is about and how it attempts to communicate that. In the priestly narrative, Yahweh's word is potent, and it is imbued with world-creating power. This is demonstrated right from the very beginning of the story when Yahweh speaks the world into its finished form. This motif continues more subtly after the creation of human beings, who then become the agents that carry out those commands. But carry them out they do. Human beings, and later, specifically the Israelites, repeatedly and enthusiastically fulfill Yahweh's commands. When Yahweh commands them to bring materials to build his Dwelling Place, for example, they respond so enthusiastically that Moses is faced with more materials than he could possibly ever use. When the priestly narrative is cut off at the death of Moses, a significant problem is created: some of

[26] There is a significant amount of scholarly debate about where the priestly narrative may have originally ended. This debate is far too complex to summarize here, but it is worth noting that the concern for identifying the end of the story is always with the oldest stratum of the priestly narrative rather than the maximalist version I have reconstructed here. For an overview of the arguments about where the priestly narrative might end, see Jason M. H. Gaines, *The Poetic Priestly Source* (Minneapolis: Fortress Press, 2015), 282–83. For a discussion of the significance of identifying the end of the priestly source, see Christophe Nihan, *From Priestly Torah to Pentateuch: A Study in the Composition of the Book of Leviticus*, Forschungen zum Alten Testament (Tübingen: Mohr Siebeck, 2007), 31.

Yahweh's most central commands and promises are left unfulfilled. Notably, the most important of these is for the Israelites to conquer the land of Canaan and return to inhabit the land of their ancestors.[27] Moses's death leaves the Israelites at the edge of the Promised Land eternally poised to conquer it; Yahweh's promise that he will give them the land of Canaan remains unfulfilled. (For examples of this promise, see Gen 28:4, 35:12; Exod 12:25; Lev 14:34; Num 13:2; 20:12, among others.) This command is explicitly fulfilled in the book of Joshua, however, when the Israelites completely conquer the entire land of Canaan.

Within the book of Joshua, one of the major contradictions has to do with this issue of conquest. In some texts, it appears as though the entire land of Canaan has been conquered and is the Israelites' posession. But in other texts, there are indications that certain areas—most notably Jerusalem—were never conquered. According to the pentateuchal priestly source, the Israelites were commanded to conquer everything, and to leave no Canaanite settlement untouched. This corresponds nicely with the strand in Joshua that tells of the complete and utter conquest of the land. Similarly, there is a very particular ideology of warfare advanced in one priestly text that describes the war with the Midianites. The ideology in this text (Num 31), from details such as the marching order to the imposition of something called *herem* (loosely translated as a ban) on conquered cities, matches the details of specific battle stories in the book of Joshua. Finally, when we leave the Israelites at the end of Deuteronomy in the priestly narrative, they are in the steppes of Moab. But the priestly narrator repeatedly offers one extra detail every time their location is mentioned: that they are opposite Jericho. Jericho is mentioned by name only in priestly texts in the Pentateuch, and the narrator reminds the reader over and over again that the Israelites are just across the Jordan River from Jericho for the final scenes before Moses's death. Perhaps not surprisingly, the very first city conquered in the book of Joshua is Jericho and it is completely and utterly destroyed, entirely in line with priestly ideologies of warfare. This is one of the reasons that my account of priestly

[27] This promise is reiterated several times in the story, beginning with Yahweh's introduction of himself to Moses in Exodus 6:4. The clearest expression of Yahweh's command to conquer Canaan comes in the story of the Reubenites and Gadites in Numbers 32.

warfare in Joshua begins with the conquest of Jericho and ends with the complete conquest of Canaan described in Joshua 11:23. This is followed only by the apportionment of the land to the various tribes by lot, exactly as commanded by Yahweh in Numbers 26:55–56.

It is worth reiterating at this point that the texts I have included in this appendix are not meant to be understood as purely "priestly" texts in the same way as the texts I included in the main body of the translation. These texts have been edited, revised, and rewritten by the people who created the book of Joshua, and in some cases, this alters details of claims made in certain stories to bring them more into line with other nonpriestly sources or stories in Joshua. What I have included in this appendix is thus tentative but guided by the command-fulfillment pattern established in the pentateuchal priestly source. Where I have identified priestly texts in Joshua it is because they can be understood as a fulfillment of commands given by Yahweh somewhere in the pentateuchal priestly source. By no means do I intend to claim that these texts in their current forms are written by the same authors as the pentateuchal priestly texts, but rather that they reflect a particular storyline that is consistent with the priestly source and inconsistent with nonpriestly and Deuteronomic sources. What I have identified in Joshua may or may not reflect something approaching the end of the priestly source. At the very least, it can be said that by the end of the texts I've included in this appendix, all of the narrative threads have been tied up and all of Yahweh's commands have been fulfilled. The world looks just as Yahweh seems to have envisioned it in the aftermath of the flood in the priestly source: the Israelites have flourished; they are living on their own land; and Yahweh is living in an elaborate tent shrine in their midst.

How Is the Priestly Narrative Different from the Canonical Story?

There are dozens of small differences between the priestly narrative and what we find in the Pentateuch as a whole. These are signaled in the notes to the translation and edition. For now, it is useful to mention just a few of them to give a sample of some of the ways in which this story differs or makes use of particular motifs. For instance, the idea that God changes the names of some characters (Abram to Abraham, Sarai to Sarah, Jacob to Israel) appears almost entirely in the priestly narrative. (There is one nonpriestly text in Gen 33:22–30 in which "the man," typically understood as God, changes Jacob's name to Israel.) Similarly, references to the promised land as "Canaan" are unique to this story. In the priestly narrative, several familiar characters from the Pentateuch never appear, including both Miriam and Dinah. Similarly, in the priestly narrative Moses is presented as a singular figure—an anomaly in the larger systems created in the narrative. He is not a priest, but at times he offers sacrifices. He is not ordained or consecrated, yet he is allowed to repeatedly enter spaces that only consecrated individuals are allowed to enter. He alone is allowed to see Yahweh. Perhaps because of his unique status in the story, Moses also never marries, and he has no children. He is truly a one-of-a-kind, one-time prophet in the priestly narrative.

It is also worth pausing at this point to underscore the fact that I have been calling this text the "priestly narrative" throughout this introduction. In this section of the introduction, I will discuss five major ways in which this text differs from the compiled pentateuchal story, or even the stories presented in other strands of the Pentateuch. The point I am making here is a simple one: despite its differences, this is a story. In fact, the reason this story is so interesting is precisely because of these differences. My presentation of this text in this edition is itself an argument that we should not simply refer to this as a "priestly source" or understand it as an impoverished version of another story. It is a fully developed narrative that can—and must—be understood on its own terms. It has a distinct theology, worldview, and as I will discuss in a subsequent section, a distinct style of storytelling. There are five major differences between the priestly narrative and the compiled Pentateuch that shape the worldview of this narrative as a whole: (1) the idea that creation is fundamentally good, (2) the utilitarian approach to the patriarchal stories, (3) the centrality and visuality of the Sinai episode, (4) the focus of the wilderness complaints against the leaders, not Yahweh, and (5) the lack of conquest for the purpose of settlement outside the land of Canaan.

1. Creation Is Good.   In the story of the creation of the world in the priestly narrative, there is a kind of refrain at the end of each day of creation. The narrator tells us that God looked at what he created and declared that "it was good." This declaration is a small detail in the creation story itself, but it frames much of how humanity and creation more broadly is presented in the priestly narrative. In this story, male and female human beings are created simultaneously. There is no sense at all that there is any power differential between them or any discord at all. They are one part of God's creation, and while they are empowered to "rule over" the rest of creation (Gen 1:26), it is clear from God's speech that this rulership is meant to be benevolent and mutually beneficial.

From the beginning, human beings are imagined as living in a kind of harmonious existence with the land. There is no explicit struggle between humans and the land. Humans do not need to toil and labor to make the soil produce plants and leafy vegetables; these simply spring up. Animals do not attempt to trick or coerce human beings into poor behavior; no snakes offer promises of knowledge. Knowledge is never off-limits in the priestly narrative. It is also worth noting that according to this creation story, humans and animals alike should be herbivores. Yet the consumption of animals is never expressly prohibited; it is simply never considered a possibility.

When this vegetarian ideal falls apart several generations after creation, God elects to destroy the world in a flood and start again with a single family of his choosing. What is interesting about this part of the priestly story is that the blame for disorder is not placed solely on human beings. Instead, it is the earth as a whole that is described as corrupt. Blame cannot be placed only on sinful or disobedient humans, but is instead assigned to creation as a whole and is imagined as something that God did not foresee. Indeed, the priestly narrative very much entertains the possibility that God does not know everything; that he can create the world but not necessarily control everything within it. And in this story, we are presented with a God who accepts that reality and adapts to it. After washing the earth clean of the bloodshed, he begins again with Noah and with a new set of rules, permitting bloodshed while also limiting it in important ways. God in the priestly narrative learns and adapts to his creation, while continually presenting his outlook as optimistic: these people will follow the rules he lays out, so long as he lays them out clearly. And the people do! Throughout this story, humans are portrayed as enthusiastically following Yahweh's instructions. This differs quite significantly from the compiled pentateuchal story, which contains scene after scene of human beings struggling with each other, with the earth, and with God. In the priestly narrative, human beings and creation more broadly are almost uniformly good, and in the rare cases when they are not, human disobedience takes God almost entirely by surprise.

2. *The Patriarchal Stories.*   In the case of the compiled Pentateuch, the stories of the patriarchs—Abraham, Isaac, Jacob, and Joseph—loom large. There is family drama, adventure, rivalry, betrayal, and reconciliation, along with a significant, recurring motif of the younger sibling usurping the place of the older sibling. Somewhat unbelievably, almost none of this is present in the priestly narrative.

In fact, the patriarchal stories themselves are surprisingly sparse—enough so that it is worth offering a quick outline of what, exactly, the patriarchs do in the priestly narrative. We are introduced to Abram (later Abraham) in Genesis 12 when he leaves Haran with his wife and nephew (Lot). They all arrive in Canaan and realize that the land is not large enough to support them all. So Lot chooses to settle in the cities in the plain while Abram settles in Canaan. Sarai (later Sarah) has difficulty conceiving so she has her servant Hagar sleep with Abram to bear a son for her, which Hagar does. Thirteen years later, God visits Abram, makes a covenant with him, and changes his name to Abraham and Sarai's name to Sarah. In the process, he promises Abraham a son from Sarah, while also commanding him to circumcise all the males in his family. Abraham does this and Sarah bears a son shortly thereafter. Then we fast forward to Sarah's death and burial. Of Isaac, Sarah and Abraham's son, we are only told that he married Rebekah when he was forty and fathered twins. The story picks up with a short notice about Jacob's wealth, and is followed by a discussion of Esau's marriage to two Hittite women. Upset about this, Rebekah sends Jacob to her family to find a wife. He acquires two wives, Rachel and Leah, and fathers twelve sons with them. Later, God changes Jacob's name to Israel and promises him numerous descendants and an assembly of nations for those descendants. Esau, in turn chooses to settle in the hill country while Jacob stays in Canaan. (Note here the parallels to Abraham and Lot.) The story then picks up with Joseph, the son of Jacob, moving to Egypt where he marries into the family of Pharoah and acquires a good deal of power. When famine hits the land of Canaan, Joseph's family comes to him for help, which he readily grants, giving his family some of the best lands in Egypt to settle. Finally, Jacob dies in Egypt, and his sons bring his body to Canaan for burial before then returning to Egypt.

This is the entirety of the priestly patriarchal story. There are relatively few scenes, and those that do exist have very specific functions in the narrative. Whether it is establishing a covenant with Abraham through circumcision, ensuring the continuity of the family line through Jacob, or moving the entire family to Egypt via Joseph, all these stories act as a bridge to get the family of Jacob (Israel) into Egypt, where their story truly begins.

Egypt is where the sons of Israel become the Israelites, growing from a small family of seventy into a group so numerous that the "land was filled with them" (Exod 1:7) and the Egyptians in turn enslaved them— possibly from fear of their power. The priestly narrative is fundamentally concerned with telling the story of the Israelites, and particularly the relationship of the Israelites with their god Yahweh. The Israelites as a group only come into being in Egypt, and Yahweh is (re)introduced as their God only in Egypt. The main focus of the priestly narrative begins in Egypt, but the stories the narrative does choose to tell of the time before Egypt, sparse though they are, set the stage for much of what is to come.

Even though the patriarchal stories are sparse, there are several elements worth highlighting, particularly as they tie into the framing conceit of the priestly narrative that creation (and humanity) is "good." In the priestly narrative there is never any hint of sibling rivalry. The story of Cain and Abel is not a part of the priestly narrative. Isaac and Ishmael are never set at odds with each other. In fact, they join together to bury their father. Jacob never tricks Esau or takes his birthright; the two brothers get along harmoniously and again come together to bury Isaac. There is no hint of discord between Joseph and his brothers either. They do not sell him into slavery or attempt to kill him. Instead, we find Joseph making his own way to Egypt and using his success there to support his family. While it is true that in some cases one son is included in the direct line of the promise made to Abraham, this does not mean that the other son is ignored or cast aside. Isaac may inherit the promise given to Abraham in Genesis 17, but Ishmael's story is included as well, and we are told that the latter had twelve sons of his own who became leaders of their people near Egypt (Gen 25:12–18). Similarly, while Jacob inherits the promise from his father Isaac, Esau is not ignored. His story is told, too, and he has five sons of his own and his family grew too large for the land of Canaan to support, so he willingly moved to the hill country of Se'ir (Gen 36). Brothers are never at war with each other in the priestly narrative; they live harmoniously and part ways only when their families grow too large for the area they are currently living.

This family accord extends to the women of these families as well. In the compiled Pentateuch, we find stories of Sarah's jealousy of Hagar and of a rivalry between Jacob's two wives, Rachel and Leah. In the compiled Pentateuch, it is Sarah who demands that Hagar and her son be cast out into the wilderness. It is Leah who taunts Rachel with her fertility and Rachel who steals the mandrake plant from her sister. In the priestly narrative, Hagar and Ishmael are never expelled; it seems as though they continue to live alongside Abraham, Sarah, and Isaac until Sarah and, ultimately, Abraham's death. (Hagar's death is never narrated.) Similarly, there is no trace of animosity between Rachel and Leah, though it is worth noting that the account of Jacob's marriage to them is missing from the story. This is almost certainly because the nonpriestly story of Jacob's attempt to marry Rachel, of his being tricked into marrying Leah, and subsequently of his working another seven years to marry Rachel supplanted a formulaic notice of Jacob's fulfillment of his mother's command and his marriage to these sisters. At no point in the very limited priestly story of Jacob, Rachel, and Leah, is there any hint that the two sisters are at odds with each other. The closest we come to sibling rivalry or family discord in the priestly narrative is in Esau's choice to marry two Hittite women. This is a decision, we are told, that upsets his mother, Rebekah. This incident in many ways foreshadows a strong concern to prevent relationships with foreign women that appears in at least one important scene later in the priestly narrative, and thus it is less about family discord than a concern with the preservation of family lines.

3. *Sinai.*   Perhaps one of the most significant differences between the priestly narrative and the compiled story in the Pentateuch comes at Mount Sinai. In the compiled Pentateuch, Sinai is fundamentally a place for lawgiving. It's where the Israelites receive the Ten Commandments, and it's where they are given a series of laws governing their newly formed, newly freed society. The lawgiving event at Sinai is, in short, the creation of a polity. In the priestly narrative, Yahweh's revelation to Moses on Mount Sinai is not explicitly about polity, but rather about the creation of a place. Specifically, it is about the creation of a Dwelling Place for Yahweh to live in the midst of the Israelite com-

munity. The polity—that which forms the basis of social order in the priestly narrative—can only come after, only from this Dwelling Place. The Ten Commandments do not exist in the priestly narrative at Sinai; neither do any of the extensive laws found in the compiled version. What Moses gets from Yahweh on Mount Sinai is not law. It is a set of instructions that constitutes a kind of blueprint for Yahweh's Dwelling Place. It includes detailed measurements, discussion of materials, arrangement of furniture, and building techniques. It is not law.

It is also worth noting here that there is no indication that it takes Yahweh forty days and forty nights to reveal this blueprint to Moses. Indeed, it seems as though it took only one day. We are told in Exodus 24:16 that "the presence of Yahweh dwelled on Mount Sinai. The cloud covered it for six days, and on the seventh day, Yahweh summoned Moses into the midst of the cloud." Despite the fact that Yahweh's speech to Moses covers seven chapters in the priestly narrative (Exod 25–31), it appears as though it takes only a day for Yahweh to deliver. This makes sense, particularly because the pacing of the story at this point is what is known as a "scene":[28] the amount of time that elapses is identical to the amount of time it takes to speak the words in these six chapters. This can be easily accomplished in one day.

When Yahweh finishes speaking, he gives Moses something called the *edut*. It is far from clear what, exactly, the *edut* are imagined to be, but they are very clearly not tablets. When Moses descends from Sinai, he comes down with the *edut*. Perhaps contrary to the expectations of canonical readers, Moses is not met with a disobedient group of people. He does not destroy the *edut*. Instead, he is met with people who are afraid of him because his face is radiating a kind of light that they've never seen before—an aftereffect of his time in Yahweh's presence. There is no hint of disobedience among the people while Moses was on Sinai, no hint of them doubting him or questioning whether he will return. There was hardly time since he was only gone for part of a day. The golden calf episode has no home in the priestly narrative. The people have been patient and obedient. That obedience is further emphasized when Moses begins to relate the instructions Yahweh gave

[28] For a more detailed discussion of pacing in narrative, see Seymour Benjamin Chatman, *Story and Discourse: Narrative Structure in Fiction and Film* (Ithaca, NY: Cornell University Press, 1978), 68–78.

him for the people and the people respond enthusiastically and without reservation.

One of the final elements that is worth noting about Sinai in the priestly narrative is that it is a critical turning point in this story. In the compiled Pentateuch, there have been a number of instances when characters have built altars and offered sacrifices. One of the most famous of these is with Noah at the end of the flood story. Readers might be surprised to learn that this scene is not a part of the priestly narrative. In fact, there are absolutely no sacrifices in the priestly narrative prior to the construction of Yahweh's Dwelling Place at Mount Sinai. Sacrifice is imagined in the priestly narrative as something that can only occur in one place—at the Meeting Tent when Yahweh is dwelling in it. If this Meeting Tent does not exist, sacrifice cannot happen; and in fact, sacrifice does not need to happen. Sacrifice is understood in the priestly story as existing, in part, to facilitate the ongoing existence of this Dwelling Place. Similarly, categories like "pure" and "impure" (sometimes translated as "clean" and "unclean") have not been relevant in the priestly narrative to this point. In the priestly narrative, "pure" and "impure" are categories that exist for the sake of ritual practice; they define things that can and cannot be used, encountered, or consumed in proximity to the Dwelling Place. They should not be understood as having any kind of moral value. Something that is "impure" is not bad or sinful—remember, all creation is good. Those things that are "impure" are simply those things that cannot be a part of ritual practices in Yahweh's Dwelling Place. This is a fundamentally different understanding of sacrifice, purity, and impurity than what is presented in the nonpriestly stories in the Pentateuch.

4. Complaint in the Wilderness.   A major plot point in the compiled Pentateuch is continual complaints of the Israelites in the wilderness in the book of Numbers. These complaints begin almost immediately after they leave Sinai and continue for most of the book. The Israelites seemingly complain about anything and everything: food, water, leadership. Even the leaders themselves lodge complaints, with Moses grumbling against Yahweh in Numbers 11. While stories of complaint are part of the priestly narrative as well, they take on a slightly different focus. In the priestly narrative, the motif of complaint appears only after the Israelites are condemned to wander for forty years in the wilderness. This differs from the nonpriestly stories, where complaints arise even before this event. Complaint arises in the priestly narrative precisely at the point in the story when the expectations and future of the community change. Faced with this new reality, the Israelites start to worry about their survival, both individually and as a whole.

The complaint motif in the priestly narrative is confined to one extended episode made up of four different scenes. In the first scene (Exod 16), the Israelites complain to Moses and Aaron, charging that they will not have enough food to eat now that they must survive in the wilderness for forty years. Yahweh solves this problem by providing manna and quail for them to eat each day. In response to this, a subgroup of the Israelite community, Korah and his followers, rise up against Moses and Aaron and question their leadership. If Yahweh will answer their complaints directly and resolve the problem, what need do they have for these leaders? Yahweh responds decisively, sending Korah and his followers to a fiery death. When the Israelites see this, the community complains again, accusing Moses and Aaron of causing these deaths, and suggesting they will lead the rest of the Israelites to such an end. Yahweh responds a third time in anger with a plague, which Aaron quickly stops. Yahweh then organizes a demonstration to prove to the Israelites that his chosen leaders for the community are Aaron and Moses. Finally, the Israelites, accepting Moses and Aaron as their leaders, complain one last time about the lack of water in the wilderness. Moses gets angry and chastises the people for all their complaining, but still does as Yahweh tells him, and brings water forth from a rock for the community. Unfortunately (and perhaps exasperated with their uprisings), Moses seems to take credit himself for this solution to their problem, rather than giving credit where it is due—to Yahweh.

The complaints in the priestly narrative are notable in one specific way: they are all directed at the human leadership in the story—Moses and Aaron. The Israelites never lodge complaints against Yahweh himself, but rather question the authority of their leaders. Complaint, then, is not about the dissatisfaction of the Israelites with their god as it is in the compiled account, but with their distrust in Moses and Aaron's ability to lead them through the wilderness and to the Promised Land. This is one example of how Yahweh's generally optimistic perspective on the obedience and enthusiasm of the people for him is upheld. Almost nowhere in this story are the people to be found complaining against

Yahweh or leveling charges against him. The notable exception here is in the story of the spies, and the response is swift and devastating. Yahweh has faith in the Israelites just as the Israelites seem to have unwavering faith in Yahweh. Their leaders, on the other hand, are fair game for critique, and criticize them they do. In the end, however, once Yahweh affirms the leadership of Moses and Aaron in front of the Israelites, the people accept them as their leaders and subsequent complaints are directed at physical conditions the people face (like lack of water) rather than communal hierarchies.

5. *Wilderness Conquest (or Lack Thereof).*   During their forty years of wandering in the wilderness, the Israelites travel from place to place, occasionally engaging in battles, conquering existing cities, and establishing new ones. Whether it is the area of Hormah, the land of the Amorites, or the regions of Bashan, Yazer, or Gilead, the Israelites are constantly fighting battles and conquering land in the wilderness. The wilderness, it seems, is filled with settled areas that the Israelites pass through, peoples to converse with, and sometimes to conquer. This, of course, is the compiled pentateuchal story. When the priestly narrative is read on its own, a very different and unexpected picture emerges.

In the biblical priestly narrative, the wilderness is an uninhabited place. As the Israelites wander, they move from the wilderness of Sinai to the wilderness of Paran to the wilderness of Sin to Mount Hor to the steppes of Moab. In the course of their movements, there are almost no named cities at all.[29] The Israelites in the priestly narrative seem to be on their own in the wilderness, set apart from other peoples and settlements. If the Israelites do not encounter any settled areas, then they do not need to conquer any settled areas. And in fact, this is exactly how the story unfolds. All the tales of conquest in the wilderness period are part of the nonpriestly strands of the Pentateuch. The priestly narrative has no interest whatsoever in conquest for the sake of settlement out-

---

[29] There is the possible notable exception of a brief itinerary notice that has them passing Obot and the Hills of Abarim on their way to the Steppes of Moab. In both cases, these are unknown places somewhere near the wilderness to the east of Moab (Num 21:10–11). See Baruch A. Levine, ed., *Numbers 21–36: A New Translation with Introduction and Commentary,* Anchor Yale Bible 4B (New Haven, CT: Yale University Press, 2000), 90.

side the land of Canaan; it is laser-focused on the Promised Land in a way that the compiled Pentateuch is not.

There is only one battle scene in the priestly narrative in the wilderness period, and that is the story of the Midianite war. What is notable about this story is that the war is framed as Yahweh exacting revenge for the behavior of the Midianites. When the Israelite soldiers win the battle and kill or capture the Midianites, they bring them back to the rest of the Israelite community, which is camped in the steppes of Moab (Num 31:12). They destroyed all the Midianite cities and settlements, but they did not then take them as their own possession. This is quite different from the nonpriestly stories, where conquest leads to possession. Here, conquest is revenge on the people, and the land is left behind. There is only one scene in the priestly narrative where the possibility of settlement outside the land of Canaan is raised, and that is in the scene right after the Midianite war. In this scene, two of the tribes look around and realize that the land they are camped on is good land (Num 32). They ask Moses to allow them to settle there, rather than in Canaan. This is an important story in the priestly narrative for a number of reasons, most of which do not need to be discussed here. What is worth highlighting, though, is that in the priestly strand in this chapter, there is absolutely no indication that this land has been or currently is inhabited.[30] It is presented as an open place to be settled; no battle is necessary to gain control of it. Indeed, once their request is granted, they build up a number of cities for their wives, children, and livestock (Num 32:34–38).

There is an apparent throwaway line at the end of one of the stories of complaint, where the narrator says, "The Israelites ate the manna for forty years, until they entered a settled land; they ate the manna until they came to the border of the land of Canaan" (Exod 16:35). This type of statement is indicative of priestly style. On the surface it seems straightforward, perhaps even unimportant. But this verse underscores the idea that the Israelites do not encounter settled land until they reach Canaan. The manna does not cease to appear until they cross the border into the land of Canaan in the first verses I have identified as priestly in the book of Joshua (5:12). In the priestly narrative, the disappearance of the manna marks the appearance of settled land

---

[30] Num 32:3. The list of cities is almost certainly a later redactional insertion to harmonize the priestly story with the nonpriestly one.

and heralds the need for conquest. One of the more notable elements of the possible priestly materials I have identified in the book of Joshua is that they are replete with specific place names. From the sites of battles to the overwhelming number of named settlements that are used to describe the borders of each tribe's territory, the book of Joshua in many ways marks itself as the antithesis of the wilderness period.

More broadly speaking, the relative emptiness of the wilderness in the priestly narrative is also a reflection of this story's framing of polity during the wilderness period. As I suggested earlier in the discussion of the Sinai story, the priestly narrative is more concerned about establishing a place for Yahweh in the midst of the people (or more specifically, a Dwelling Place) than in creating a full-fledged polity. The wilderness period in this story reflects a time of transition and instability, when a community is waiting for one generation to die out and another to come of age so that it can truly establish itself in its land. Polity, to the extent that it exists in the priestly narrative in the wilderness period, exists only with respect to maintaining the presence of Yahweh among the Israelites. The Israelites encounter almost no other polities (with the notable exception of the Midianites) in the wilderness. They avoid settled areas and established peoples for nearly forty years. The establishment of the Israelites as a political entity in the priestly narrative requires them to have their own land and to have settled it. This is the goal that the community pushes toward throughout the wilderness period, and the goal that they achieve only in the book of Joshua.

The Literary Profile of the Priestly Narrative

In the ancient world as in the modern world, every author has their own style of storytelling. These individual styles are perhaps even more pronounced in a text such as the biblical priestly narrative for at least three reasons. First, as I discussed earlier, this text is not the product of one author, but many. This has the potential to multiply idiosyncrasies or peculiarities in the way that the story is told. Second, this story relies heavily on literary forms that are unfamiliar to many modern readers. Lists permeate the discourse of the biblical priestly narrative in the form of genealogies, laws, ritual instructions, and descriptions of land regions. Finally, there are certain expectations that modern readers tend to have of biblical narrative form. Sometimes these expectations are set by other biblical stories, at other times they are unconsciously imported from what readers know of modern literature. This is, in part, as I argued earlier, where the claim that the priestly narrative is "impoverished" originated. I have suggested throughout this introduction that we should not understand the biblical priestly narrative as impoverished, but instead attempt to encounter it in all of its peculiarities and assess it on its own terms. In this section, I will discuss the literary style of the priestly narrative and some of its peculiarities in storytelling as a way of introducing some of its distinctive literary profile while also touching on some of the major motifs in the story.[31] Finally, in a third subsection I will discuss a rare but repeated phenomenon of out-of-place texts in the priestly narrative.

Literary Style.   The literary style of the biblical priestly narrative is quite distinct. This is one of the elements that has made the identification of this source one of the most agreed-on conclusions in pentateuchal scholarship. The identification of the priestly narrative has often been done on the basis of its use of distinctive words or phrases. For example, the use of the phrase "community" (*'edah*) has long been seen as specific to this source. Entire word lists have been developed by multiple scholars, not only for the priestly source as a whole but for layers within it.[32] I prefer not to rely on word lists of this kind when it comes to identifying the biblical priestly narrative. They can be imprecise, and there is always the possibility that other authors chose to use the same word, even if they did so with less frequency. Instead, I prefer to look to the literary style more broadly, to the ways in which the story itself is constructed and its forms of discourse.

One of the most frequently identified elements of the priestly narrative is its affinity for lists of all kinds. At times these lists are easy to identify: lists of materials needed to construct the Dwelling Place, for example, or lists of animals that are pure or impure. At other times the list form is more subtle. The priestly creation story is itself a list of God's activities on each day for seven days. Its structure is clear, with a

---

[31] I am indebted to the extensive and excellent analysis of priestly style written by Meir Paran in Hebrew: Meir Paran, *Forms of the Priestly Style in the Pentateuch: Patterns, Linguistic Usages, Syntactic Structures* (Jerusalem: Magnes Press, 1989). A brief summary of his main points in English is available in on pages v–xvi.

[32] See, for example, Knohl, *Sanctuary of Silence*, 108–10.

coda at the end of each subsection of the list ("Then it was evening, then morning—the first day"). This list is more elevated in style than some of the others in this narrative, but it nevertheless participates in this form. Genealogies are also a central element of the priestly narrative, and they too are structured as lists. Indeed, right after creation is complete, the story continues with a genealogy that accounts for the first human beings up through the time of Noah. Lists not only serve as structuring devices for narrative scenes; they also provide a way for the story to move forward quickly. If we understand the events of creation as having taken place in a hypothetical year zero, the genealogical list found in Genesis 5 covers just over 1,500 years within the world of the story. In roughly the same number of verses that it takes to tell about God's creation of the world in seven days, the narrator fast-forwards the reader through 1,500 years to get to the time of Noah and makes use of a genealogical list to do so.

So why these lists? What is the priestly narrative's interest in list-making all about? It is impossible to pin down exactly what the authors of this text intended with their extensive use of the list form. What can be said is that in the ancient world, list-making was one form of scientific discourse.[33] This ties directly into one of the major motifs of the biblical priestly narrative: separation and categorization, which are themselves other elements of ancient scientific discourse. One of the primary sites of separation and categorization in the biblical priestly narrative is in its lists. Lists are a way of recording, sorting, ordering, and creating knowledge. They are a means of describing the world and an individual's perception of it.[34] It has been famously argued that biblical narrative is "fraught with background."[35] What Erich Auerbach meant by this statement is that biblical narrative tends to lack robust descriptions, and things like time or place are left vague and undefined in contrast to something like Homeric epic, which revels in such detail.

[33] Wolfram von Soden, "Leistung und Grenze sumerischer und babylonischer Wissenschaft," *Die Welt als Geschichte* 2 (1936). For a more recent summary of his arguments and an insightful analysis of the literary functions of list-making in biblical literature, see Jacqueline E. Vayntrub, "Tyre's Glory and Demise: Totalizing Description in Ezekiel 27," *Catholic Biblical Quarterly* 82 (2020): 214–36.

[34] Eva von Contzen, "The Limits of Narration: Lists and Literary History," *Style* 3 (2016): 245–47.

[35] Auerbach, "Odysseus' Scar," 11–12.

What I would suggest (and indeed have argued elsewhere) is that the biblical priestly narrative is not fraught with background in the same way as nonpriestly pentateuchal materials. That background is generated by its lists.[36] It is the lists that offer an anchoring in time by providing the chronological backbone to the story. It is the lists that create a sense of space and place through their detailed instructions for creating the Dwelling Place and its surroundings. It is the lists that offer unexpected moments of insight and describe relationships between various characters. In short, the lists in the biblical priestly narrative are the background. They are what we might understand as "description" in modern novels. In the biblical priestly narrative, lists are a literary form used to create, describe, categorize, and finally understand the world.

One of the effects of the priestly narrative's use of lists is that it results in a very uneven pacing across the story. Lists are used in the form of genealogies (in part) to speed up the story and advance hundreds or even thousands of years in the timeline very quickly. On the other hand, lists are also used in the form of ritual instructions or building instructions to slow down the pace of the storytelling. Pacing is a very important element in the priestly narrative, and paying attention to changes in the pace of storytelling can help to highlight particular moments of importance in the story.[37] Pace is essentially the relationship between two elements: the amount of time that elapses in the world of the story (known as "story time") and the amount of time it takes to narrate that event (often measured in the physical length of the text and known as "discourse time").[38] For example, in the case of the genealogical list from creation to Noah, just about 1,500 years pass in the world of the story but it is only thirty-two verses long and takes someone no more than ten minutes to read it. This is known as a "summary" or a "fast-forward," and it is used frequently in the priestly narrative. The lists of instructions or laws in the priestly narrative are almost all framed as direct speech. Direct speech in a story has a more

[36] Liane M. Feldman, *The Story of Sacrifice: Ritual and Narrative in the Priestly Source,* Forschungen zum Alten Testament (Tübingen: Mohr Siebeck, 2020), 10–18.

[37] See figure 2 for an overview of the pacing in the priestly narrative.

[38] For a discussion of pacing in biblical narrative specifically, see Jean Louis Ska, *"Our Fathers Have Told Us": Introduction to the Analysis of Hebrew Narratives* (Rome: Editrice Pontificio Istituto Biblico, 2000), 7–16.

natural pacing, and the time elapsed in the world of the story matches the discourse time. An example of this in the priestly narrative is Yahweh's speech to Moses on Mount Sinai. From Exodus 25 to 31, Yahweh gives a long and detailed speech with instructions for building his Dwelling Place. The time elapsed in the story is the same as the time elapsed in the discourse. Because the priestly narrative more often favors summary—though not always covering 1,500 years in just a few verses—these moments of direct speech effect a kind of marked slowing down of the pacing in the story. They draw attention to themselves and force the reader to listen to Yahweh's speech just as Moses listens to it in the story: in real time. This type of pacing—a constant push and pull between rushing forward and slowing down—is a distinctive characteristic of the biblical priestly narrative.

Finally, there is the issue of repetition. The biblical priestly narrative is filled with repetition, both on large and small scales. When thinking about repetition in the biblical narrative, the example that comes to mind for most people is the instructions for building Yahweh's Dwelling Place. Yahweh gives these instructions to Moses in Exodus 25–31. Moses then repeats them to the Israelites, and the Israelites carry out the instructions in Exodus 35–39. While this kind of repetition might seem unnecessary—why can't the narrator simply say that they did everything?—it actually serves as an illustration of one of the central motifs of the priestly narrative: command and fulfillment. Throughout this story, there is a strong emphasis on the absolute fulfillment of each and every one of Yahweh's commands. Not a single command is left unfulfilled. This large-scale repetition in Exodus 25–31 and 35–39 is perhaps the most visible example of this. Nearly every instruction given by Yahweh on Sinai is fulfilled by the Israelites. The instructions that are not fulfilled by the Israelites in Exodus 35–39 are explicitly fulfilled by Moses in either Exodus 40 or Leviticus 8–9. This repetition has a literary purpose: it helps to construct the characterization of the Israelites as enthusiastically and wholly obedient and it serves to further emphasize the world-creating power behind Yahweh's words.

Repetition exists on a smaller scale as well, sometimes within individual scenes in the story. One of the best examples of repetition within a single scene in the priestly narrative is found in the story of the Israelite leaders bringing gifts for the inauguration of Yahweh's

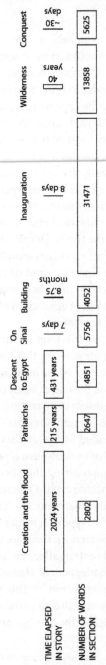

FIGURE 2. Plot pacing in the priestly narrative.

	Creation and the flood	Patriarchs	Descent to Egypt	On Sinai	Building	Inauguration	Wilderness	Conquest
TIME ELAPSED IN STORY	2024 years	215 years	431 years	7 days	8.75 months	8 days	40 years	~30 days
NUMBER OF WORDS IN SECTION	2802	2647	4851	5756	4052	31471	13858	5625

Dwelling Place found in Numbers 7. This chapter is a staggering eighty-nine verses long. What strikes most readers when they encounter this story is the incredible amount of repetition. In this text, each of the twelve tribes sends a leader to bring a series of gifts to the entrance of the Meeting Tent. One tribe appears at the entrance of the Meeting Tent each day for twelve days. Each leader brings exactly the same gifts. Each paragraph of this text is nearly identical; the only differences are the numbering of the day and the name of the leader and his tribe. Everything else is exactly the same. Some might call this passage a narrative failure because of this kind of repetition. It is anything but that. The authors of the priestly narrative have deployed repetition in this case for an important rhetorical end: to demonstrate the ideal of absolute equality between the tribes. Despite the fact that they are different sizes, the tribes are all equally responsible for and invested in maintaining Yahweh's Dwelling Place and serving Yahweh. No tribe is any less important than another; no tribe is any more important either. This chapter represents a kind of egalitarian ideal in this story, and it does so through the use of repetition.

Repetition also occurs on the level of individual verses or even clauses. There are many different forms that this type of repetition can take in the priestly narrative. One of the most frequent is represented by a short phrase that appears at the end of many of the fulfillment notices in this story. When they finish constructing the component of the Dwelling Place, for example, the narrator says: "The Israelites did everything that Yahweh commanded Moses, so they did" (Exod 39:32). The appearance of "so they did" or its equivalent is pervasive throughout the story as a kind of coda emphasizing the obedience of the Israelites. Other forms of repetition include explicit repetition in laws and instructions, particularly of the kind that termed a "circular inclusio" by one scholar. A circular inclusio is a type of sentence structure specific to the priestly narrative. In these sentences, there are typically two independent clauses. The first presents a straightforward instruction or command of some kind; the second independent clause repeats that command while also adding more information.[39] This phenomenon is easiest to identify in the Hebrew as it is tied to particular verbal patterns, but it is best explained in English by offering an example. Among the

---

[39] Paran, *Priestly Style*, viii. For a full discussion in Hebrew, see 47–97.

instructions for building the Dwelling Place, Yahweh commands the Israelites to build an incense altar: "Make an altar, a place for burning incense; make it of acacia wood" (Exod 30:1). The second independent clause here—"make it of acacia wood"—is somewhat repetitive. It would have been more succinct to say, "Make an altar of acacia wood, a place for burning incense." Yet, that is not typical priestly style. Instead, it is far more common to encounter something like we do in Exodus 30:1, where the main command is repeated with some specific detail added to the instruction. As far as possible, I have preserved these types of syntactical repetition in my translation of this story.

Storytelling Peculiarities.   The biblical priestly narrative contains a number of peculiarities in the way in which it tells its story. The most readily apparent element of priestly storytelling is its concern with chronology and timekeeping. Readers will notice a concern for marking the age of characters at significant moments in the story, headings marking the month, day, and sometimes year in which events occurred, and later in the story full-fledged calendars setting out specific dates for the Israelites to mark with offerings and festivals. This concern with marking time permeates the entirety of this story. It is worth noting that time is marked in two different ways in the priestly narrative. Sometimes time is absolute: "In the seventh month, on the first day of the month, you will have a complete cessation, a declared holy day marked with horn blasts" (Lev 23:23). This kind of statement assumes that there is a fixed calendar with established months. In other cases, time appears to be relative: "On the fifteenth day of the second month after their departure from Egypt" (Exod 16:1). In this case, time is marked as relative to the exodus from Egypt, as if counting the duration of the Israelites' freedom. These two forms of marking time weave their ways throughout this story and serve as a foundation for the unfolding of its plot.

Another distinctive element worth highlighting here is the relative absence of drama or narrative tension in the story. This is not to say that drama is entirely absent, but on the whole this story does not tend to leave its reader in a state of suspense wondering what is going to happen. This is in large part because the narrative nearly always unfolds precisely as Yahweh commands. There is a high level of regularity and order in this story. Things almost always go according to

Yahweh's plans, plans that Yahweh has laid out in great detail. As a result, the few moments in the story where things do not go according to plan are exceptional and highly marked. This particular feature of the story may seem to a modern reader as if it is simply poor storytelling, but the way that this plot unfolds communicates some of the central themes of the priestly narrative as a whole: the priestly world is ordered, sorted into recognizable categories, stable, predictable, and easily navigable so long as one follows Yahweh's commands.

Finally, modern readers may feel like the priestly narrative has a tendency to jump into a story immediately, without seemingly introducing its main characters or offering a back story for their lives. Noah gets more of an introduction than most just prior to the flood story: "This is the story of Noah; Noah walked with God.[10] Noah fathered three sons, Shem, Ham, and Yafet" (Gen 6:9–10). From here, the narrator moves immediately to describing how the earth has become corrupt. Questions are left unanswered here: what does it mean that Noah walked with God? What did he do? But at least we are given some background about Noah here. In the case of two other major characters, Abraham and Moses, we are given no background about their lives at all. In Genesis 12:4, we are told "Abram was seventy-five when he left Haran." From here, we are launched into the story of Abram/Abraham. Similarly in Exodus 6:2 we are told "God spoke to Moses and said to him, 'I am Yahweh.'"

It is not entirely true, of course, that these characters are not introduced at all. They are simply introduced differently than many modern readers expect them to be: the priestly narrative tends to introduce its main characters through genealogies, and their back story is communicated through listing their lineage. The genealogy in Genesis 5 points directly to Noah; the genealogy in Genesis 11 points to Abraham; the genealogy found later in Exodus 6 leads to Moses. The priestly narrative introduces its characters by tying their lineage to characters we have already encountered. When compared with the compiled Pentateuch, or even many other texts in the Hebrew Bible, it is still notable that the characters who seem to loom large in the priestly narrative appear almost entirely without fanfare or formal introduction. In most cases in the Hebrew Bible, major characters are given a backstory or formal introduction: Jacob's nonpriestly birth story features him wrestling with his brother Esau in the womb, foreshadowing the later struggles between the brothers (Gen 25); David is introduced as the overlooked youngest son of a shepherd (1 Sam 17); and Jeremiah is told that God knew him before he was even created in the womb, consecrated before he was born (Jer. 1). This is not the style of the priestly narrative. Major characters appear and act almost immediately; what backstory they are given comes through the identification of their family lineage.

Out-of-Place Stories.   The last issue that I want to address in this section on the literary context of the priestly narrative has to do with stories that are out of place. Or to be more precise, they appear in the independent priestly narrative at a different point than they do in the compiled Pentateuch. The most significant example of this phenomenon is in the story of Yahweh providing the Israelites with manna for their time in the wilderness. In the compiled version of the Pentateuch, this story is found in Exodus 16. At this point in the compiled story, the Israelites have just left Egypt and are on their way to Mount Sinai. The story in Exodus 16 is itself composite, made up of an intertwined priestly and nonpriestly story. Once separated from the nonpriestly story, there are a number of elements of the priestly version that are anachronistic at this point in the story. Most notably, it references the *edut,* something that is only introduced by Yahweh on Mount Sinai; it describes the Israelites as being "in front of Yahweh," which is a technical designation in the priestly narrative indicating that they are present at the entrance to the Meeting Tent, something that does not yet exist in the story; and finally it mentions the appearance of the presence of Yahweh, something that happens only at Mount Sinai and the Meeting Tent in this story.[40]

Yahweh can only give the manna to the Israelites once in the compiled Pentateuch. It is presented as a miraculous kind of food that sustains them throughout their time in the wilderness; such a sustained miracle cannot occur twice. In the nonpriestly story, the manna is given prior to Sinai, in part because in the nonpriestly story of the exodus from Egypt, the Israelites leave under the ruse that they are taking only a three-day journey to worship their god. This means that

[40] Joel S. Baden, "The Original Place of the Priestly Manna Story in Exodus 16," *Zeitschrift für die alttestamentliche Wissenschaft* 122 (2010): 496–99.

they could only carry enough provisions for three days and would be in immediate need of sustenance. In the priestly story of the exodus from Egypt, the Israelites leave openly and defiantly. They could have brought with them whatever provisions they wanted. The anachronisms in the priestly manna story suggest that this scene occurred after the establishment of the Meeting Tent and after the Israelites departed from Mount Sinai. In other words, this scene can only occur in the priestly story sometime in the book of Numbers, and most logically it occurs when the Israelites encounter an unexpected extension of their time in the wilderness after the episode with the spies.[41] Once they were faced with wandering for forty years in the wilderness, the Israelites raised their concern about starving to death, and Yahweh responded with the giving of manna. In this case, the redactors responsible for combining the priestly and nonpriestly stories together into the Pentateuch privileged the nonpriestly timeline and moved the priestly story of the giving of the manna from its place after the spies' rebellion to the period between the exodus and Sinai. In this edition, I have chosen to include the story of the manna in the location that I believe it originally occurred in the independent priestly narrative: after the episode of the spies in Numbers 13–14.

There are at least three other cases in the priestly narrative in which a redactor or redactors relocated elements of the independent priestly story in the process of combining them with nonpriestly materials. For the sake of space, I will not discuss these three cases in the same amount of detail here as I did with the story of the manna. But I will note that similar principles apply and a pattern can be identified among all of these. In every case, the priestly materials are relocated in order to conform to the timeline or narrative constraints presented in the nonpriestly stories. This happens with priestly itinerary notices in what is now Numbers 21 and 22, with reports of the birth of Jacob's children in what is now Genesis 35:22–26, and with a brief notice of Lot's rescue from the impending destruction of the cities of the plain in what is now Genesis 19:29. In all cases, these stories would have been found in a different place in the independent priestly narrative and would have been moved to accommodate the new chronology created in the combina-

---

[41] Ibid., 499–500. For a fuller argument of this point, see Joel S. Baden, "The Structure and Substance of Numbers 15," *Vetus Testamentum* 63 (2013): 351–67.

tion of priestly and nonpriestly elements in the Pentateuch. In this edition I have moved all three of these passages to what I think was their original location in the independent priestly narrative, and I have marked each instance with a footnote indicating that they appear to be "out of place" given the conventional numbering of chapters and verses.

HISTORICAL CONTEXT

Some of the most frequent questions I am asked about the biblical priestly narrative are historical in nature. Who wrote it? When? For whom was it written? Does it reflect actual ritual practices in the First Temple in Jerusalem? What about the Second Temple? The short answer to most of these questions is an unsatisfying one: we simply don't know. Historical questions surrounding the biblical priestly narrative are some of the most hotly argued issues among biblical scholars who work on this material.

My focus in this book is primarily on the literary shape and characteristics of the priestly source. Nevertheless, I do not want to ignore historical questions entirely. While I cannot offer definitive answers to the level of detail that might satisfy many readers, in this section I want to at least outline some of the possible historical contexts for the production of the priestly narrative.

Dating

The question of when the biblical priestly narrative was written is still debated by scholars. Some argue that the text was written during the reign of Hezekiah in the late eighth to early seventh century BCE,[42] while others argue that it originates centuries later during the Persian period (fifth–fourth centuries BCE).[43] To put it differently, there is a division between scholars about whether this text should be understood as a "First Temple" or a "Second Temple" period work.

The contours of these debates can be quite complex, but there are a few hard boundaries that constrain the possibilities. We know that a version of the compiled Pentateuch broadly resembling the one we

---

[42] Menahem Haran, "Behind the Scenes of History: Determining the Date of the Priestly Source," *Journal of Biblical Literature* 100 (1981): 321–33.

[43] Schmid, *The Old Testament: A Literary History*, 147–52.

have today existed in the third or second century BCE. This is because the Pentateuch was famously translated into Greek in a diaspora Jewish community in Egypt.[44] Therefore, most if not all of the priestly narrative must have been written prior to the third or second century BCE. It is more difficult to pinpoint the earliest possible date for this text, but no scholar has suggested a date prior to the late eighth century. This leaves us with a roughly 500-year period in which the biblical priestly narrative could have been written. It is worth recalling at this point that the biblical priestly narrative is itself a composite text that was likely written over the course of multiple centuries, though almost certainly not over the course of the entirety of this 500-year time frame.

Why is it so hard to date the composition of this text? The challenge of situating this story arises from the material it covers and the way it is told. Unlike materials found in the biblical book of Kings, for example, in the priestly narrative, there are no explicit references to known historical figures, and there no clear references to wars that can be corroborated by external evidence. There are no historical details that can be seized on to situate this text historically. Instead, the authors of the biblical priestly narrative maintain a strong conceit of timelessness and a retelling of the distant past throughout.

The priestly narrative constructs the past in a way that removes the Israelites from interactions with other political entities for the vast majority of the story. What entities they do interact with (the Egyptians, for example) are set far enough in the past that they predate the invention of biblical Hebrew, the language this story is written in.[45] The biblical priestly narrative is self-consciously set primarily in the wilderness period. It eschews any simplistic transposition into a setting within the borders of ancient Israel and Judah until the book of Joshua, and because the priestly materials in Joshua are so heavily edited by other later authors, materials in that book cannot be used to determine dating.

[44] This translation project is described in a second-century BCE text known as the *Letter of Aristeas*. For a discussion of the *Letter of Aristeas* and the origins of the Septuagint, including an overview of the theories about why the Pentateuch was translated in the first place, see Benjamin G. Wright III, "The Letter of Aristeas and the Question of Septuagint Origins Redux," *Journal of Ancient Judaism* 2 (2011): 303–25.

[45] The first evidence of narrative prose written in biblical Hebrew can be dated to the ninth century BCE. For a discussion of this and its relationship to biblical literature, see Seth L. Sanders, *The Invention of Hebrew* (Urbana: University of Illinois Press, 2009), esp. 159–66.

It is worth at least briefly summarizing the arguments on both sides of this debate, even if in the end a definitive conclusion remains elusive. Scholars who have argued for a First Temple period date (around the eighth–seventh century BCE) for the biblical priestly narrative have done so on the basis of a few different kinds of evidence. Some have pointed to the relationship between the pentateuchal priestly materials and the book of Ezekiel, which was almost certainly written in the late sixth century BCE. They argue that Ezekiel knows and draws on the pentateuchal priestly materials and therefore must be earlier.[46] Others have turned to comparing the ritual materials in Leviticus to ritual materials from other areas in ancient Mesopotamia, Anatolia, and the Levant.[47] Still others have looked to lexical and syntactic patterns in order to argue that the Hebrew of the biblical priestly narrative is what is known as "Standard Biblical Hebrew," which is commonly dated to the eighth– through sixth centuries BCE.[48] In my view, this linguistic approach to the dating of the biblical priestly narrative is the most compelling and well-supported argument for an earlier date for parts of this text. That being said, it is not without its difficulties, especially since the priestly narrative is a composite text and other parts of it seem to have been written in a later form of biblical Hebrew, dated to the late sixth–through fourth centuries BCE.

Scholars who have argued that this is a Persian period text have done so by linking historical events to the perceived theological

[46] Menahem Haran, "Ezekiel, P, and the Priestly School," *Vetus Testamentum* 58 (2008): 211–18.

[47] Moshe Weinfeld, "Social and Cultic Institutions in the Priestly Source Against Their Ancient Near Eastern Background," in *Proceedings of the Eighth World Congress of Jewish Studies—Bible Studies and Hebrew Language* (Jerusalem: World Union of Jewish Studies, 1984), 95–129.

[48] This line of argumentation originated with a series of studies by Avi Hurvitz in the 1980s: see Avi Hurvitz, *A Linguistic Study of the Relationship between the Priestly Source and the Book of Ezekiel* (Paris: Gabalda, 1982); Avi Hurvitz, "The Language of the Priestly Source and Its Historical Setting—The Case for an Early Date," in *Proceedings of the Eighth World Congress of Jewish Studies: Panel Sessions—Bible Studies and Hebrew Language*. This argument was advanced by Jacob Milgrom in the 1990s and early 2000s: see Jacob Milgrom, *Leviticus 1–16: A New Translation with Introduction and Commentary,* Anchor Bible 3 (New Haven, CT: Yale University Press, 1991), 3–13. Most recently, this line of argumentation has been picked up in Samuel Boyd, *Language Contact, Colonial Administration, and the Construction of Identity in Ancient Israel,* Harvard Semitic Monographs (Leiden: E. J. Brill, 2021), 229–303.

concerns of the priestly narrative. These scholars put a strong emphasis on the identification of elements of the priestly narrative that are
seen as reflecting the experience of exile and the construction of Israelite (or Jewish) identity in a diaspora setting. One example that is
often used in this case is that of circumcision.[49] The emphasis in the
biblical priestly narrative on the recovery of the land, the unhappiness
of the people wandering in the wilderness, and—above all—the focus
on the details of constructing a sanctuary points to a Persian period
origin for many scholars.[50] Taking the idea that the beginning of the
Persian period saw a return of Jews to the land and the building of
multiple temples (one in Jerusalem and one in Samaria), some of these
scholars see the detailed accounts of sanctuary-building in the priestly
narrative as scribal attempts to negotiate between multiple Jewish
communities.[51] The difficulty with these approaches is that they
assume there is a clear correlation between historical events and literary responses. As Benjamin Sommer has argued, "it is always possible
that an author at one period came up with ideas that turned out to be
peculiarly relevant at another period."[52] Indeed, questions of exile,
return, and sanctuary construction could be relevant at several points
in the history of ancient Israel, starting in the eighth century BCE.
Still, this Persian period date for the biblical priestly narrative remains
the predominant conclusion among scholars.

Identifying a precise date for the composition of this text is extraordinarily challenging, and it is my belief that this is in large part by
design. The way the biblical priestly narrative is constructed is meant to
complicate simple ideas of historicity. The project of the biblical priestly
narrative is the construction of what Mikhail Bakhtin has called epic

[49] Carr, *Formation of the Hebrew Bible*, 297.

[50] This line of argumentation is largely accepted among biblical scholars, and an
example of this can be found in Schmid, *The Old Testament: A Literary History*, 141–47.

[51] Christophe Nihan, "The Torah between Samaria and Judah: Shechem and Gerizim in Deuteronomy and Joshua," in *The Pentateuch as Torah: New Models for Understanding Its Promulgation and Acceptance*, ed. Gary N. Knoppers and Bernard M. Levinson (Winona Lake, IN: Eisenbrans, 2007), 187–224.

[52] Benjamin D. Sommer, "Dating Pentateuchal Texts and the Perils of Pseudo-
Historicism," in *The Pentateuch: International Perspectives on Current Research*, ed. Thomas B. Dozeman, Konrad Schmid, and Baruch J. Schwartz (Tübingen: Mohr Siebeck,
2011), 85.

time, which is "an 'absolute past,' a time of founding fathers and heroes, separated by the unbridgeable gap from the real time of the *present day* (the present day of the creators, the performers and audience of epic songs)."[53] While the biblical priestly narrative should not be understood as an epic like Homer, it does make use of epic time. It is meant to be a story about the origins of the Israelite cult—something that by design occurred long ago in the past. The biblical priestly narrative is constructed in such a way as to render the gap between its imagined historical context in the story and the real historical context of its composition unbridgeable. This has not, of course, stopped scholars from attempting to bridge that gap. The most likely scenario, given the evidence we have, seems to be that the earliest layers of the biblical priestly narrative were written sometime in the late seventh to early sixth centuries BCE in a form of Standard Biblical Hebrew. The text was then almost certainly supplemented, edited, and revised well into the Persian period (fifth to fourth centuries BCE). The story itself, however, resists this form of concrete historical dating at every turn. In my view, this is an important feature of the narrative, and it is worth keeping that in mind when attempting to pinpoint a date for its composition.

Authorship and Audience

Thankfully, the question of authorship is somewhat more straightforward than that of dating. It is a broad consensus among pentateuchal scholars that the scribes responsible for the composition of the biblical priestly narrative were almost certainly themselves priests. While the Meeting Tent in the biblical priestly narrative is itself a work of fiction, its architecture is quite similar to the descriptions of Solomon's Temple in the book of Kings, and conforms to what is known as a tripartite, or three-room, style of temple common in ancient Israel and the broader Levant. This suggests that those responsible for writing the biblical priestly narrative were familiar with the architecture of temples in and around ancient Israel, and this suggestion logically points to the involvement of priests. The high level of detail found in the ritual instructions and the concern with the establishment of the priesthood and the ongoing support of the sacrificial cult further support these

[53] M. M. Bakhtin, *The Dialogic Imagination: Four Essays,* trans. Caryl Emerson and Michael Holquist (Austin: University of Texas Press, 1981), 218.

conclusions. Questions have arisen about which groups of priests might have been responsible for this text and whether any sort of polemic against other priestly groups might be at play in this text, but these issues remain unsettled and are somewhat speculative at best.

Still debated, however, is the issue of the intended audience for the biblical priestly narrative, in part because it is largely tied to the question of when this text was composed. Broadly speaking, there are two possible audiences for this text: other priests, on the one hand, or the Israelite community more generally, on the other. To put it differently, the debate among scholars is whether the priestly narrative was meant to be an "internal" document circulated only among the priests, or whether it was meant to be a public-facing text.

Scholars who see it as an internal document tend to point to the high level of detail in the ritual instructions and assume that these are meant to be a kind of instruction manual for priests.[54] Most of these arguments assume that the ritual instructions in the priestly narrative are a clear reflection of historical ritual practice, and in some cases are actually forms of shorthand notes for the performance of these rituals. Menahem Haran and Israel Knohl both go so far as to imagine that chapters 1–16 from Leviticus were originally sixteen different scrolls stored by priests in the Temple and used for reference when needed.[55]

Other scholars—myself included—have argued that the intended audience for the biblical priestly narrative was the Israelite community more broadly. We think that it was meant to be an outward-facing document.[56] From beginning to end, after all, this story is concerned with convincing nonpriests of the importance of the cult, and this makes most sense if we think of its aim as convincing its implied audience—ancient Israelites/Jews themselves—of the importance of the participation of the ordinary people in that cult.[57] If so, this also helps to explain the importance of its written form, as more than just the record of what could be passed down orally among priests. In my view,

[54] Two prominent examples of this are Menahem Haran and Israel Knohl (Haran, "Behind the Scenes," 328–329; Knohl, *Sanctuary of Silence*, 223.)

[55] Haran, "Book Scrolls," 115; Knohl, *Sanctuary of Silence*, 68.

[56] James W. Watts, *Ritual and Rhetoric in Leviticus: From Sacrifice to Scripture* (Cambridge: Cambridge University Press, 2007); Feldman, *The Story of Sacrifice*.

[57] Feldman, *The Story of Sacrifice*, 195–200.

as noted above, the ritual instructions should not be understood as transparent reflections of historical practice. Instead, they are best understood as a literary composition that is an integral part of the priestly narrative as a whole. The ritual instructions in the priestly narrative are presented as Yahweh's direct speech to Moses. In the construction of this story, the implied audience is granted the same point of view as Moses; readers of the story "hear" Yahweh speak to Moses in real time, as it happens in the story. The characters in the story are not afforded this privilege; they must wait for Moses to come down the mountain or come out of the Meeting Tent and repeat the instructions to them. In the world of the story, the Israelites are not allowed into the Meeting Tent or up to Mount Sinai because of issues surrounding ritual impurity. But the biblical priestly narrative itself is self-consciously textual.[58] It recognizes its medium and creatively makes use of it. This story allows the implied audience direct access to Yahweh and permits that audience to "see" and enter into Yahweh's Dwelling Place. These are things that Israelites within the story world could never have done, but one need not be concerned with ritual purity when it comes to reading texts. The textual medium of the priestly narrative creates a way to open up the otherwise closed world of the sacrificial cult to all Israelites.

Whether the implied audience consisted of ancient Israelites in the First Temple period or ancient Jews in the Persian period also remains an open question. For the form of the biblical priestly narrative that I have presented here—a text in its fullest possible form with

[58] In making the case for a nonpriestly audience of the priestly narrative, the most important question is one of ancient literacy beyond priests. Literacy in the ancient world was not nearly as widespread as it is today. Indeed, it was likely confined to an elite class of scribes, many of whom would have also been priests. That being said, "reading" in antiquity should be understood as an act of hearing. Throughout the Hebrew Bible, as well as early Jewish and Christian texts, there are repeated descriptions of texts being read aloud to audiences. (The book of Ezra is a prime example of this phenomenon.) This practice allows for the possibility of a nonelite, nonpriestly audience for this narrative. For a more detailed discussion of the relationship between textuality and oral performance in ancient Israel, see William M. Schniedewind, *How the Bible Became a Book* (Cambridge: Cambridge University Press, 2004), esp. 165–94; David M. Carr, *Writing on the Tablet of the Heart: Origins of Scripture and Literature* (Oxford: Oxford University Press, 2005).

all identifiable supplements and revisions included—it seems most likely that the intended audience would have been early to mid-Persian period Jews (ca. late sixth to late fifth century). It is possible that earlier versions of the priestly narrative had a different intended audience, but the form of the story presented here is its latest possible form prior to its inclusion with the nonpriestly and Deuteronomic materials into the Pentateuch, which likely happened in the late Persian period (ca. late fifth to late fourth centuries). Given that one of the main points of this story seems to be to motivate the participation and investment of ordinary people in the activities of the sacrificial cult, it seems most likely to me that this text was meant for Jews who were living in the land, and not those living in diaspora communities. Indeed, the importance of a Temple and its priesthood in this period of ancient Israel's history cannot be overstated, especially in light of the absence of a continued kingship. Priests in this period were granted more authority by virtue of Persian imperial treatment of them as leaders of their people. This may help to make sense of the more positive, optimistic outlook advanced by this story.[59]

[59] This positive, optimistic outlook present in the priestly narrative is markedly different from the doom-and-gloom approach of the Deuteronomistic texts. The world described in the biblical priestly narrative is one in which the Israelite cult and its priesthood are defined by their claim of radical continuity with the past. This stands in stark contrast to the focus on the rupture of social order found in many of the Deuteronomistic texts in the Hebrew Bible. This focus on priestly continuity is one that is picked up and developed in a number of later Hellenistic-era texts, such as the Aramaic Levi Document.

1

Creation and the Flood

^{Genesis 1:1}When God began to create the heavens and the earth, ² the earth was mire and murk with darkness over the deep waters and the breath of God hovering[1] over the surface of the waters. ³ God said, "Let there be light!" Then there was light. ⁴ God saw that the light was good, and God separated[2] the light from the darkness. ⁵ God called the light "day" and the darkness he[3] called "night." Then it was evening, then morning—the first day.[4]

^{1:6} God said, "Let there be a canopy[5] between the waters that it may separate water from water." ⁷ Then God made the canopy and it

[1] In this story, God's preference is nearly always to be at rest. In these first moments of creation, God can be imagined as resting, as lingering over the unformed mass beneath him, and as breath hovering in anticipation of his world-creating speech.

[2] The word used here in the Hebrew becomes increasingly important throughout the story, as the separation and classification of objects, people, and parts of the world becomes integral to the ongoing maintenance of the priestly world.

[3] In the Hebrew, male pronouns are consistently used to refer to God in this story.

[4] The first day (and all days) end when the sun comes up; biblical days run from sunrise to sunrise, not sunset to sunset as in later Jewish tradition.

[5] This word is typically translated as "firmament." I have avoided that translation here in part because it obscures the imagery: God is described as placing a physical object between the waters to separate them. I have chosen to render this as canopy in part because one of the most significant images in the priestly narrative as a whole is that of the Meeting Tent, and there are a number of literary connections between the creation of the Meeting Tent and the story of the creation of the world

separated between the waters below the canopy and the waters above the canopy. So it was. [8] God called the canopy "sky." Then it was evening, then morning—the second day.

[1:9] God said, "Let the waters below the sky be gathered to one place so that dry land may appear." So it was. [10] God called the dry land "earth" and the gathered waters he called "seas," and God saw that it was good. [11] God said, "Let the earth sprout plants: seeded plants, fruit trees of every kind with seeded fruits on the earth." So it was. [12] The earth produced plants: seeded plants of every kind and fruit trees with seeded fruits of every kind and God saw that it was good. [13] Then it was evening, then morning—the third day.

[1:14] God said, "Let there be lights in the canopy of sky to separate between the day and the night. Let them be signs for the appointed times, the days, and the years. [15] Let the lights in the canopy of the sky illuminate the earth." So it was. [16] God made two large lights, the larger light to govern the day and the smaller light to govern the night, along with the stars. [17] Then God set them in the canopy of sky to illuminate the earth, [18] to direct the day and the night and to separate between light and darkness, and God saw that it was good. [19] Then it was evening, then morning—the fourth day.

[1:20] God said, "Let the waters swarm with swarming creatures and let birds fly over the earth and across the canopy of sky." [21] Then God created the large sea monsters, living creatures of every kind that swarm in the waters, and winged birds of every kind, and God saw that it was good. [22] God blessed them: "Be fertile and multiply[6] and fill the waters of the seas; let the birds multiply on the land." [23] Then it was evening, then morning—the fifth day.

---

as a whole. Thinking about the divider between the heavens and the earth as a kind of canopy helps to foreshadow the tent that will create a living space for God later in the story.

[6] Despite its imperative form, this is not so much a command as an empowering statement, encouraging creation to continue until the earth and waters are filled (similarly, see Gen 27:29).

1:24 God said, "Let the earth produce living creatures of each kind: four-legged animals, creeping creatures, and wild land animals of every kind." So it was: 25 God created wild animals of every kind: four-legged animals of every kind, and ground-creeping creatures of every kind, and God saw that it was good. 26 Then God said, "Let us make human beings in our image,[7] looking like us, and let them rule over the fish of the sea, the birds of the sky, all land animals, and all creeping creatures on the earth." 27 God created human beings in his image; in the image of God he created them; male and female he created them. 28 Then God blessed them and God said to them, "Be fertile and multiply and fill the earth and subdue it; rule over the fish of the sea and the birds of the sky and every animal that moves on land." 29 God said, "I am giving you all the seeded plants on the earth and all fruit trees with seeded fruits to be your food. 30 For every land animal, every bird of the sky, and every living thing that creeps on the earth: all the green plants for food." So it was. 31 God saw all that he had made: it was very good. Then it was evening, then morning—the sixth day.

2:1 The heavens and the earth were finished with all their divisions.[8] 2 On the seventh day, God finished the work he was doing; on the seventh day he ceased from the all work he had done. 3 God blessed the seventh day and sanctified it because he ceased from all the labor[9] of creation he had done on it.

[7] This first person plural speech should not be understood as a "royal we" but rather as God speaking with his council of other divine and semidivine beings. This story does not presuppose a monotheistic worldview. Other gods exist and are even explicitly referred to at times. One of the key points of the story, however, is that the Israelites should only worship this particular god.

[8] The term used here is a typically military term denoting various groupings of soldiers. While this is often translated as "host," I am using "divisions" to preserve the military character of the language and to link this usage to the descriptions of the Israelites later in the story as traveling in their divisions.

[9] The use of the term "labor" here parallels the language used later in the story of the physical construction of Yahweh's Dwelling Place. Just as Yahweh has labored to build the earth for his creation, the Israelites will labor to build Yahweh's home for him.

²:⁴ This is the story of heaven and earth once they were created.[10]

⁵:¹ These are the descendants of Adam.[11] When God created humans, he made them in the image of God; ² male and female he created them, and he blessed them and called them human when they were created.[12]

⁵:³ When Adam was 130, he fathered a son in his likeness, looking like him, and he named him Seth. ⁴ After the birth of Seth, Adam lived 800 years and fathered sons and daughters. ⁵ Adam lived a total of 930 years and then he died.

⁵:⁶ When Seth was 105, he fathered Enosh. ⁷ After the birth of Enosh, Seth lived 807 years and fathered sons and daughters. ⁸ Seth lived a total of 912 years and then he died.

⁵:⁹ When Enosh was 90, he fathered Kenan. ¹⁰ After the birth of Kenan, Enosh lived 815 years and he fathered sons and daughters. ¹¹ Enosh lived a total of 905 years and then he died.

[10] There is a regular refrain in the priestly narrative that punctuates the first few parts of this story. In Hebrew it is *elleh toledot,* literally translated as "these are the descendants of . . ." This translation is not always apt in English, however. In this case, the heavens and the earth cannot have "generations" in the same way that human beings can. When this refrain is deployed in the story, it serves as a kind of funnel that begins with the broadest possible category (the whole world) and slowly serves to focus the attention on a particular family within a specific group of people. It moves from the world, to human beings, to the family of Abraham, and so on until the last use of this refrain, which points to the family of the Levites, and specifically the characters of Moses and Aaron.

[11] The proper name "Adam" is the same Hebrew word as "human being" used in the story of creation. This section plays on the double meaning of the word to pivot from the general creation of human beings to the tracing of a single family line.

[12] Genealogies appear quite frequently in the priestly narrative and serve a number of literary functions. First, they help to move the timeline of the story forward quickly. In this case, we move from the first week of creation to a specific individual (Noah) just over 1,500 years later. Second, the genealogies give a sense of continuity and connection between main characters in the story. Finally, these genealogies also frame large segments of the story. Note that this genealogy only follows one specific family line. Many other sons and daughters are born to these figures, but their names and stories are not followed.

^{5:12} When Kenan was 70, he fathered Mahalalel. ¹³ After the birth of Mehalalel, Kenan lived 840 years and he fathered sons and daughters. ¹⁴ Kenan lived a total of 910 years and then he died.

^{5:15} When Mehalalel was 65, he fathered Yared. ¹⁶ After the birth of Yared, Mehalalel lived 830 years and fathered sons and daughters. ¹⁷ Mehalalel lived a total of 895 years and then he died.

^{5:18} When Yared was 162, he fathered Enoch. ¹⁹ After the birth of Enoch, Yared lived 800 years and he fathered sons and daughters. ²⁰ Yared lived a total of 962 years and then he died.

^{5:21} When Enoch was 65, he fathered Methuselah. ²² After the birth of Methuselah, Enoch walked with God for 300 years and he fathered sons and daughters. ²³ Enoch lived a total of 365 years. ²⁴ Enoch walked with God, and then he no longer existed because God took him.

^{5:25} When Methuselah was 187, he fathered Lamech. ²⁶ After the birth of Lamech, Methuselah lived 782 years and fathered sons and daughters. ²⁷ Methuselah lived a total of 969 years and then he died.

^{5:28} When Lamech was 182, he fathered [Noah].[13] ³⁰ After the birth of Noah, Lamech lived 595 years and fathered sons and daughters. ³¹ Lamech lived a total of 777 years and then he died.

^{5:32} When Noah was 500, he fathered Shem, Ham, and Yafet.

^{6:9} This is the story of Noah; Noah walked with God. ¹⁰ Noah fathered three sons, Shem, Ham, and Yafet.[14] ¹¹ The earth became corrupt in front of God; the earth was filled with violence. ¹² When God saw the earth: it was corrupt, because all flesh had corrupted their assigned

[13] The compiled text here reads "a son" and is followed by an etymology of the name of Noah connecting it with a nonpriestly creation story. This verse is clearly redactional and is meant to harmonize the two stories. The formula in the priestly narrative's genealogy is well established, and so I have emended the text to follow that formula here.

[14] The repetition here is both typical priestly style and also possibly a catchphrase to link this genealogical portion of the story with the following tale of the flood.

roles on earth.[15] 13 God said to Noah, "I will bring an end to all flesh, as the earth has been filled with violence because of them; I am about to destroy them along with the earth. 14 Make for yourself an ark of *gofer* wood;[16] with reeds you will make the ark; cover it inside and out with pitch.[17] 15 This is how you will make it: the length of the ark, 300 cubits, its width 50 cubits, its height 30 cubits. 16 Make a roof for the ark and finish it a cubit higher; the entrance of the ark put on its side, and make lower, second, and third levels. 17 I am about to bring a flood of waters on the earth to destroy all flesh that has the breath of life[18] in it under the heavens; everything on earth will die, 18 and then I will establish my covenant with you. You will enter the ark, you and your sons and your wife and your sons' wives with you. 19 From every living thing, from all flesh, you will bring two of each into the ark to keep alive with you; they will be male and female—20 birds of every kind, land animals of every kind, and creeping land creatures of every kind; two of each kind will come to you in order to stay alive. 21 Now, take for yourself the provisions[19] that you will eat and store it because it will be provisions for you and for them." 22 Noah did everything that God commanded him. So he did.

7:6 Noah was 600 when the floodwaters came on the earth. 7 Noah, with his sons, his wife, and his sons' wives, entered the ark because of

[15] The problem God sees here is one of violence and bloodshed. The Hebrew verb in this verse is a homophone: *shaḥaṭ/shaḥat*. The verb used here means to corrupt or ruin, but the homophone means to slaughter, and indeed the root for slaughter is used much more frequently later in this story. Undoubtedly the use of this verb is meant to call to mind the more common verb for slaughter and to underscore the problem—both human beings and animals were supposed to eat only plants and vegetation. Clearly, they have not adhered to this ordering of creation and have begun to kill each other.

[16] The specific type of wood has not been identified.

[17] In the Hebrew, the word for "pitch" (*kofer*) rhymes with the word for the unknown type of wood (*gofer*).

[18] Contrast this use of breath with the previous use in Gen 1:3, when God's breath lingered in anticipation of creation. Here, the same God uses his breath to take away the breath and life of that creation.

[19] I am using the term "provisions" and not "food" here to make it clear that what Noah brings on the ark is meant to feed both his family and the animals. Indeed, here is it worth recalling that humans and animals are both meant to be vegetarians and that Noah's food cannot be the animals themselves.

the floodwaters. [11] In the 600th year of Noah's life, on the seventeenth day of the second month, on that very day all of the fountains of the deep[20] split apart, and the windows of the sky opened. [13] On that very day Noah, and Shem, Ham, and Yafet (Noah's sons), Noah's wife, and the three of his sons' wives entered the ark, [14] they and all the living creatures according to their kind, every kind of land animal, creeping creature on the earth, and bird, every winged animal. [15] They came to Noah, to the ark, two of all flesh with the breath of life in it. [16] The ones who entered were male and female of all flesh; they entered just as God had commanded.

[7:17] The waters multiplied[21] and they carried the ark, and it rose high above the earth. [18] The waters intensified and multiplied greatly on the earth and the ark drifted over the surface of the waters. [19] The waters intensified even more over the earth and all the high mountains beneath the sky were covered. [20] The waters rose fifteen cubits higher as the mountains were covered. [21] All flesh that moved on the earth died, from birds to land animals, wild animals, and everything that swarms over the earth, and all humans. [22] Everything that had the breath of life in its nostrils, everything that was on dry land, died.

[7:24] The waters rose over the earth for 150 days. [8:1] Then God remembered Noah[22] and all the living creatures and animals that were with him in the ark. God caused a wind[23] to move over the earth and the waters subsided. [2] He closed the fountains of the deep and the windows of the sky [3] and the waters decreased at the end of 150 days. [4] The ark came to rest on the mountains of Ararat on the seventeenth day of the seventh month. [5] The waters continued to diminish until the tenth month. On the first day of the tenth month, the tops of the mountains appeared. [6] Then Noah opened the window of the ark that he had

[20] This is the same deep that was covered in darkness at the beginning of creation.

[21] This is the same word used after the creation of animals and humans to encourage them to be fertile and increase their population.

[22] This is not meant to convey that God is forgetful in this story, but rather that he turns his attention to Noah and the ark at this point.

[23] The word for wind is the same word as breath, and the double meaning is almost certainly intentional here. God's breath was lingering and static before the act of creation, and it begins to move here in the act of restoration after destruction.

made ⁷ and he sent out a raven. It went back and forth until the waters dried up from the surface of the earth.

⁸:¹³ In the 601st year, on the first day of the first month, the waters began to dry up on the earth, ¹⁴ and on the seventeenth day of the second month, the earth was dry.

⁸:¹⁵ God spoke to Noah: ¹⁶ "Go out of the ark, you and your wife and your sons and your sons' wives with you. ¹⁷ Bring out every living thing of all flesh that is with you: birds, land animals, and everything that moves on the earth. Let them swarm on the earth and be fertile and multiply on the earth." ¹⁸ Noah, along with his sons and his wife and his sons' wives, went out. ¹⁹ Every animal, all the creeping creatures, every bird—everything that moves on the earth—came out of the ark according to their families.

⁹:¹ Then God blessed Noah and his sons and said to them, "Be fertile and multiply and fill the earth. ² Fear and the terror of you will come over every animal of the earth and over every bird of the sky, and over everything that moves along the ground, and over all the fish of the sea; they are hereby given into your hand. ³ Every moving thing that lives will be yours to eat; just like the green plants, I am giving everything to you. ⁴ However, you must not eat the flesh with its life—that is, its blood. ⁵ I will now avenge your blood—that is, your lives. From every animal, I will avenge it and from every human, each for another. I will avenge human life. ⁶ As for one who sheds human blood—because of that human his blood will be shed because God made humans in his image. ⁷ As for you, be fertile and multiply, swarm over the earth and multiply on it!"

⁹:⁸ God said to Noah and to his sons, ⁹ "I am establishing my covenant with you and with your descendants after you, ¹⁰ and with every living creature that is with you—birds, domestic animals, and every land animal—those who came out of the ark with you, every living creature on earth. ¹¹ I am establishing my covenant with you: never again will all flesh be cut off by the floodwaters, and never again will a flood destroy the earth."

⁹:¹² God said, "This is the sign of the covenant that I am making between me and you, and between every living creature with you for all time.

[13] I have set my bow in the clouds. It will be a sign of the covenant between me and the earth. [14] When I bring clouds over the earth and the bow appears in the clouds, [15] I will remember my covenant between me and you and every living creature, all flesh, and never again will the floodwaters destroy all flesh. [16] When the bow is in the clouds, I will see it and remember the perpetual covenant between God and all living beings, all flesh that is on the earth." [17] God said to Noah, "This is the sign of the covenant that I have established between me and all flesh on the earth."

[9:28] After the flood, Noah lived 350 years. [29] Noah lived for a total of 950 years and then he died.

[10:1] These are the descendants of Noah's sons, Shem, Ham, and Yafet.[24]

[10:2] The sons of Yafet: Gomer, Magog, Madai, Yavan, Tuval, Meshek, and Tiras. [3] The sons of Gomer: Ashkenaz, Ripath, and Togarmah. [4] The sons of Yavan: Elishah, Tarshish, Kittim, and Dodanim. [5] The coastal peoples extended from these, according to their lands, each with its language, their families and their nations.

[10:6] The sons of Ham: Kush, Mitzrayim, Put, and Canaan. [7] The sons of Kush: Seva, Havilah, Savtah, Ramah, and Savteka. The sons of Ramah: Sheva and Dedan. [20] These are the sons of Ham according to their families and languages, by their lands and nations.

[10:22] The sons of Shem: Eilam, Ashur, Arpakhshad, Lud, and Aram. [23] The sons of Aram: Utz, Hul, Geter, and Mash. [31] These are the sons of Shem according to their families and languages, by their lands and nations.

[10:32] These are the families of the sons of Noah, according to their generations, by their nations. From them the nations spread out across the earth after the flood.

[24] The function of this genealogy isn't temporal; it is geographical. This genealogy traces the descendants of Noah as they repopulate and fill the various parts of the earth: coastal lands (Yafet's line) and inland areas; Ham's line covering the western area; and Shem's line covering the central and eastern areas of the Mediterranean.

11:10 These are the descendants of Shem.[25] Shem was 100 when he fathered Arpakhshad, two years after the flood. 11 After the birth of Arpakhshad, Shem lived 500 years and fathered sons and daughters. 12 When Arpakhshad was 35 he fathered Shelah. 13 After the birth of Shelah, Arpakhshad lived 403 years and fathered sons and daughters. 14 When Shelah was 30, he fathered Ever. 15 After the birth of Ever, Shelah lived 403 years and fathered sons and daughters. 16 When Ever was 34, he fathered Peleg. 17 After the birth of Peleg, Ever lived 430 years and fathered sons and daughters. 18 When Peleg was 30, he fathered Re'u. 19 After the birth of Re'u, Peleg lived 209 years and fathered sons and daughters. 20 When Re'u was 32, he fathered Serug. 21 After the birth of Serug, Re'u lived 207 years and fathered sons and daughters. 22 When Serug was 30, he fathered Nahor. 23 After the birth of Nahor, Serug lived 200 years and fathered sons and daughters. 24 When Nahor was 29, he fathered Terah. 25 After the birth of Terah, Nahor lived 119 years and fathered sons and daughters. 26 When Terah was 70, he fathered Abram and Haran.

[25] This genealogy, following immediately on the heels of the last one, serves to propel the narrative forward in time and bridge the gap between Noah's sons and the patriarch Abraham. It also serves as an introduction to the character of Abraham by explaining his origins.

2

The Era of the Patriarchs

Genesis 11:27 These are the descendants of Terah. Terah fathered Abram and Haran; Haran fathered Lot. [28] Haran died before Terah, his father. [31] Terah took his son Abram and Lot, the son of Haran (his grandson), and his daughter-in-law Sarai, his son Abram's wife, and set out with them to go to the land of Canaan. They arrived at Haran[1] and settled there. [32] Terah lived a total of 205 years, and he died in Haran.

12:4 Abram was 75 when he left Haran. [5] Abram took his wife Sarai, his nephew Lot, and all their belongings and people they had acquired in Haran and set out for the land of Canaan. When they arrived in Canaan, 13:6 the land could not support them settling together; because their possessions were so numerous, they could not settle together. [12] Abram settled in the land of Canaan and Lot settled in the cities of the plain. 19:29 When God destroyed the cities of the plain, God remembered Abram.[2] He sent Lot away from the midst of the upheaval when he overthrew the cities where Lot had been living.[3]

[1] Despite the similar spelling in English, this Haran is spelled differently in Hebrew.

[2] While the original Hebrew text reads "Abraham" here, that is almost certainly because, in the canonical text, this passage comes after Abram's name is changed to Abraham in Genesis 17. In its original place here in the priestly story, the name almost certainly read "Abram."

[3] This is one of the passages that has been relocated in the compiled text from this point in the priestly narrative. The nonpriestly story of the destruction of the cities of

^{16:1} Now Sarai, Abram's wife, had not borne him children, but she had an Egyptian slave whose name was Hagar. ³ After Abram had lived in Canaan for ten years, Abram's wife Sarai took her Egyptian slave Hagar and gave her to her husband Abram as a wife. ¹⁵ Hagar bore Abram a son and Abram named the son that Hagar bore him Ishmael. ¹⁶ Abram was 86 when Hagar bore Ishmael.

^{17:1} When Abram was 99, Yahweh appeared to Abram and said to him, "I am El Shaddai. Walk before me and be uncorrupted.[4] ² I will make my covenant between you and me and I will cause you to multiply many times over." ³ Abram prostrated himself[5] and God spoke with him: ⁴ "As for me, this is my covenant with you, that you will be a father of a multitude of nations. ⁵ But you will never again be called Abram. Your name will be Abraham because I have made you the father of a multitude of nations.[6] ⁶ I will make you abundantly fertile and make nations of you; kings will descend from you! ⁷ I will establish my covenant between me and you, and your descendants after you, as a perpetual covenant, to be God for you and your descendants after you. ⁸ I will give the land where you are now living as migrants, the land of Canaan, to you and your descendants as a perpetual holding. I will be their God."

^{17:9} Then God said to Abraham, "As for you, you and your descendants throughout the generations must guard my covenant. ¹⁰ This is the covenant that you will guard, between me, you, and your descendants after you: all your males will be circumcised. ¹¹ You will circumcise the flesh of your foreskin; it will be a sign of the covenant between me and

---

the plain (i.e., Sodom and Gomorrah) is much more robust, and in the compiled Pentateuch this notice is found there. In the priestly narrative, the destruction of these cities is only a sidenote, and the reason for their destruction is never given.

[4] The word used here is the same one that is used to describe animals that are fit for sacrifice on the altar later in this story. While Yahweh's first attempt with humanity ended in the corruption of the world through violence, this attempt through a single family starts off with an explicit command to avoid corruption.

[5] Literally, the idiom used here is "he fell on his face," which is best understood as him prostrating himself on the ground before Yahweh.

[6] Abraham's name change is a wordplay in the Hebrew on the phrase "father of a multitude"—that is, *av hamon*.

you. [12] At eight days old, each of your males will be circumcised throughout your generations. In the case of a slave born in your household or one purchased from any foreigner who is not your descendant, [13] he too must be circumcised, whether born in your household or purchased. My covenant will be in your flesh as a perpetual covenant. [14] As for an uncircumcised male who does not circumcise the flesh of his foreskin, that person will be cut off from his people; he has broken my covenant."

[17:15] God said to Abraham, "As for Sarai, your wife—you will no longer call her Sarai, but her name will be Sarah. [16] I will bless her, and moreover, I will give you a son by her. I will bless her, and she will become nations; kings of peoples will come forth from her. [17] Abraham fell on his face[7] and laughed. He said to himself, "Can a son be born to a 100-year-old man? Can Sarah give birth at 90?"[8] [18] Abraham said to God, "Let Ishmael prosper before you!" [19] God said to Abraham, "Nevertheless, your wife Sarah will bear you a son, and you will name him Isaac.[9] I will establish my covenant with him as a perpetual covenant for his descendants.[10] [20] As for Ishmael, I have heard you. I will bless him and make him fertile. I will multiply him many times over. He will be the father of twelve princes; I will make him a great nation.[11] [21] But my covenant I will establish with Isaac, whom Sarah will bear to you at

[7] This is the same idiom as earlier in the chapter, but in this case the reverence implied by prostration seems to be lacking, given Abraham's simultaneous laughter at God's promise.

[8] Here is one of the first indications that lifespans are decreasing in the priestly narrative. If we look at the earlier genealogies, fathering children at this age was quite common.

[9] The name Isaac comes from the same Hebrew root as the verb "to laugh." God is making clear at this moment that he is aware of Abraham's reaction to his promise.

[10] This exchange between God and Abraham helps to define "covenant" in the priestly narrative. Covenant is not linked with prosperity in terms of progeny or land—Ishmael receives both those things despite the fact that only Isaac is a part of the covenant. The covenant is explicitly about the fact that Ishmael will have a different God, because this God will be the God of Isaac and his descendants.

[11] Compared to the promise to Abraham earlier in this chapter, it becomes clear that while Ishmael is also blessed by God, his blessing is lesser than Abraham's. Ishmael is to father princes to Abraham and Isaac's kings. He is to produce a single great nation, rather than Abraham's multitude of nations.

this time next year." ²² When he had finished speaking with him, God ascended from Abraham.[12]

¹⁷:²³ Abraham took his son Ishmael and all the homeborn, and purchased slaves, every male in Abraham's household, and he circumcised the flesh of their foreskins that very same day, just as God had instructed him. ²⁴ Abraham was 99 when he circumcised the flesh of his foreskin, ²⁵ and Ishmael was 13 when he circumcised the flesh of his foreskin. ²⁶ That very day Abraham and his son Ishmael were circumcised, ²⁷ and all the men of his household, homeborn and purchased slaves, were circumcised along with him.

²¹:² Sarah conceived and bore a son for Abraham in his old age, at the appointed time that God had told him. ³ Abraham named his son, the one Sarah bore him, Isaac. ⁴ Abraham circumcised his son Isaac at eight days, just as God had commanded him. ⁵ Abraham was 100 when his son Isaac was born to him.

²³:¹ Sarah's lifetime, the duration of Sarah's life, was 127 years. ² Sarah died in Kiryat Arba—that is, Hebron—in the land of Canaan. Abraham went to mourn for Sarah and to weep for her. ³ When Abraham arose from his dead, he spoke to the Hittites: ⁴ "I am a stranger and an immigrant among you.[13] Give me a permanent burial site among you so that I may bury my dead." ⁵ The Hittites answered Abraham, saying to him, ⁶ "Hear us, my lord. You are a great leader in our midst. In the best of our tombs, you can bury your dead; no one will withhold his tomb from you for burying your dead." ⁷ Abraham then bowed down to the people of the land, to the Hittites. ⁸ He said to them, "If you desire the burial of my dead, hear me and appeal for me to Ephron, son of Zohar, ⁹ so that he might give me the cave of Machpelah, which

[12] This verse provides a rare hint about where this story imagines God living at this stage. The use of the word "ascend" here strongly suggests that God is currently dwelling somewhere in the heavens.

[13] Before the birth of Isaac, God promised Abraham that he would inherit the land of Canaan. His self-description as a foreigner and an immigrant here is an indication that this land does not yet belong to him. The purchase of a burial plot is significant: burial sites remained in families for generations and established a long-term connection to a particular area.

he owns; it is at the edge of his field. Let him give it to me in your midst, for the full price, as a permanent burial site."

23:10 Now Ephron was there among the Hittites, so Ephron the Hittite answered Abraham within earshot of the Hittites, all who entered the gate of his city, 11 "No, my lord. Hear me! The field I am giving to you; the cave that is on it—I am giving it to you! In the presence of my people, I am giving it to you. Bury your dead!" 12 Abraham bowed down before the people of the land. 13 He said to Ephron within earshot of the people of the land, "If only you would hear me! I will give you the price of the field. Take it from me so that I may bury my dead there." 14 Ephron answered Abraham, 15 "My lord, hear me! A piece of land is 400 shekels of silver. Between you and me, what is that? Bury your dead!" 16 Abraham heard Ephron. Abraham paid Ephron the price that he quoted within earshot of the Hittites—400 shekels of silver, at the current rate. 17 With that, Ephron's field in Machpelah, near Mamre, and its cave, and every tree within its confines was established[14] 18 for Abraham as a purchase in the presence of the Hittites, all who entered the gate of his city.

23:19 After this, Abraham buried his wife Sarah in the cave in the field of Machpelah, near Mamre—that is, Hebron—in the land of Canaan. 20 The field and the cave and everything that was in it was established for Abraham as a permanent burial site from the Hittites.[15] 25:7 The length of Abraham's life was 175 years. 8 Abraham died at an advanced age as a content old man, and he was gathered to his people.[16] 9 His sons Isaac and Ishmael buried him in the cave of Machpelah in the

[14] The Hebrew verb used here—*qwm*—is the same verb used to describe God's establishment of a perpetual covenant with Abraham earlier in the story. In this context, it suggests the permanence of Abraham's ownership and the beginning of the fulfillment of God's promise of land.

[15] It is worth noting here that the establishment of this permanent burial site in Hebron might be prompted by the death of Sarah, but it is ultimately not for Sarah; it is for Abraham.

[16] The idiom "gathered to his people" in the priestly narrative is actually quite literal. The permanent burial site that Abraham purchases includes a cave, which would have served as a tomb for multiple generations of his family. When a family member died, they would have been placed in the cave with those who had predeceased them.

field of Ephron son of Zohar the Hittite, near Mamre, [10] the field that Abraham bought from the Hittites. There Abraham was buried with Sarah his wife. [11] After Abraham died, God blessed his son Isaac.

[25:12] These are the descendants of Ishmael, son of Abraham, whom Hagar, Sarah's Egyptian slave bore to Abraham. [13] These are the names of the sons of Ishmael, by their names and in order of their birth. The firstborn of Ishmael was Nevayot, then Kedar, Adbe'el, and Mivsam, [14] Mishma, Dumah, and Massa, [15] Hadad, and Tema, Yetur, Naphish, and Kedmah. [16] These, then, are the sons of Ishmael, and these are their names by their villages and by their camps; twelve leaders of their people. [17] Ishmael lived 137 years, and he died and was gathered to his people. [18] They settled from Havilah to Shur, which is near Egypt, along the way to Asshur. They settled down with all their people.

[25:19] These are the descendants of Isaac, son of Abraham; Abraham fathered Isaac. [20] Isaac was 40 when he married Rebekah, daughter of Betu'el the Aramean from Paddan Aram, sister of Lavan the Aramean. [Rebekah gave birth to twin sons. Isaac named his sons Esau and Jacob.][17] [26] Isaac was 60 when they were born.[18] [26:13] Now the man grew abundantly wealthy and [14] he had flocks of sheep, herds of cattle, and a large household, such that the Philistines envied him.[15] (The Philistines who had closed and filled the wells that the servants of his father had dug during the life of his father Abraham.) [18] Isaac again dug the wells that had been dug during the lifetime of his father Abraham, which the Philistines had closed up after Abraham's death. He called them by the same names that his father had given them.

[26:34] When Esau was 40, he married Judith daughter of Be'eri the Hittite, and Basemat daughter of Elon the Hittite. [35] These wives were a source of bitterness for Isaac and Rebekah. [27:46] Rebekah said to Isaac,

---

[17] The announcement of the births of Esau and Jacob is missing from the priestly narrative, most likely because the nonpriestly version of this story is quite detailed and dramatic. The priestly version, if it followed the pattern of other birth announcements, would have been terse and to the point, similar to what I have reconstructed here.

[18] Note that in the priestly narrative, there is no indication that there is any sense of rivalry or animosity between Esau and Jacob. The same goes for Isaac and Ishmael. The two sets of brothers appear to get along harmoniously in this story.

"I abhor my life because of the Hittite women. If Jacob marries a Hittite woman like these, from the women in this land, why should I even live?" [28:1] So Isaac summoned Jacob. He blessed him and commanded him: "You will not marry a Canaanite woman. [2] Go to Paddan Aram, to the house of Betu'el, your mother's father. You will pick a wife from there, from among the daughters of your uncle Lavan. [3] May El Shaddai bless you and cause you to be fertile and multiply, so that you will become an assembly of nations. [4] May he give you the blessing of Abraham, to you and to your descendants, to inherit the land where you are now living as migrants which God gave to Abraham." [5] Isaac sent Jacob, and he went to Paddan Aram, to Lavan son of Bethuel the Aramean (the brother of Rebekah, Jacob and Esau's mother). [6] When Esau saw that Isaac had blessed Jacob and sent him to Paddan Aram to find a wife there, blessing him and commanding him, "you will not marry a Canaanite woman," [7] and that Jacob obeyed his father and mother and went to Paddan Aram, [8] Esau understood that Canaanite women were bad in his father Isaac's opinion. [9] Esau went to Ishmael and, in addition to the wives he already had, he married Mahalat daughter of Ishmael son of Abraham, sister of Nevayot.

[When Jacob was 40 years old,[19] he married Rachel daughter of Lavan and Leah daughter of Lavan.][20]

[30:43] Now the man grew abundantly rich, and he owned flocks and large numbers of female and male slaves, along with camels and donkeys.[21]

---

[19] This age is purely conjecture, based on the age of Esau when he married and the fact that it appears as though little to no time has passed in the story since Esau's marriages.

[20] Like the announcement of Jacob and Esau's birth, the announcement of Jacob's marriage to Rachel and Leah is absent in the priestly narrative. Such an announcement was likely parallel to the one for Esau in 26:34. We do not, however, know how old Jacob was when he married Rachel and Leah.

[21] This parallels the similar announcement given by the narrator about Isaac earlier in the story. The phrasing here highlights the generational wealth that this family is accumulating.

35:22 Jacob had twelve sons.[22] 23 The sons of Leah: the firstborn of Jacob—Reuben, Simeon, Levi, Judah, Issachar, and Zevulun. 24 The sons of Rachel: Joseph and Benjamin. 25 The sons of Bilhah, Rachel's slave Dan and Naphtali. 26 The sons of Zilpah, Leah's slave Gad and Asher. These are the sons that Jacob fathered in Paddan Aram.

31:17 Jacob set his children and wives on camels, 18 and he led all his livestock and moveable goods that he had purchased in Paddan Aram, going to his father Isaac in the land of Canaan. 33:18 Jacob came to [Luz],[23] (which is in the land of Canaan) when he was coming from Paddan Aram and he settled in front of the city. 35:9 God appeared to Jacob and he blessed him.[24] 10 God said to him, "Your name is Jacob. You will no longer be called Jacob. Rather, Israel will be your name." So he named him Israel. 11 God said, "I am El Shaddai. Be fruitful and multiply. A nation—an assembly of nations—will come from you. Kings will come forth from your loins. 12 The land that I gave to Abraham and to Isaac—I will give it to you, and to your descendants after you I will give the land." 13 Then God ascended from the place where he was speaking with him.

35:15 Jacob named the place where God spoke with him Beit El.[25] 16 They left Beit El. When they were a distance from Ephrat, 19 Rachel died. She was buried there on the way to Ephrat—that is, Beit Lehem. 27 Jacob came to his father Isaac at Mamre—that is, Kiryat Arba, now Hebron—where Abraham and Isaac had been living. 28 Isaac was 180

[22] This is another passage that has been moved by a redactor in the compiled Pentateuch to align with the chronology of the nonpriestly story. It would have belonged here in an independent priestly narrative.

[23] In the compiled version of Genesis, Jacob camps at Shechem, not Luz. This is almost certainly a change made by the editors, who combined the priestly and nonpriestly accounts in order to harmonize their geographic claims.

[24] In the canonical Hebrew text, the phrase, "when he was coming from Paddan Aram," appears again here. I have omitted it from this edition because it is most likely a scribal error made when copying an independent priestly text; the scribe's eye saw the phrase on the line above and inadvertently copied it a second time at this point in the text (known as vertical dittography).

[25] This literally translates to "the house of God"; the idea that the place where human beings and God meet is called a house of God is a critical plot point.

[29] when he died, and he was gathered to his ancestors as a content old man. His sons Esau and Jacob buried him.

[36:1] These are the descendants of Esau—that is, Edom.

[36:2] Esau selected his wives from the women of Canaan, Adah the daughter of Eilon the Hittite, Oholibamah daughter of Anah daughter of Zibeon the Hivite, [3] and Basemat daughter of Ishmael, sister of Nevayot.[26] [4] Adah gave birth to Eliphaz for Esau, Basemat gave birth to Reu'el, [5] and Oholibamah gave birth to Ye'ush, Yalam, and Korah. These are the sons that were born to Esau in the land of Canaan.

[36:6] Then Esau took his wives, his sons and daughters, and all the people in his household, along with his flocks and herds and all the possessions he had acquired in the land of Canaan, and he left the land because of his brother Jacob. [7] Their possessions were too abundant to settle together, and the land where they were living as migrants was not able to sustain both of them with their livestock. [8] So Esau settled in the hill country of Se'ir. (Esau is Edom.)[27]

[36:9] These are the descendants of Esau, father of the Edomites, in the hill country of Se'ir. [10] These are the names of Esau's sons: Eliphaz son of Esau's wife Adah, and Reu'el son of Esau's wife Basemat. [11] The sons of Eliphaz[28] were Teman, Omar, Zepho, Gatam, and Kenaz. [12] Now Timnah was the mistress of Eliphaz (son of Esau) and she gave birth to Amalek for Eliphaz. These are the sons of Esau's wife Adah.

[26] Careful readers of these genealogies will recognize right away that the names of Esau's wives in this genealogy do not match the names given earlier in the story in chapters 26–28. It is possible that these two genealogies represent two different priestly traditions about Esau's lineage that agree as to the nationality of the women he married—two Canaanite women and then a daughter of Ishmael—but disagree as to their names.

[27] The parting of the brothers here is entirely amicable and parallels the parting of Abraham and Lot earlier in this story in chapter 13.

[28] By going to the third generation here—Esau's grandchildren born in Se'ir—the narrator creates a structure that parallels the genealogy of Ishmael in Gen 25. Both Ishmael and Esau are said to settle outside the land of Canaan (to the south near Egypt for Ishmael, and to the east over the Jordan for Esau) and they have twelve descendants from which their regions are populated and ruled.

^{36:13} These are the sons of Reu'el: Nahat, Zerah, Shammah, and Mizzah. These are the children of Esau's wife Basemat.

^{36:14} These were the sons of Esau's wife Oholibamah daughter of Anah daughter of Zibeon: she gave birth to Ye'ush, Yalam, and Korah for Esau.

3

The Descent to Egypt

^{Genesis 37:1} Meanwhile, Jacob settled in the land where his father lived, in the land of Canaan. ² These are the descendants of Jacob.

[Joseph descended to Egypt.][1]

^{41:45} Pharaoh renamed Joseph Zaphenat-Panea and he gave him Asenat daughter of Poti-Phera, priest of On, as a wife. In this way Joseph gained authority over the land of Egypt. ⁴⁶ Joseph was 30 when he began serving Pharaoh, king of Egypt.

^{41:54} Now there was a famine in all lands, but in Egypt there was bread. ^{46:6} So they gathered their cattle and their moveable possessions that they acquired in the land of Canaan, and Jacob and all his descendants went to Egypt. ⁷ His sons and grandsons, his daughters and granddaughters, all his descendants he brought with him to Egypt.

^{46:8} These are the names of the descendants of Israel who came to Egypt, Jacob and his descendants. The firstborn of Jacob was Reuben.

[1] The birth notices for all of Jacob's sons have been given already in chapter 31. There is certainly something missing here in the priestly narrative, likely notice of Joseph's decision to migrate to Egypt. In the nonpriestly story, this is famously the tale of his brothers selling him to passing traders. There is no such priestly story, and it appears as though Joseph goes to Egypt of his own accord.

⁹ The sons of Reuben were Enoch, Pallu, Hezron, and Karmi. ¹⁰ The sons of Simeon were Yemu'el, Yamin, Ohad, Yachin, Zohar, and Sha'ul son of a Canaanite woman. ¹¹ The sons of Levi were Gershon, Kahat, and Merari. ¹² The sons of Judah were Er, Onan, Shelah, Perez, and Zerah. The sons of Perez were Hezron and Hamul. ¹³ The sons of Issachar were Tolah, Puvah, Yov, and Shimron. ¹⁴ The sons of Zevulun were Sered, Elon, and Yahle'el. ¹⁵ These were the sons that Leah birthed for Jacob in Paddan Aram. His sons numbered 33 people.

⁴⁶:¹⁶ The sons of Gad were Zipheyon, Haggai, Shuni, Ezbon, Eri, Arodi, and Areli. ¹⁷ The sons of Asher were Yimnah, Yishvah, Yishvi, and Beriyah, and their sister Serah. The sons of Beriyah were Hever and Malki'el. ¹⁸ These are the children of Zilpah, whom Lavan gave to his daughter Leah; she birthed these children for Jacob, 16 people.

⁴⁶:¹⁹ The sons of Jacob's wife Rachel were Joseph and Benjamin. ²⁰ Born to Joseph in the land of Egypt, birthed by Asenat, daughter of Poti-Phera, priest of On, were Manasseh and Ephraim. ²¹ The sons of Benjamin were Bela, Becher, Ashbel, Gera, Na'aman, Ehi, Rosh, Muppim, Huppim, and Ard. ²² These are the sons of Rachel that were born to Jacob, all told 14 people.

⁴⁶:²³ The son of Dan was Hushim. ²⁴ The sons of Naphali were Yahze'el, Guni, Yezer, and Shillem. ²⁵ These were the sons of Bilhah, whom Lavan gave to his daughter Rachel; she birthed these children for Jacob, 7 people.

⁴⁶:²⁶ All Jacob's people who went to Egypt, those who came from his loins aside from his sons' wives, numbered 66, ²⁷ and Joseph's sons who were born in Egypt were 2 people. The total number of all of Jacob's household that came to Egypt was 70.

⁴⁷:⁵ Pharaoh said to Joseph, "Your father and your brothers have come to you. ⁶ The land of Egypt is before you; settle your father and your brothers in the best part of the land." ⁷ Joseph brought his father Jacob and presented him before Pharaoh, and Jacob blessed Pharaoh. ⁸ Pharaoh said to Jacob, "How many are the years of your life?" ⁹ Jacob replied to Pharaoh, "The years of my living as a migrant are 130. Few and bad

have the years of my life been, and they do not approach the lifetimes of my ancestors during their migrations." [10] Then Jacob blessed Pharaoh and departed from Pharaoh's presence. [11] Joseph settled his father and his brothers, and he gave them a holding in the land of Egypt, from among the best lands, the region of Ramses, just as Pharaoh had commanded. [27] Thus Israel lived in the land of Egypt, [in the region of Ramses]; they held land in it, and they were fertile and multiplied abundantly. [28] Jacob was in the land of Egypt for 17 years, so that Jacob's life came to 147 years.

[48:3] Jacob spoke to Joseph: "El Shaddai appeared to me at Luz in the land of Canaan and he blessed me. [4] He said to me, 'I will make you fertile. I will cause you to multiply, and I will make you an assembly of people. I will give this land to your descendants who come after you as a permanent holding.' [5] Now, your two sons who were born to you in the land of Egypt before I came to you, to Egypt, they are mine. Ephraim and Manasseh, just like Reuben and Simeon, will be mine. [6] But the children that you had after them will be yours. They will be recorded in the place of their brothers with respect to their inheritance. [7] For when I was coming from Paddan, Rachel died in the land of Canaan on the road when there was still some way to go to Ephrat. I buried her there on the way to Ephrat, which is now Beit Lehem." [20] Then he blessed them on that day, "by you, may Israel invoke a blessing: may God make you like Ephraim and Manasseh."

[49:1] Jacob summoned his sons [28] and he blessed them; each with his own blessing he blessed them. [29] Then he commanded them and said to them, "I am going to be gathered to my people. Bury me with my fathers in the cave that is in the field of Ephron the Hittite. [30] The cave that is in the field of Machpelah, which is near Mamre in the land of Canaan, the field which Abraham bought from Ephron the Hittite as a burial plot. [31] There they buried Abraham and his wife Sarah. There they buried Isaac and his wife Rebekah. And there I buried Leah— [32] the field and the cave in it, purchased from the Hittites." [33] When Jacob finished his instructions to his sons, he died and was gathered to his people. [50:12] His sons did everything that he had commanded. [13] His sons carried him to the land of Canaan and buried him in the cave in the field of Machpelah, near Mamre, which Abraham had bought as a burial site from Ephron the Hittite.[14] Joseph returned to Egypt with his brothers. [22] Joseph lived 110 years [26] and then Joseph died.

Exodus 1:1 These are the names of the Israelites who came to Egypt with Jacob (each man came with his household): [2] Reuben, Simeon, Levi, and Judah; [3] Issachar, Zebulun, and Benjamin; [4] Dan and Naphtali, Gad and Asher. [5] All Jacob's descendants amounted to 70 people; Joseph was already in Egypt.

1:7 The Israelites were fertile. They swarmed[2] and increased and became extraordinarily numerous, so much so that the land was filled with them. [13] The Egyptians ruthlessly enslaved the Israelites. [14] They made their lives bitter with hard labor using mortar and bricks, and with every kind of field labor. They ruthlessly imposed all their labors on them. [2:23] The Israelites were groaning under their labor and cried out; their pleas for relief rose to God from their enslavement. [24] God heard their cries and remembered his covenant with Abraham, Isaac, and Jacob.

2:25 God saw the Israelites and recognized them.[3] 6:2 God spoke to Moses and said to him, "I am Yahweh.[3] I appeared to Abraham, to Isaac, and to Jacob as 'El Shaddai,' but my name is Yahweh; I chose not to make it known to them. [4] I established my covenant with them in order to give them the land of Canaan, the land where they were living as migrants. [5] I have heard the groans of the Israelites who are now enslaved by the Egyptians, and I remembered my covenant.

[2] The word used here is rare in the Hebrew Bible and typically refers to swarms of insects or other animals physically covering the land. It is used several times in the beginning of the priestly narrative to describe animals spreading out over the land at the time of creation and after the flood. This is the only place where it is used to refer to humans, but the image this verb evokes is one of the Israelites increasing so rapidly that they spread out over the land of Egypt and almost entirely cover it.

[3] The phrasing in this verse mimics that found early on in the creation story when "God saw" the parts of the world that he created and deemed them good, and again when "God saw" the corruption of the earth prior to the flood. This phrase indicates a kind of divine perception that leads to or marks some change of state. Here, "God saw" the Israelites enslaved in Egypt, and so he begins the process of the exodus.

6:6 "Therefore, tell the Israelites, 'I am Yahweh. I will release you from the burdens imposed by the Egyptians and I will deliver you from their enslavement. I will redeem you with an outstretched arm and with great acts. 7 I will take you as my people, and I will become your God. You will know that I, Yahweh, am your God, the one who released you from the burdens of the Egyptians. 8 I will bring you to the land that I raised my hand[4] to give to Abraham, to Isaac, and to Jacob. I will give it to you as a possession. I am Yahweh.'"

6:9 When Moses told this to the Israelites, they did not listen to Moses because of their wearied spirits and due to their hard labor. 10 Yahweh said to Moses, 11 "Go! Tell Pharaoh, king of Egypt, that he must send the Israelites out of his land!" 12 But Moses replied to Yahweh, "Even the Israelites will not listen to me. How will Pharaoh ever listen to me? I am a clumsy speaker." 13 In response, Yahweh spoke to both Moses and Aaron and instructed them about the Israelites and about Pharaoh, king of Egypt, so that he would release the Israelites from the land of Egypt.

6:14 Now these were the heads of the Israelites' ancestral houses:

The sons of Reuben, Israel's firstborn, were Enoch and Pallu, Hetzron and Carmi. These are the Reubenite households.

6:15 The sons of Simeon were Yemu'el and Yamin, Ohad and Yakhin, and Tzohar, and Sha'ul, the son of a Canaanite woman. These are the Simeonite households.

6:16 These are the names of the sons of Levi by their generations: Gershon, Kehat, and Merari. (Levi lived 137 years.)

6:17 The sons of Gershon were Livni and Shimi, by their households.

---

[4] This idiom, "to raise one's hand," typically means to do so in the process of swearing an oath. In this case, the idiom can also be read literally as foreshadowing the raising and outstretching of hands that will happen in the various plagues to demonstrate Yahweh's power and control over the situation of the Israelites.

6:18 The sons of Kehat were Amram and Yitzhar, Hevron and Uzzi'el. (Kehat lived 133 years.)

6:19 The sons of Merari were Mahli and Mushi. These are the families of Levi by their generations.

6:20 Now, Amram married Yocheved, his father's sister, and she gave birth to Aaron and Moses.[5] (Amram lived for 137 years.)

6:21 The sons of Yitzhar were Korah and Nefeg and Zikhri.

6:22 The sons of Uzzi'el were Misha'el and Elzaphan and Sitri.

6:23 Now Aaron married Elisheva, daughter of Amminadav and sister of Nahshon, and she gave birth to Nadav, Avihu, Eleazar, and Ithamar.

6:24 The sons of Korah were Assir and Elkanah and Aviasaph.[6] These are the Korahite families. 6:25 Aaron's son Eleazar married one of the daughters of Puti'el, and she gave birth to Phineas.[7] These are the heads of the ancestral houses of the Levites by their generations.

6:26 This is the same Aaron and Moses to whom Yahweh said, "Bring out the Israelites from the land of Egypt in their divisions!"[8] 27 This is

[5] Nearly all the names from this point forward in the genealogy introduce characters who will make an appearance later in the priestly narrative. This section functions as a kind of priestly family tree, explaining how the various factions of the tribe of Levi are related to each other.

[6] In each case, the narrator here is concerned with providing the genealogical line for the firstborn son, so while Amram was the father of Aaron and Moses, because Aaron is older, his line is followed. Similarly, Korah is the eldest son of Yitzhar, and so his line is followed.

[7] This one line of the genealogy actually traces a younger son, in this case the third-born son. This is a moment of foreshadowing, as Aaron's eldest two sons die almost immediately after being made priests later in the story, and Eleazar becomes the oldest living son of Aaron.

[8] The word used in the Hebrew here is identical to the word in Gen 2:4 (there translated as "array") used to describe everything that had been created within the heavens and earth.

the same Aaron and Moses who spoke to Pharaoh, king of Egypt, so that he would release the Israelites from Egypt.[9]

6:28 When Yahweh spoke to Moses in the land of Egypt, 29 Yahweh said to Moses, "I am Yahweh. Tell Pharaoh, king of Egypt, everything that I command you." 30 Now Moses had responded to Yahweh, claiming, "I am a clumsy speaker! How will Pharaoh ever listen to me?" 7:1 So Yahweh replied to Moses, "Look, I will set you up in the role of a god to Pharaoh, and your brother Aaron will serve as your prophet. 2 You will tell him everything that I command you and then Aaron, your brother, can speak to Pharaoh so that he sends the Israelites out of his land. 3 However, I will make Pharaoh act stubbornly so that I can perform many signs and wonders in the land of Egypt. 4 When Pharaoh refuses to listen to you, I will set my hand against Egypt, and I will bring about the release of my divisions, my people, the Israelites, from the land of Egypt with great acts. 5 When I stretch out my hand over Egypt and bring forth the Israelites from their midst, then the Egyptians will know that I am Yahweh!"

7:6 Moses and Aaron did what Yahweh commanded them to do; so they did. 7 (Moses was 80 years old and Aaron was 83 years old when they spoke to Pharaoh.)

7:8 Yahweh said to Moses and Aaron, 9 "When Pharaoh says to you 'perform your wonder!' you should tell Aaron, 'Take your staff and throw it before Pharaoh!' It will become a crocodile."[10] 10 So Moses and Aaron came before Pharaoh and did just as Yahweh had commanded. Aaron threw his staff before Pharaoh and his servants, and it turned into a crocodile. 11 Then Pharaoh summoned his wise men and his sorcerers, and the Egyptian magicians performed the same feat with their magic.

[9] One of the major purposes of this genealogy in the middle of this story is to introduce the characters of Moses and Aaron. They seemingly come from nowhere otherwise, and this genealogy traces their roots for the reader. Abraham is introduced in a similar way earlier in the story.

[10] The exact meaning of the Hebrew *tannin* is unclear, but typically it is understood to mean something like snake or water-dwelling monster. Given the proximity to the River Nile (a location heavily populated with crocodiles), the most likely translation here is crocodile.

[12] Each man threw down his staff and they turned into crocodiles, but then Aaron's staff swallowed all their staffs. [13] Pharaoh became stubborn and would not listen to them, just as Yahweh had said.

7:19 So Yahweh said to Moses, "Say to Aaron, 'Stretch out your hand[11] over the waters of Egypt—their rivers, streams, and pools—over every bit of gathered water so that they become blood.' There will be blood throughout the entire land of Egypt, even in vessels and in stone!" [20] Moses and Aaron did as Yahweh commanded, [21] and there was blood throughout the entire land of Egypt. [22] Then the Egyptian magicians did the same thing with their magic, and Pharaoh became stubborn and did not listen to them, just as Yahweh had said.

8:1 Then Yahweh said to Moses, "Say to Aaron, 'Stretch out your hand over all the rivers and the streams and the pools, and make frogs come up over the land of Egypt.'" [2] Aaron stretched out his hand over the waters of Egypt and brought up frogs and they covered the land of Egypt. [3] But then the Egyptian magicians did the same with their magic and brought frogs up over the land of Egypt. [11] Pharaoh became stubborn and did not listen to them, just as Yahweh had said.[12]

8:12 Next Yahweh said to Moses, "Say to Aaron, 'Stretch out your hand and strike the dust of the land. It will turn into lice throughout the whole land of Egypt.'" [13] So they did: Aaron stretched out his hand and struck the dust of the land. It was all over the humans and the animals; all the land's dust became lice throughout the land of Egypt. [14] The Egyptian magicians tried to remove the lice with their magic, but they could not do it; the lice remained all over the humans and the

[11] In the compiled text, Moses is described as stretching out his hand with a staff at various points in this plague story. Moses does not have a staff in the priestly story; only Aaron does. In the nonpriestly story of the plagues, Moses does have a staff. A redactor most likely added a staff to some of these verses to harmonize the priestly materials with the nonpriestly ones. The harmonization is incomplete, however, because there is never any mention of a staff in Moses's hand in the fulfillment notices, only in Yahweh's commands.

[12] The Hebrew in this passage is not quite the same as elsewhere, a remnant of the two plague narratives being combined at this point. The English translation has been modified to match the standard priestly notice of Pharaoh's stubbornness.

animals. [15] The magicians said to Pharaoh, "This is the finger of God!" But Pharaoh became stubborn and would not listen to them, just as Yahweh had said.

9:8 Yahweh again spoke to Moses and to Aaron: "Take a handful of soot from the oven. Have Moses toss[13] it toward the sky in the sight of Pharaoh. [9] It will become dust over the entire land of Egypt. It will cause erupting boils on both humans and animals throughout the whole land of Egypt!" [10] So they took a handful of soot and stood before Pharaoh. Moses flung it toward the sky, and it caused erupting boils to appear on both humans and animals. [11] The magicians were not able to come near Moses because of the boils, since the boils were on the magicians along with all the other Egyptians. [12] But Yahweh caused Pharaoh to become stubborn and he would not listen to them, just as Yahweh had said to Moses.

9:22 Then Yahweh spoke to Moses: "Stretch out your hand toward the sky so that hail will come down over the whole land of Egypt, on humans and on animals, and on all the vegetation in the fields across the land of Egypt." [23] Moses stretched out his hand toward the sky [24] and there was hail and lightning in the midst of the hail. [25] The hail struck everything throughout the whole land of Egypt. The hail struck all the open spaces, humans, animals, and all the vegetation in the fields. It shattered all the trees in the fields. [31] The flax and the barley were struck down; the barley was fresh, and the flax was budding. [32] (The wheat and the rye were not struck because they are late to ripen.) [35] Yet still, Yahweh caused Pharaoh to become stubborn and he would not release the Israelites, just as Yahweh had said through Moses.[14]

10:12 Yahweh then said to Moses, "Stretch out your hand over the land of Egypt so that locusts come up over Egypt. They will eat all the

[13] The word used for "toss" here (zaraq) will become a technical term for one of the ways blood is manipulated in sacrificial procedures later in the story. Its use here is atypical and may hint at thematic connections between this scene and the sacrificial system that is established later in the story.

[14] This added clause "through Moses" at the end of this sentence is a reminder that Moses continues to serve as an intermediary between Yahweh and Aaron, passing along Yahweh's messages to Aaron so that Aaron may perform them publicly.

vegetation of the land that was not destroyed by the hail!" [13] So Moses stretched out his hand over the land of Egypt [14] and locusts came up over the whole land of Egypt. [15] They ate all the vegetation of the land and all the fruit-bearing trees that remained after the hail. There was nothing left, not a single bit of grass or tree or vegetation in any field throughout the whole land of Egypt. [20] But Yahweh again caused Pharaoh to become stubborn and he would not release the Israelites.

[10:21] Finally, Yahweh said to Moses, "Stretch out your hand toward the sky so that it becomes dark over the whole land of Egypt, a darkness so thick it can be felt!" [22] Moses stretched out his hand toward the sky and there was a thick darkness over the whole land of Egypt for three days. [23] People could not even see each other. They could not stand or move from their places for three days, but the Israelites had light in their dwellings. [27] Still, Yahweh caused Pharaoh to become stubborn and he would not agree to release them.

[11:9] At this point, Yahweh reminded Moses, "Pharaoh would not listen to you so that my wonders could be multiplied in the land of Egypt." [10] Even as Moses and Aaron performed all these wonders before Pharaoh, Yahweh continued to cause Pharaoh to grow stubborn so that he would not release the Israelites from his land.

[12:1] Now Yahweh said to Moses and to Aaron in the land of Egypt, [2] "This new moon is the beginning of months for you.[15] It will be your first month of the year. [3] Speak to the whole Israelite community:

'On the tenth day of this month, each of them should take a lamb for their immediate family, a lamb per household. [4] But if the household is too small for a lamb, they shall join with their nearest neighbor. The lamb should be divided up according to the number of people who will eat it. [5] Your lamb should be an unblemished year-old male lamb, and you may take it from either the sheep or the goats.

---

[15] This is the first time in the story that the idea of calendrical timekeeping is introduced. Timekeeping in the priestly narrative literally begins with the Israelites' escape from Egyptian slavery.

12:6 'You should guard it until the fourteenth day of this month. Then the entire community of Israelites should slaughter it at dusk. 7 They should take some of the blood and smear it on the two doorposts and on the lintel of the houses in which they will eat. 8 They should eat the meat of the lamb that evening; roasted in fire with unleavened bread and bitter herbs they should eat it.

12:9 'Do not eat it raw or even boiled in water, but only fire-roasted, with its head, legs, and innards.[16] 10 You should not allow any of it to be leftover in the morning, but if there are leftovers, they should be burned in a fire.

12:11 'This is how you should eat it: with your loins girded, your sandals on your feet, and your staff in your hand. You should eat it hurriedly. It is Yahweh's passover.

12:12 'I will pass through the land of Egypt on that night and I will strike down every firstborn in the land of Egypt, from human to animal. Against all the gods of Egypt I will perform great acts. I am Yahweh! 13 The blood will be your sign on the houses in which you are dwelling. I will see the blood and I will protect you when I strike the land of Egypt.

12:14 'This day will become a day of remembrance for you. You will celebrate it as a festival to Yahweh throughout your generations. You will celebrate it in perpetuity. 15 For seven days you will eat unleavened bread. On the first day you will remove leaven from your houses because whoever eats leavened bread, from the first day to the seventh, that person will be cut off from the Israelites. 16 On the first day and on the seventh day, there will be a proclaimed holy day for you. You shall not do any work on them except for what is required for everyone to eat—that alone may be prepared for you.

12:17 'You will mark the celebration of unleavened bread, for on this very day I brought your divisions out of the land of Egypt. You should mark this day throughout your generations in perpetuity. 18 In the first month,

[16] While the passover lamb is not technically a sacrifice, the terminology used here is similar to sacrificial terminology.

from the fourteenth day of the month at dusk until the twenty-first day of the month at dusk you should eat unleavened bread. [19] For seven days, no leaven should be found in your houses; indeed, anyone who eats a leavened thing, that person will be cut off from the Israelite community, whether they are a foreigner or native-born. [20] You should eat nothing leavened; in all your settlements you should eat unleavened bread.

[12:21] 'Now, go and take a lamb for your families and slaughter the passover. [22] Take a bunch of hyssop, dip it in the blood that is in the basin, and touch it to the lintel and the two doorposts. And as for you—no one is to go outside of their house until morning. [23] Yahweh will pass by to strike the Egyptians and he will see the blood on then lintel and two doorposts and Yahweh will protect the door. He will not permit the destruction to enter your homes to strike them.

[12:24] 'You will keep this as a perpetual law for you and your children. [25] When you enter the land that Yahweh will give to you, as he has promised, you shall keep this ritual. [26] When your children say to you, 'What is this ritual to you?' [27] you should say: 'It is Yahweh's passover sacrifice,[17] because he passed over the houses of the Israelites in Egypt when he struck the Egyptians, while he spared our houses.'"

[12:28] The Israelites went and did so; just as Yahweh commanded Moses and Aaron, so they did.

[12:37] Then the Israelites set out from Ramses to Succot. [40] Now, the Israelites had lived in Egypt for 430 years. [41] At the end of the 430 years, on that very day, all the divisions of the Israelites departed from the land of Egypt.

---

[17] It is worth noting that the specific term "sacrifice" (*zevakh*) appears for the first time here, in the context of laws about what the Israelites should do after they have inherited their land in Canaan.

[12:42] For Yahweh it was a night of watching to bring them out of the land of Egypt. This night was a night of watching for all the Israelites throughout their generations.[18]

[12:43] Yahweh said to Moses and to Aaron, "This is the regulation for the passover. No foreigner may eat it. [44] But any slave a man has purchased, you must first circumcise him and then he may eat it.[19] [45] No immigrant laborer[20] or hired laborer may eat it. [46] In one house it must be eaten; you cannot take any meat outside the house, and you may not break its bones. [47] The entire Israelite community will do this.

[12:48] If an immigrant who lives among you wants to offer a passover to Yahweh, all his men must be circumcised, and then he may approach to offer it; he is equal to a citizen of the land. But any who are uncircumcised cannot eat it. [49] There will be one law for the native-born and the immigrant who lives among you."

[12:50] All the Israelites did so; just as Yahweh commanded Moses and Aaron, so they did. [51] On that very day, Yahweh brought out the Israelites in their divisions from the land of Egypt.

[13:3] Moses said to the people, "Remember this day when you went out from Egypt, from slave quarters! Yahweh brought you out of this with great strength.

[18] This translation differs a bit from the compiled text, which almost certainly reflects a text critical corruption (an error introduced by a scribe into a version of the text during the process of copying); the second sentence should probably be read as *hu halayla hazeh leil shimmurim*, which is what I have translated here. The compiled *lyhwh* ("to Yahweh") is almost certainly a scribal mistake influenced by the first sentence in the verse.

[19] These instructions are still imagining future passover observances, once the Israelites are settled in the land of Canaan, as it is unlikely that slaves would have owned slaves. Even before the Israelites have escaped their own enslavement in Egypt, Yahweh envisions a situation in which they themselves might own slaves in Canaan.

[20] What seems to be imagined here is a seasonal immigrant worker—someone who is temporarily living with the Israelites, but is not explicitly a part of their community.

[13:3] "Leavened bread should not be eaten! [4] Today you depart, in the month of Aviv.[21] [5] When Yahweh has brought you into the land of the Canaanites, the Hittites, the Amorites, the Hivites, and the Jebusites, which he promised to your ancestors to give to you—a land flowing with milk and honey—you should practice this ritual in that month: [6] for seven days you will eat unleavened bread, and on the seventh day there will be a festival for Yahweh.[22] [7] Unleavened bread will be eaten for seven days. No leavened bread should be in your possession, and no leaven should be found within your borders. [8] On that day you will declare to your children, 'This is because of what Yahweh did for me when I went out from Egypt.' [9] This will be a sign for you on your hand and a reminder on your forehead that Yahweh brought you out of Egypt with great strength. [10] You will keep this law at its appointed time every year.

[13:11] "When Yahweh has brought you into the land of the Canaanites, as he promised to you and to your ancestors, and he has given it to you, [12] then you will transfer[23] every firstborn to Yahweh. Every firstborn male offspring of your cattle will be Yahweh's, [13] and every firstborn donkey you will redeem with a sheep.[24] If you do not redeem it, you must break its neck. And every firstborn among your sons you must redeem.

[13:14] "When your children eventually ask you 'What is this?' you should tell them 'with great strength Yahweh brought us out of Egypt, out of slave quarters. [15] When Pharaoh stubbornly refused to free us, Yahweh

[21] Aviv is a springtime month and was marked by the appearance of new grain crops. Baking this new grain into leavened bread would have been a reasonable expectation at this time of year, but Moses now tells the people that they should refrain from doing this. In the immediate story this is a practical concern: there is no time to bake bread before their departure.

[22] These instructions are concerned with marking the departure from Egypt itself. First Yahweh gave instructions for the lamb, and now he is giving instructions about the unleavened bread.

[23] Literally: pass over, from the same Hebrew root used to describe Yahweh's passover in the previous chapter.

[24] A donkey is not an acceptable sacrificial animal, and so the sheep must be substituted for it.

killed all the firstborn of the land of Egypt, from the human firstborn to the firstborn of the animals. Therefore, I sacrifice every male firstborn to Yahweh, but every firstborn of my sons I redeem. [16] It is a sign on your hand and a symbol on your forehead because with great might Yahweh brought us out of Egypt!'"

[13:20] Then the Israelites set out from Succot and set up camp in Eitam, at the edge of the wilderness.

[14:1] Yahweh spoke to Moses: [2] "Tell the Israelites to turn back and set up camp at Pi-Hahirot, between Migdal and the sea, in front of Ba'al Zafon. You should set up camp opposite it, next to the sea. [3] Pharaoh will say about the Israelites 'they are confused by the land! The wilderness has closed in on them!' [4] Then I will make Pharaoh become stubborn and he will pursue you so that I can have glory over Pharaoh and all his army, so that the Egyptians know that I am Yahweh!"

[14:7] The Israelites did so, [8] and Yahweh made Pharaoh, king of Egypt, become stubborn while the Israelites were defiantly departing. [9] The Egyptians pursued them and all Pharaoh's chariot horses and his horsemen and his army overtook them camping along the sea at Pi-Hahirot, in front of Ba'al Zafon.

[14:10] The Israelites cried out to Yahweh, [15] and Yahweh said to Moses, "Why do you cry out to me? Tell the Israelites to depart! [16] And as for you, stretch out your hand over the sea and split it so that the Israelites can go into the midst of the sea on dry land! [17] As for me, I am about to make the Egyptians even more stubborn so that they go after them, so that I can gain glory against Pharaoh and all his army, his chariots, and his horsemen, [18] so that the Egyptians know that I am Yahweh when I win glory over Pharaoh, his chariots, and his horsemen."

[14:21] So Moses stretched out his hand over the sea and split the waters. [22] The Israelites went into the midst of the sea on dry land and the waters were like walls on their right and on their left. [23] The Egyptians pursued and went after them—all the horses of Pharaoh, his chariots, and his horsemen—into the midst of the sea.

¹⁴:²⁶ Then Yahweh said to Moses, "Stretch out your hand over the sea so that the waters come down on the Egyptians, on their chariots and horsemen."

¹⁴:²⁷ Moses once again stretched out his hand over the sea, ²⁸ and the waters returned and covered the chariots and the horsemen and all of Pharaoh's army who were coming after them in the sea. ²⁹ But the Israelites walked on dry land in the midst of the sea, with the waters forming a wall for them on their right and on their left. ¹⁵:²² They traveled three days into the wilderness but they did not find water. ²⁷ Then they came to Elim, where there were twelve springs of water and seventy palm trees. They set up camp there beside the water.

4

At Mount Sinai

Exodus 16:1 They set out from Elim, and on the fifteenth day of the second month, after their departure from Egypt, the whole community of Israelites came to the wilderness of Sin, which is between Elim and Sinai. 17:1 From the wilderness of Sin, the entire Israelite community set out and traveled in stages according to Yahweh's command. 19:1 On the day of the third new moon after the Israelites' departure from Egypt, they entered the wilderness of Sinai 2 and they set up camp there.

24:15 A cloud covered the mountain, 16 and the presence of Yahweh dwelled on Mount Sinai. The cloud covered it for six days. On the seventh day, he summoned Moses into the midst of the cloud. 17 To the Israelites, the presence of Yahweh looked like a consuming fire on the top of the mountain. 18 Moses went into the midst of the cloud and ascended the mountain.

25:1 Then Yahweh spoke to Moses: 2 "Tell the Israelites to bring gifts for me. From each person who would freely offer, you should take my gifts. 3 These are the gifts that you should take from them: gold and silver and copper; 4 blue, purple, and earthy-red yarns, fine linen and goats' hair; 5 reddened rams' skins, dyed green-blue leather,[1] and

[1] The meaning of this Hebrew word (*tehashim*) is unclear, but on the basis of Akkadian and West Semitic cognates, it has been suggested that this material is likely similar to materials described in the construction of other tent-shrines and thus should

acacia wood; [6] lamp oil, spices for the anointing oil and for incense; [7] onyx stones and setting stones for the *ephod*[2] and for the breastplate.

[25:8] "They will make me a sanctuary so that I can dwell among them. [9] Just as I show you—the blueprint of the Dwelling Place and the blueprint of all its components—that is how you should make it.[3]

[25:10] "They will make an ark of acacia wood, 2.5 cubits long, 1.5 cubits wide, and 1.5 cubits tall.[4] [11] You will overlay it with pure gold, both inside and out you should overlay it. Make a gold border around it. [12] Cast 4 gold rings for it and fix them on its 4 feet, 2 rings on one side and 2 rings on the other side. [13] Make acacia wood bars and overlay them with gold. [14] Put the bars into the rings on the side of the ark to carry the ark with. [15] The poles should remain in the rings of the ark. They should not be removed from it. [16] Then put the *edut*[5] that I will give you into the ark.

---

be identified as a dyed leather with a green-blue color to it. Contextually, it is highly unlikely to be dolphin skins, which is how this is typically translated.

[2] This is a specialized garment worn by the high priest, perhaps to be understood as a kind of mantle or shoulder-piece garment.

[3] Yahweh is launching into a very lengthy speech in which he provides Moses with exceptionally detailed instructions for how to build each component of this new sanctuary. If we look past the repetitive, list-like nature of this section of the story, a vivid picture of the priestly sanctuary emerges and different zones of holiness are delineated through the use of different types of materials: gold for the holiest sections; silver for the intermediate holy sections; and bronze for the outer courtyard areas. The use of fabrics, too, mimics this pattern. This section of the story conveys a good deal about the personality and aesthetic preferences of Yahweh.

[4] The lengthy description of the Dwelling Place and its furniture that follow take the form of a list, a genre that evoked scientific and mathematical thinking in the ancient world. In order to draw attention to some of these lists' mathematical and architectural qualities, I have used numerals for the various measurements described rather than spell them out as is the more common practice in translations.

[5] The exact translation of this word is hard to pin down. It is some kind of memorial object, but there is no indication that it should be understood as having writing of any kind on it, or that it is similar to the tablets discussed in the nonpriestly Sinai stories. For a more substantive discussion of my rationale for leaving this term untranslated, see the to the translator's note in this volume.

[25:17] "Make a pure gold cover, 2.5 cubits long by 1.5 cubits wide. [18] Make 2 gold *keruvim*[6]—make them hammered—at the two ends of the cover. [19] Make one *keruv* at one end and the other *keruv* at the other end. Make the *keruvim* of one piece with the cover on its two ends. [20] The *keruvim* should have wings spread upward, covering the cover with their wings. They should face one another, with the faces of the *keruvim* toward the cover. [21] Then you will put the cover on the top of the ark after you put the *edut* that I will give you in the ark. [22] There I will meet with you, and I will tell you—from above the cover, between the two *keruvim* that are on the ark of the *edut*—everything that I am instructing you concerning the Israelites.

[25:23] "Make an acacia wood table, 2 cubits long, 1 cubit wide, and 1.5 cubits tall. [24] Overlay it with pure gold and make a gold border around it. [25] Make for it a handsbreadth-sized rim around it and make a gold border around the rim. [26] Make for it 4 gold rings and put the rings on the 4 corners of its 4 legs. [27] The rings should be next to the rim in order to house the bars to carry the table. [28] Make the acacia wood bars and overlay them with gold. With these, the table will be carried. [29] Make its bowls, ladles, jars, and libation jugs; make them of pure gold. [30] You will set the display bread on the table to be before me regularly.

[25:31] "Make a pure gold lampstand; of hammered work you should make the lampstand: its base, and its stalk, its cups, its bulbs, and its petals should be made of one piece. [32] Six branches should come out from its side; 3 branches from one side of the lampstand and 3 branches from the other side of the lampstand. [33] Three almond blossom-shaped cups on one branch with a bulb and a petal, and on the next branch 3 almond blossom-shaped cups with a bulb and a petal. And so on for the 6 branches that come out from the lampstand. [34] On the lampstand, 4 almond blossom-shaped bowls, each with its bulb and its petals. [35] A bulb under a pair of branches, of one piece with it; a bulb

[6] Unlike the *edut*, we know quite well what the *keruvim* are—they are fearsome-looking animal statues, typically containing the parts of more than one type of animal. I have chosen to leave the term untranslated here because in modern English, the term "cherub" or "cherubim" (how this is typically translated) has largely become identified with artistic portrayals of chubby infants with wings.

under a pair of branches, of one piece with it; and a bulb under a pair of branches, of one piece with it—for all 6 branches coming out of the lampstand. [36] Their bulbs and their branches should be of one piece with it, all made of a single piece of hammered pure gold. [37] Make its 7 lamps (mount the lamps to shine on the front side), [38] its tongs and its firepans of pure gold. [39] It should be made, along with all these vessels, with a talent of pure gold. [40] Look—make them according to their blueprints that are being shown to you on the mountain.

[26:1] "As for the Dwelling Place itself, make it out of 10 curtains; of fine twisted linen, blue, purple, and earthy-red yarn, with an embroidered *keruvim* pattern you should make them. [2] The length of each curtain: 28 cubits, the width: 4 cubits for each curtain; the same measurements for all the curtains. [3] Five of the curtains will be connected to each other, and the other 5 curtains connected to each other. [4] Make loops of blue on the edge of one curtain at the end of a set. Do the same on the edge of the curtain at the end of the other set. [5] Fifty loops you will make on one curtain, and 50 loops you will make on the end of the second set of curtains, one opposite the other. [6] Make 50 gold clasps and join the curtains to each other with the clasps so that there is a single Dwelling Place.

[26:7] "Make goat hair curtains for the tent around the Dwelling Place. Make 11 curtains. [8] The length of one curtain: 30 cubits; width: 4 cubits for each curtain; the same measurements for all 11 curtains. [9] Connect 5 of the curtains by themselves, and then 6 curtains by themselves. Fold over the sixth curtain at the entrance to the tent. [10] Make 50 loops on the edge of one curtain, at the end of one set, and 50 loops on the edge of the end of the other curtain set. [11] Make 50 copper clasps and bring the clasps into the loops. Connect the tent so that it is one piece. [12] As for the overlapping remainder of the curtains of the tent, the half-curtain excess should hang down over the back of the Dwelling Place. [13] The excess cubit on each end of the tent should overlap the sides of the Dwelling Place on both sides to cover it. [14] Make a covering for the tent out of tanned rams' skins, and a covering of dyed green-blue leather over that.

[26:15] "Make the boards for the Dwelling Place out of acacia wood, upright. [16] A board is 10 cubits long, and the width of one board is

1.5 cubits. [17] There should be 2 tenons on each board to join the boards together. Make all the Dwelling Place boards in this way. [18] Make the boards for the Dwelling Place: 20 boards for the south side, [19] and make 40 silver receptacles[7] under the 20 boards, 2 receptacles under one board for its two tenons, and two receptacles under the next board for its two tenons. [20] For the second wall of the Dwelling Place, on the north side: 20 boards. [21] And 40 silver receptacles, 2 receptacles under the first board, and 2 receptacles under the next board. [22] For the back of the Dwelling Place, to the west, make 6 boards. [23] Make 2 boards for the corners of the Dwelling Place in the back. [24] They should be twins along the bottom, but together they should be undivided[8] at the top, to the first ring. This is for both of them; they will become the 2 corners. [25] There will be 8 boards with their silver receptacles: 16 silver receptacles, 2 receptacles under the first board, and 2 receptacles under the next board.

26:26 "Make acacia wood bars: 5 for the boards on one side of the Dwelling Place, [27] and 5 bars for the other side of the Dwelling Place, and 5 bars for the side of the Dwelling Place to the rear, to the west. [28] The middle bar, in the center of the boards, will run from end to end. [29] Overlay the boards with gold and make their rings of gold, to house the bars. Then overlay the bars with gold. [30] Then you will erect[9] the Dwelling Place according to its plan that you were shown on the mountain.

26:31 "Make a curtain of blue, purple, and earthy-red yarns, and of fine twisted linen; it should be made with a design of embroidered *keruvim* on it. [32] Put it on the 4 acacia wood pillars overlaid with gold, and their gold hooks which are on the 4 silver receptacles. [33] Hang the curtain under the clasps and bring the ark of the *edut* there, inside the curtain, so that the curtain will establish a separation for you between the

[7] Often translated "sockets," but the image here is of a kind of base or pedestal with holes to insert the tenons into.

[8] The Hebrew here is quite unclear, but there is a play on the similar sounding *to'amim* (twins) and "undivided" (*tamim*).

[9] The term used here is the same verb used to describe the establishment of a covenant between Yahweh and the people, which implies that the creation of this sanctuary is itself a type of covenant within the story.

outer sanctuary and the inner sanctuary.[10] 34 Then put the cover on the ark of the *edut* in the inner sanctuary. 35 Put the table outside the curtain, along with the lampstand opposite the table on the south wall of the Dwelling Place. Put the table on the north wall.

26:36 "Make a screen for the entrance to the tent of blue, purple, and earthy-red yarns, and of fine embroidered twisted linen. 37 Make 5 acacia wood pillars for the screen. Overlay them with gold, with their gold hooks. Cast 5 copper receptacles for them.

27:1 "Then you should make an acacia wood altar: 5 cubits long and 5 cubits wide—the altar will be a square—and 3 cubits tall. 2 Make its horns on its 4 sides. Its horns should be of one piece with it. Then overlay it with copper. 3 Make buckets for its ashes, along with its shovels, basins, forks, and fire pans. All its utensils you will make of copper. 4 Make for it a grate of copper mesh, and on the mesh make 4 copper rings on its 4 corners. 5 Put it below the ledge of the altar so that the mesh continues halfway up the altar. 6 Make bars for the altar, acacia wood bars, and overlay them with copper. 7 The bars should be brought through the rings so that the bars are on the 2 sides of the altar when it is carried. 8 With hollow planks you should make it; just as you were shown on the mountain, so you should do.[11]

27:9 "Make the courtyard of the Dwelling Place. On the southern side: fine, twisted-linen curtains for the courtyard, 100 cubits long for that side, 10 and its 20 pillars and their 20 receptacles of copper, with the pillars' hooks and bands of silver. 11 So too on the north side with 100 cubits of curtains, and 20 pillars and their 20 receptacles of copper, with the pillars' hooks and bands of silver. 12 The width of the western side of the courtyard: 50 cubits of hangings, and 10 pillars and their 10 receptacles. 13 The width of the front, the eastern side of the courtyard: 50 cubits. 14 Fifteen cubits of curtains on one side, their 3 pillars and

[10] Literally: between holy and most holy.

[11] These repeated appeals to Moses having been shown plans on Mount Sinai appear at moments when the descriptions are the least clear. They are a reminder that Moses was shown blueprints by Yahweh on Mount Sinai, and that these verbal instructions are imagined as accompanying the visual depiction.

3 receptacles, [15] and on the other side 15 cubits of curtains, their 3 pillars and 3 receptacles. [16] For the gate of the courtyard: a screen of 20 cubits, of blue, purple, and earthy-red yarns and fine twisted, embroidered linen, their 4 pillars and their 4 receptacles.

[27:17] "All the pillars surrounding the courtyard are banded with silver, their hooks silver, but their receptacles copper. [18] The length of the courtyard is 100 cubits, and the width 50 and 50,[12] and a height of 5 cubits of twisted linen with their copper receptacles. [19] All the Dwelling Place's vessels for all its ritual work, and all its tenons and all the tenons of the courtyard are of copper.[13]

[27:20] "You will command the Israelites to bring pure beaten olive oil to you for the lampstand for lighting the lamp regularly. [21] In the Meeting Tent, outside the curtain that is in front of the *edut*, Aaron and his sons will tend it from evening until morning before Yahweh. This will be a perpetual law throughout their generations, from the Israelites.[14]

[28:1] "Then bring forward your brother Aaron, with his sons, from the Israelites to serve me as priests: Aaron, Nadav and Avihu, Eleazar and Ithamar, Aaron's sons.[15] [2] Make the sacred garments for your brother

[12] This is a bit opaque, but seems to indicate that the width remains consistent for the whole length of the structure, fifty cubits in the front and fifty cubits in the back.

[13] This marks the end of the description of the structures themselves. There are two main components: a large outer rectangle, known as the courtyard, that measures 100 × 50 cubits, and a smaller inner rectangular structure, known as the Dwelling Place or sanctuary. The text never provides clear measurements for this inner structure. The instructions themselves contain contradictory measurements and it is nearly impossible to calculate its intended size. We know only that it fits within the 100 × 50 courtyard, and that it contains an inner sanctuary ("holy of holies") and an outer sanctuary that are separated by the curtain.

[14] These instructions are repeated nearly verbatim by Yahweh in Lev 24:2–3 when he reminds Moses of these requirements after the Meeting Tent has been inaugurated (just over a year from now in the story's chronology).

[15] It is easy to imagine that there are dozens or even hundreds of priests working in Yahweh's sanctuary, but this is the first clear indication that, at least at this point in the story, Yahweh only intends there to be five: Aaron and his four sons.

Aaron, for presence[16] and for adornment. ³ You will instruct everyone who is skilled, those whom I have filled with skill, to make Aaron's garments to consecrate him to make him a priest for me. ⁴ These are the garments that they will make: a breastplate, an *ephod,* a robe, a woven tunic, a turban, and a sash. When they make the sacred garments for your brother Aaron and his sons, so that they can serve me as priests, ⁵ they should take gold, blue, purple, and earthy-red yarns, and fine linen.

²⁸:⁶ "They will make the *ephod:* gold, blue, purple, and earthy-red yarns and fine twisted embroidered linen.[17] ⁷ It should have 2 connected shoulders joined to its 2 sides. ⁸ The embroidered band that is on it should be like it, of one piece with it: gold, blue, purple, and earthy-red yarns and fine twisted linen. ⁹ Then take 2 onyx stones and engrave on them the names of the sons of Israel: ¹⁰ 6 of their names on one stone, and the names of the remaining 6 on the second stone, in their birth-order.[18] ¹¹ Like an engraver's work of stone, like engraved seals, you should engrave the 2 stones with the names of the sons of Israel; surrounded with settings of gold you will make them. ¹² Then you will put the two stones on the *ephod's* shoulder pieces: memorial stones[19] for the Israelites. Aaron will bear their names before Yahweh on his two shoulders as a reminder.[20] ¹³ Make gold settings ¹⁴ and 2 pure gold chains. Make them like rope and put the rope-like chains on the gold settings.

²⁸:¹⁵ "Make the breastplate of judgment of embroidered work, like the *ephod's* style you will make it. Of gold, blue, purple, and earthy-red yarn

[16] The word used here is *kavod,* which is typically mistranslated as "glory." This translation is likely because of a reticence to admit an anthropomorphic god in the story. In reality, the word *kavod* is used in this story to describe the physical presence of Yahweh. Here it is used to describe the function of Aaron's garments (those of the high priest): to enable his presence before Yahweh and for his adornment, like the rest of the Meeting Tent.

[17] Notice that the fabrics for this *ephod* match the fabric for the curtain that divides the inner sanctuary from the outer sanctuary.

[18] This list is found in Genesis 35:22–26.

[19] The motif of memory and remembering is one that appears repeatedly throughout this story, most often in connection with physical objects like this one that serve as a memory aid.

[20] This reminder, importantly, is for Yahweh, not for Aaron.

and fine twisted linen you will make it. [16] It will be square and doubled; its length a span and its width a span. [17] You will fill it with set stones, 4 rows of stone. The first row of carnelian, topaz, and emerald;[21] [18] The second row: turquoise, sapphire, and a *yahalom* stone.[22] [19] The third row: a jacinth, an agate, and an amethyst. [20] The fourth row: a beryl, an onyx, and a jasper. They will be set in gold settings. [21] The stones will equal the names of the sons of Israel: 12, according to their names, each engraved like seals with its name for the 12 tribes.[23]

[28:22] "Make for the breastplate twisted corded chains of pure gold, [23] Make 2 rings on the breastplate, and put the 2 rings on the 2 sides of the breastplate. [24] Put the 2 gold cords in the 2 rings at the ends of the breastplate. [25] Then the 2 ends of the 2 cords put in the 2 gold settings. Then attach it to the shoulders of the *ephod* in the front. [26] Make 2 gold rings and put them on the 2 ends of the breastplate on its inner edge next to the *ephod*. [27] Make 2 gold rings and put them on the 2 shoulders of the *ephod*, in the lower part in the front, near the seam but above the *ephod's* band. [28] They will bind the breastplate from its rings to the rings of the *ephod* with a blue cord, so that the *ephod* is on the band and the breastplate does not detach from the *ephod*.

[28:29] "Aaron will bear the names of the Israelites on the breastplate of judgment, over his heart, when he enters the sanctuary as a regular reminder before Yahweh.

[28:30] "You will put the *urim* and the *tummim* on the breastplate of judgment, so that they are over Aaron's heart when he goes in before Yahweh. Aaron will bear the judgment of the Israelites over his heart in front of Yahweh regularly.

[21] Carnelian is a red stone and the underlying Hebrew word (*odem*) is a consonantal cognate ('-d-m) with the word used for "human being" in this story (*adam*). word here is .

[22] The identity of this stone is unknown and widely disputed. It contains the Hebrew root for "hammer," suggesting that it is a particularly hard stone.

[23] A shift is made here from the literal twelve sons of Jacob (Israel) to the more abstract understanding of the "sons of Israel" as the twelve tribes—that is, the entirety of the Israelites.

²⁸:³¹ "Make the robe of the *ephod* entirely of blue. ³² The opening for his head will be in the middle of it; it will have a woven edge around its opening, like the opening of a coat of mail, so that it will not tear. ³³ Make on its hem pomegranates of blue, purple, and earthy-red yarns, all around its hem, with gold bells between them all around: ³⁴ golden bell and pomegranate, golden bell and pomegranate all around the hem of the robe. ³⁵ Aaron will wear it for serving so that its sound will be heard when he enters the sanctuary before Yahweh and when he leaves it so that he does not die.[24]

²⁸:³⁶ "Make a pure gold blossom diadem and engrave on it a seal inscription: "holy to Yahweh." ³⁷ Then put it on a blue cord and attach it to the turban; it will be on the front of the turban. ³⁸ It will be on Aaron's forehead, so that Aaron can remove sin incurred from the sacred objects that the Israelites will consecrate, from any of their sacred gifts. It will be on his forehead regularly for their acceptance before Yahweh.[25]

²⁸:³⁹ "You will make a woven tunic of fine linen. You will make a turban of fine linen, and a sash you will make of embroidery. ⁴⁰ For Aaron's sons you will make tunics; make for them sashes; headdresses you will make for them for presence and for adornment.[26] ⁴¹ You will clothe

[24] There is a fascinating detail revealed by this garment about the character of Yahweh: he does not like to be startled. It is important that Yahweh hears Aaron coming and knows when he has left. The golden bells on the bottom of Aaron's robe act as a kind of doorbell alerting Yahweh to Aaron's presence.

[25] The gold blossom diadem has a very specific purpose in this story. The Israelites have been charged with giving all sorts of gifts to Yahweh in order both to construct this sanctuary and, later, so that they can be instructed to give gifts for its ongoing upkeep. Once these gifts are given to Yahweh, they become his property, they become sancta. Transgressions against sancta are some of the most severe in this story in part because those are transgressions against Yahweh's own property. The golden blossom on Aaron's headband serves as a kind of failsafe. If one or more of the Israelites commits some kind of transgression against the sancta, this golden blossom is designed to enable Aaron to mitigate those transgressions with Yahweh and to secure Yahweh's acceptance of their offerings and perhaps even their presence in the vicinity. In short, it is form of protection against divine anger and subsequent punishment.

[26] Aaron's sons' garments are said to serve the same purpose as his—that is, to enable them to serve in Yahweh's presence. The sons' garments, however, are much less ornate than Aaron's.

them, Aaron and his sons with him, anoint them, ordain them, and consecrate them to serve me as priests. [42] Make for them linen underwear to cover their naked flesh. They will go from their loins to their thighs. [43] Aaron and his sons will wear them when they enter the Meeting Tent or when they approach the altar to serve in the sanctuary so that they do not incur sin and die. This is a perpetual law for him and for all his descendants after him.

[29:1] "This is what you should do to consecrate them to serve me as priests:

[29:1] "Take 1 young bull of the herd and 2 rams, unblemished, [2] along with unleavened bread, unleavened cakes mixed with oil, and unleavened wafers smeared with oil. Make them with the finest flour. [3] Put them in one basket and offer them along with the basket and the bull and the 2 rams.

[29:4] "Aaron and his sons you will bring to the entrance of the Meeting Tent, then wash them with water. [5] Take the garments and clothe Aaron: the tunic, the robe of the *ephod*, the *ephod*, and the breastplate. Then bind him with the band of the *ephod*. [6] Put the turban on his head and put the holy diadem on the turban. [7] Then take the anointing oil and pour it over his head and anoint him.

[29:8] "Then bring forward his sons, clothe them in tunics, [9] and bind them with a sash. Bind headdresses for them. The priesthood will be theirs as a perpetual law. You will ordain Aaron and his sons.

[29:10] "Bring the bull before the Meeting Tent and Aaron and his sons will lay their hands on the head of the bull. [11] You will slaughter the bull[27] before Yahweh at the entrance to the Meeting Tent. [12] Take some

[27] Note here the return to second-person address: while Aaron and his sons lay their hands on the bull, marking it as a sacrifice on their behalf, it is Moses who carries out the sacrifice, precisely because Aaron and his sons are not yet priests and cannot do so. Moses is a singular character in this story in a lot of ways, and this is one of them. He is never ordained as a priest or consecrated in the way that Aaron and his sons are, but he—unlike any other human being in the story—is able to enter Yahweh's presence, converse with him, and offer sacrifices on his altar.

of the bull's blood and smear it on the horns of the altar with your finger. The rest of the blood you should pour out at the base of the altar.

29:13 "Then take all the fat covering the innards and the lobe of the liver and the two kidneys, along with the fat on them, and turn them to smoke on the altar. 14 But the flesh of the bull, along with its skin and its dung, you should burn outside the camp. It is a decontamination offering.[28]

29:15 "Then take one of the rams. Aaron and his sons will lay their hands on the ram's head. 16 You will slaughter the ram, take its blood, and toss it all around the altar. 17 Butcher the ram and wash its innards and its legs. Then put them on its portions, along with its head, 18 and turn the whole ram into smoke on the altar. It is a burnt offering for Yahweh, a pleasing aroma; it is a food offering for Yahweh.[29]

29:19 "Take the second ram. Aaron and his sons will lay their hands on the ram's head. 20 You will slaughter the ram, take some of its blood, and put it on Aaron's right earlobe and on the right earlobes of his sons, on the thumbs of their right hands, and on the big toe of their right feet. Then toss the blood all around the altar. 21 Take some of the blood that is on the altar and some of the anointing oil and sprinkle it on Aaron and on his garments, and on his sons and on their garments,

[28] This type of sacrifice (in Hebrew the *hatta't*) is conventionally translated as "sin offering." More recently the translation, "purification offering" has also been used. The function of this type of sacrifice is to remove contamination caused by the Israelites' impurities and sins from the altar and sanctuary. Impurities are considered to be a normal part of human life and are not considered "sinful" in any way. The translation "sin offering" is patently incorrect as it obscures the fact that this sacrifice can be and often is used in cases where no sin has occurred. The translation "deconamination offering" is more correct as the purpose of this sacrifice is to decontaminate the altar so that its contaminants (caused by impurity and sin) are removed. In short, the process of decontamination effects purification. This has the advantage of being able to distinguish between this Hebrew root and *kipper*, which is most commonly recognized from the modern holiday of Yom Kippur, and which I have translated here as "purification."

[29] Unlike the decontamination offering, this burnt offering is described as having a pleasing aroma and as food for Yahweh. Purification offerings never have these descriptors in the story.

thus consecrating him and his garments and his sons and their garments. ²² Then take the ram's fat, its fatty tail, the fat that covers the
innards, the lobe of the liver, the two kidneys, and all their fats, along
with the right thigh—it is a ram of ordination—²³ and one loaf of
bread, one cake of oiled bread, and one wafer from the basket of
unleavened bread that is before Yahweh. ²⁴ Put everything in the hands
of Aaron and in the hands of his sons. Raise them as an elevation offering before Yahweh.[30] ²⁵ Take them from their hands and turn them to
smoke on the altar on top of the burnt offering as a pleasing aroma for
Yahweh; it is a food offering for Yahweh.

²⁹:²⁶ "Then take the breast of Aaron's ram of ordination and raise it as
an elevation offering before Yahweh. It will be your portion.[31] ²⁷ You
will consecrate the breast of the elevation offering and the right thigh
that was presented as a gift from Aaron and his sons' ordination ram.
²⁸ It will be a perpetual portion[32] for Aaron and his sons from the
Israelites. It is a gift.[33] The gift will be from the Israelites, from their
well-being offerings, which are their gifts to Yahweh.

²⁹:²⁹ "Aaron's sacred garments will belong to his sons after him—to be
anointed in them and ordained in them. ³⁰ For seven days the son who
will become priest in his place, the one who enters the Meeting Tent to
serve in the sanctuary, will wear them.

²⁹:³¹ "Take the ordination ram and boil its flesh in a sacred place.
³² Aaron and his sons will eat the ram's flesh and the bread that was in

[30] The Hebrew term for ordination is literally translated as "to fill his hands."
Here, we see where that idiom comes from when Moses fills the hands of Aaron and his
sons with parts of the ordination ram and the unleavened bread.

[31] In this case, it is Moses's portion because he is the one performing the sacrifices.
Once the priests finish their ordination, this portion becomes theirs because they are
then able to do the ritual work.

[32] There is a literary wordplay in the Hebrew here. Typically this phrase reads
hukkat olam, meaning "perpetual law." Here it reads *hoq olam*, meaning "perpetual
portion."

[33] The term here (*teruma*) is the same word used to describe the gifts that Yahweh
asks the Israelites to bring to build the Meeting Tent earlier in this speech. Here it
describes a gift from the Israelites to the priests instead of Yahweh.

the basket at the entrance to the Meeting Tent. [33] They will eat them—those for whom purification was made in order to ordain them and consecrate them. No stranger can eat them because they are holy. [34] If any of the flesh of the ordination offering or any of the bread is left over until the morning, you should burn the leftovers in fire; it should not be eaten because it is holy.

[29:35] "So you will do for Aaron and for his sons according to everything that I have commanded you. For seven days you will ordain them: [36] you will offer a bull for a decontamination offering each day in accordance with the purification procedure. You will perform the decontamination offering on the altar, thereby purifying it, and you shall anoint it in order to consecrate it. [37] For seven days you will purify the altar and consecrate it. The altar will be at the highest level of holiness.[34] Anyone who touches the altar must be consecrated.

[29:38] "This is what you should sacrifice on the altar: 2 one-year-old lambs daily, regularly.[35] [39] One lamb you will offer in the morning, and the second lamb offer in the evening, [40] along with a tenth measure of fine flour mixed with a quarter *hin* of beaten oil, and a libation: a quarter *hin* of wine for the first lamb. [41] The second lamb you will offer in the evening, along with the morning grain offering, and its libation you will offer it as a pleasing aroma, a food offering for Yahweh. [42] It is a regular burnt offering throughout your generations at the entrance of the Meeting Tent before Yahweh, where I will meet you to speak

[34] "The highest level of holiness" is a technical category in this story, designating those things that are of the greatest importance and that also present the greatest danger to people who are not consecrated. Later in the story, we are told that any non-priest who touches the altar will die (Num 3:38).

[35] This is a particularly important section in Yahweh's instructions. Here Yahweh emphasizes that after Moses finishes the consecration of the priests, they should begin making this daily offering, which will continue in perpetuity and serve as Yahweh's two daily meals (a meal schedule that mirrors that of the ancient Israelite diet!). Only once the priests do this will Yahweh take up permanent residence in the Meeting Tent, thus signaling the completion of a millennium-long plan to keep a closer eye on human beings in order prevent the violence and chaos that led him to send the flood, thus ensuring the continued existence of the world and the well-being of the Israelites within it.

with you.[36] 43 I will meet the Israelites there, and it will be consecrated by my presence.[37] 44 I will consecrate the Meeting Tent and the altar; Aaron and his sons I will consecrate to serve as my priests. 45 Then I will take up residence among the Israelites and I will be their God. 46 They will know that I am Yahweh their God, who brought them out from the land of Egypt in order to live among them. I am Yahweh their God.

30:1 "Make an altar, a place for burning incense; make it of acacia wood, 2 a cubit in length and a cubit in width—it will be square—and 2 cubits high; its horns are of one piece with it. 3 Overlay it with pure gold—its top, all around its sides, and its horns. Make a gold border around it. 4 Two gold rings you will make for it under its border; on its 2 opposite sides you will make them.[38] They will house the poles used to carry it. 5 Make the acacia wood poles and overlay them with gold. 6 Put it in front of the curtain that is in front of the ark of the *edut*, in front of the cover that is on the *edut* where I will meet with you. 7 Aaron will burn fragrant incense on it every morning; when he maintains[39] the lamps, he will burn it. 8 When Aaron lights the lamps in the evening, he will burn it, a regular incense offering before Yahweh throughout his generations.

[36] At some of the most critical points in his speeches, Yahweh shifts from addressing himself in the third person to speaking in the first person directly to Moses. This is one of those cases, and it comes at the moment when Yahweh first emphasizes that the Meeting Tent is meant to be the site of communication both between him and his prophet Moses and between him and the Israelites, as well as when he promises to be the god of the Israelites.

[37] These last two verses also emphasize the reason this story calls Yahweh's home a "Meeting Tent"; it is the place where Yahweh meets with his people.

[38] By now, this seemingly repetitive type of sentence structure should be somewhat familiar. This is very typical of the priestly literary style. It is a kind of parallelistic formulation known as a "circular inclusio" in which the initial command is given (here: "you will make two gold rings") and then further details about how to make them and the initial verb ("you will make") are repeated near or at the end of the clause. It is a peculiar style, but one that occurs countless times in these instructions for building the wilderness tent shrine and again in the ritual instructions later in the story.

[39] Literally: "when he makes the lamps pleasing." This likely refers to Aaron replenishing the oil and making sure the lamps are lit so that Yahweh's space contains light to see.

30:9 "Do not offer unauthorized incense on it, or a burnt offering or a grain offering; do not pour out a libation on it. 10 Aaron will perform purification on its horns once a year; with blood of the decontamination offering for purification,[40] once a year he will purify it throughout your generations. It is of the highest level of holiness to Yahweh."

30:11 Then Yahweh spoke to Moses:[41] 12 "When you take a census of the Israelites in order to muster them,[42] each man should give a ransom payment[43] for himself to Yahweh when he is mustered, so that a plague does not befall them for being mustered. 13 This is what everyone who passes through the muster should give: a half shekel according to the sanctuary weight (a shekel is 20 *gerah*), a half shekel as a gift for Yahweh. 14 All who pass through the muster, from the age of 20 and up will give Yahweh's gift. 15 A rich man will not pay more and a poor man will not pay less than a half shekel when bringing Yahweh's gift as ransom for your lives. 16 You will take the ransom money from the Israelites and give it for the ritual work of the Meeting Tent; it will be the Israelites' reminder in front of Yahweh of the ransoming of your lives.'"

30:17 Yahweh spoke to Moses: 18 "Make a copper basin and a copper stand for it for washing. Put it between the Meeting Tent and the altar and put water in it. 19 Aaron and his sons will wash their hands and feet in it; 20 when they enter the Meeting Tent they will wash with water so that they do not die. When they approach the altar to serve, to offer food offerings for Yahweh, 21 they will wash their hands and their feet so that they do not die. It will be a perpetual law for him and for his descendants throughout their generations."

---

[40] The repetitive nature of the English here reflects the repeated use of the root *k-p-r*, to purify in both verbal form and as a proper noun, which refers to the once-yearly purification ritual that will be explained later in more detail (Lev 16).

[41] The narrator's repetition of an introductory speech formula is a common tactic in this story to indicate a change of topic within a longer speech. It is not indicative of a significant lapse of time between speeches or even another speech event.

[42] In this story, the purpose of a census is always to count the number of potential troops for a military campaign.

[43] This word is from the same Hebrew root as "purification" (*kofer*), and this likely explains the link between a discussion of a yearly purification of the sanctuary and the payment for census taking.

^{30:22} Yahweh spoke to Moses: ²³ "As for you, take the best spices: 500 of liquid myrrh, half that—250—of fragrant cinnamon and 250 of fragrant cane, ²⁴ 500, by the sanctuary weight, of cassia, and a *hin* of olive oil. ²⁵ Make it into a holy anointing oil, a blended perfume like that made by a perfumer. It will be a holy anointing oil. ²⁶ With it anoint the Meeting Tent and the ark of the *edut*, ²⁷ the table and all its vessels, the lampstand and all its vessels, and the incense altar, ²⁸ the altar of burnt offering and all its vessels, and the basin and its stand. ²⁹ Consecrate them so that they are of the highest level of holiness; anyone who touches them must be consecrated. ³⁰ Anoint Aaron and his sons and consecrate them to serve me as priests. ³¹ To the Israelites, you should say: 'This will be my holy anointing oil throughout your generations. ³² On a layperson's flesh, it should not be poured; you should not make anything like it with its proportions. It is holy; it will be holy for you. ³³ Anyone who blends something like it or who puts some of it on a layperson will be cut off from their people.'"

^{30:34} Yahweh spoke to Moses: "Take spices: stacte, onycha, and galbanum, spices with pure frankincense, an equal part of each, ³⁵ and make a blended incense like that made by a perfumer; salted,[44] pure, and holy. ³⁶ Beat some of it into a powder and put it before the *edut* in the Meeting Tent, where I will meet with you. It will be of the highest level of holiness for you. ³⁷ But you should not make incense for yourselves according to these proportions. It is holy for you, for Yahweh. ³⁸ Anyone who makes something like it to enjoy its smell will be cut off from their people."

^{31:1} Yahweh spoke to Moses: ² "Look, I have summoned Bezalel son of Uri son of Hur, from the tribe of Judah. ³ I have filled him with the breath of God,[45] with wisdom, intelligence, and knowledge in all types

[44] The inclusion of salt here may seem odd, but later on in the ritual instructions, Yahweh says that all offerings to him must be salted. Since this incense is being kept near his ark, it makes sense that it would also include salt.

[45] This phrase (*ruah elohim*) is sometimes translated as "divine spirit." I have translated it as "breath of God" here to highlight the echo with Genesis 1:2, when the breath of Yahweh moves across the formless emptiness of the world to begin the process of its creation. Here, too, God's breath is imagined as the force behind creation, this time of his Meeting Tent and through the human conduit of Bezalel.

of physical labor—[4] in creating designs in gold, silver, and copper, [5] in cutting stone for setting, and in carving wood—to do all types of physical labor. [6] I have appointed with him Oholiab son of Ahisamakh of the tribe of Dan. I have given skill to all the skillful so that they will create everything I have instructed you: [7] the Meeting Tent, and the ark of the *edut,* the cover that is on it, and all the tent's vessels, [8] the table and its vessels, and the pure lampstand and its vessels, the incense altar, [9] and the burnt offering altar with all its vessels, the basin and its stand, [10] the woven garments and the sacred garments of Aaron the priest, and the garments of his sons for their work as priests, [11] the anointing oil, and the aromatic incense for the sanctuary. They will create everything just as I instructed you."

[31:12] Yahweh spoke to Moses: [13] "Speak to the Israelites: 'However, my sabbaths you must keep, because it is a sign between me and you throughout your generations, so that you know that I am Yahweh who consecrates you. [14] You will keep the sabbath because it is holy for you. Anyone who profanes it will be put to death; anyone who does physical labor on it, that person will be cut off from among their people.[46] [15] For six days, physical labor can be done, but on the seventh day: a cessation,[47] a sacred cessation for Yahweh. Anyone who does physical labor on the sabbath day will be put to death. [16] The Israelites will keep the sabbath, performing the cessation throughout their generations, a perpetual covenant [17] between me and the Israelites. It is a perpetual sign, that in six days Yahweh made the heavens and the earth, and on the seventh day he ceased and was refreshed."

[31:18] When he finished speaking with him on Mount Sinai, he gave Moses the *edut.*

[34:29] Moses descended Mount Sinai. The *edut* was in Moses's hand when he descended the mountain, but he did not know that the skin of his face

---

[46] This provision helps to explain why the sabbath law appears now. Yahweh has just appointed Bezalel and Oholiab to do all the physical labor (*melakah*) of constructing the Meeting Tent. But here Yahweh wants to make clear that on one day a week, the sabbath, they are not permitted to do that physical labor (*melakah*).

[47] The literal translation of sabbath is "cessation."

was shining because he had spoken with him. [30] When Aaron and all the Israelites saw Moses, the skin of his face was shining. They were afraid to approach him. [31] Moses summoned them, and Aaron and all the leaders of the community returned to him and Moses spoke to them. [32] After this, all the Israelites approached, and he instructed them in everything that Yahweh told him on Mount Sinai. [33] When Moses finished speaking with them, he put a veil over his face.

[34:34] Whenever Moses went before Yahweh to speak with him, he removed the veil until he departed, but when he would leave to tell the Israelites what he had been commanded, [35] the Israelites would see Moses's face—that the skin of Moses's face was shining—and Moses would put the veil back over his face until he went in to speak with him.

5

Building Yahweh's Dwelling Place

Exodus 35:1 Moses gathered the entire community of Israelites and said to them,[1] "these are the things that Yahweh commanded you to do: 2 For six days physical labor can be done, but on the seventh day you will have a sacred cessation, a cessation for Yahweh; anyone who does physical labor on it will be put to death.[2] 3 You cannot burn a fire in any of your settlements on the day of cessation."

35:4 Then Moses said to the entire Israelite community, "This is what Yahweh commanded: 5 'Take gifts for Yahweh from among you; everyone whose heart is generous will bring it, a gift for Yahweh: gold, silver, and copper, 6 blue, purple, and earthy-red yarns, fine linen, and goats' hair; 7 reddened rams' skins, and dyed green-blue leather and acacia wood; 8 lamp oil, spiced for the anointing oil and for the incense; 9 onyx stones and setting stones for the *ephod* and for the breastplate. 10 Everyone who is skilled among you will come and make all that Yahweh commanded! 11 The Dwelling Place and its tent and its covering, its

[1] The speech that follows is a detailed version of the speech alluded to a few verses ago in Exod 34:32.

[2] The order of Moses's speech to the Israelites largely follows the order of Yahweh's speech to Moses on the mountain. This first section is an important exception. Moses leads off with the rules about the sabbath and the necessary cessation of labor on the seventh day before he begins to enumerate what, exactly, that labor is going to be. This gives the sabbath both a pride of place in his speech to the Israelites and a particular emphasis as the last thing Yahweh said and the first thing Moses repeats.

clasps and its boards, its bars and its pillars and its receptacles; [12] the ark and its bars and the cover, and the curtain for the screen; [13] the table and its bars and its vessels and the display bread; [14] the lampstand for the light and its vessels and its lamps, and the oil for the light; [15] the incense altar and its bars, and the anointing oil and the incense, along with the entrance screen for the entrance to the Dwelling Place; [16] the burnt-offering altar and its copper grate, its bars and its vessels, the basin and its stand; [17] the curtains for the courtyard, its pillars and its receptacles and the screen for the courtyard gate; [18] the tenons for the Dwelling Place and the tenons for the courtyard along with their cords; [19] the woven garments for serving in the sanctuary, the sacred garments for Aaron the priest, and the garments for his sons to serve as priests.'"

[35:20] The entire Israelite community left Moses's presence. [21] Everyone whose heart was moved and everyone whose spirit freely offered brought Yahweh's gifts for the physical labor of the Meeting Tent and for all its ritual labor and for the sacred garments. [22] Men and women, everyone of generous heart, came and brought ornaments, earrings, and rings, and pendants—every kind of gold object, everyone raising a gift of gold to Yahweh. [23] Everyone who had it brought blue, purple, or earthy-red yarns, fine linens, or goats' hair, reddened rams' skins, or dyed green-blue leather. [24] Everyone who could raise a gift of silver or copper brought Yahweh's gift, and everyone who had it brought acacia wood for all the labor.

[35:25] All the skilled women spun with their hands and brought what they spun: blue, purple, and earthy-red yarns and fine linen. [26] All the women who excelled in the skill spun goats' hair. [27] The leaders brought onyx stones and setting-stones for the *ephod* and the breastplate, [28] along with spices, oil for lighting and anointing oil and incense. [29] The Israelites—each man and woman whose hearts freely offered to bring anything for all the physical labor that Yahweh commanded to be done through Moses—brought it as a freewill offering to Yahweh.

[35:30] Moses said to the Israelites, "Look, Yahweh has summoned Bezalel son of Uri son of Hur, from the tribe of Judah, [31] and filled him with the breath of God, with wisdom, intelligence, and knowledge in all types of physical labor—[32] to create designs in gold, silver, and copper, [33] and in cutting stone for setting, and in carving wood—to do all the skilled physical labor. [34] He has set it in his heart to teach. He and Oholiab son of Ahisamakh of the tribe of Dan [35] have been filled with skill to do all the physical labor of an engraver, a designer, or an embroiderer, with the blue, purple, and earthy-red yarns, and in fine linen, or a weaver—doing any of the physical labor or skilled work. [36:1] Now, let Bezalel and Oholiab and every skilled person whom Yahweh has given skill and knowledge for doing all the labor of the sanctuary do everything that Yahweh has commanded."

[36:2] Moses summoned Bezalel and Oholiab and every skilled person whom Yahweh gave skill—everyone whose heart was moved to offer[3] physical labor—to do it. [3] They took all the gifts that the Israelites had brought for doing the labor of the sanctuary from Moses. But they continued to bring to him even more freewill offerings morning after morning. [4] All the skilled workers who were doing the sanctuary work came, each person from the task that they were doing, [5] and they said to Moses, "The people are bringing more than is needed for doing the work that Yahweh commanded be done." [6] So Moses commanded that a message be passed through the camp: "No man or woman should do any more labor toward the sanctuary gifts!" Then the people were stopped from bringing; [7] their labor was enough for all the work left to do and then some.

[36:8] Then everyone with skill among those doing the labor for the Dwelling Place made 10 curtains; of fine twisted line, blue, purple, and earthy-red yarn with an embroidered *keruvim* pattern they made them.[4] [9] The length of the curtain: 28 cubits, and the width: 4 cubits

[3] The Hebrew verb here is the same one that is often used to describe the offering of an animal or grain sacrifice to Yahweh (*q-r-b*).

[4] Attentive readers might notice that the order of the narrator's report about the construction of the various elements of the Meeting Tent does not follow the exact order of Yahweh's instructions from chapters 25–31. This is an issue that has been discussed at length by scholars, with many different proposed reasons for these differences ranging from intentional literary variation to multiple different authors adding to and adjusting these texts over the course of many years. It should also be noted that there is a significant difference in the ordering and even wording of these instructions in different ancient versions of Exodus, especially in the ancient Greek versions. What this tells

for each curtain; the same measurements for all the curtains. [10] They connected 5 curtains to each other, and the other 5 curtains they connected to each other. [11] They made loops of blue on the edge of the curtain at the end of the first set; they did likewise on the edge of the curtain at the end of the second set. [12] Fifty loops they made on the first curtain, and 50 loops they made on the end curtain of the second set, the loops were opposite each other. [13] They made 50 gold clasps, and they joined the curtains to each other with the clasps so that the Dwelling Place became one piece.

[36:14] They made goat-hair curtains for the tent over the Dwelling Place, 11 curtains they made. [15] The length of a curtain: 30 cubits; 4 cubits in width for a curtain; the same measurements for the 11 curtains. [16] They connected 5 of the curtains by themselves and 6 curtains by themselves. [17] They made 50 loops on the edge of the curtain at the end of the set, and another 50 loops they made at the edge of the curtain of the second set. [18] They made 50 copper clasps to connect the tent so that it would be one piece. [19] They made a covering for the tent of tanned rams' skins and a covering of dyed green-blue leather over that.

[36:20] They made boards for the Dwelling Place out of acacia wood, upright. [21] A board was 10 cubits long, and each board was 1.5 cubits in width. [22] Two tenons for each board, joining one board to another; so they did for all the boards of the Dwelling Place. [23] They made the boards for the Dwelling Place, 20 boards for the south side, [24] and 40 silver receptacles they made under the 20 boards, 2 receptacles under the first board for its 2 tenons, and 2 receptacles under the next board for its 2 tenons. [25] For the second side of the Dwelling Place, the north side, they made 20 boards, [26] and their 40 silver receptacles, 2 receptacles under the first board and 2 receptacles under the next board. [27] For the back of the Dwelling Place, to the west, they made 6 boards, [28] and 2 boards they made for the back corners of the Dwelling Place. [29] They

---

us is that this is a section of text that was given quite a bit of attention in antiquity, being written, rewritten, and edited in a number of different contexts by different ancient Jewish communities. The version translated here is that of the tenth-century CE Masoretic text. Resources to learn more about these differences can be found in the bibliography.

were twins along the bottom, but together, they were undivided, at the top, to the first ring; so they did for the both of them at the 2 corners. ³⁰ There were 8 boards with their silver receptacles—16 receptacles—2 under each board.

³⁶:³¹ They made acacia wood bars, 5 for the boards on one side of the Dwelling Place, ³² and 5 bars for the boards of the western side of the Dwelling Place. ³³ They made the middle bar, running in the middle of the boards from end to end. ³⁴ The boards they overlaid with gold and the rings they made of gold, as houses for the bars; they overlaid the bars with gold.

³⁶:³⁵ They made the curtain of blue, purple, and earthy-red yarns and fine twisted linen; they made them with an embroidered *keruvim* pattern. ³⁶ They made 4 acacia wood poles for it and overlaid them with gold, along with their gold hooks; they cast for them 4 silver receptacles.[5] ³⁷ They made the screen for the entrance to the tent of blue, purple and earthy-red yarn and of fine embroidered twisted linen, ³⁸ its 5 poles and their hooks. They overlaid their tops and their sides with gold, but their 5 receptacles were made of copper.

³⁷:¹ Then Bezalel made the acacia wood ark, 2.5 cubits long, 1.5 cubits wide, and 1.5 cubits tall. ² He overlaid it with pure gold both inside and out, and he made a gold border around it. ³ He cast 4 gold rings for it on its 4 feet and 2 rings on one side and 2 rings on its other side. ⁴ He made acacia wood bars and overlaid them with gold, ⁵ and he put the bars into the rings on the side of the ark in order to carry the ark. ⁶ Then he made a pure gold cover, 2.5 cubits long and 1.5 cubits wide. ⁷ He made 2 gold *keruvim*; he made them hammered, on the 2 ends of the cover. ⁸ The first *keruv* on one end and the second *keruv* on the other end; of one piece with the cover he made the two *keruvim* on

[5] One of the biggest differences between Yahweh's speech to Moses and the narrator's recounting of their completion is that Bezalel, Oholiab, and their workers do not assemble most of the physical structure, including which pieces to attach where and when. In part, this is because the artisans are responsible for making the components of Yahweh's Dwelling Place, but it will be Moses himself who is responsible for assembling all the components into a finished structure.

its ends. [9] The *keruvim* had wings spread upward, covering the cover with their wings, and the two of them faced each other, the faces of the *keruvim* toward the cover.

[37:10] Then he made the acacia wood table, 2 cubits long, 1 cubit wide, and 1.5 cubits tall. [11] He overlaid it with pure gold and made a border around it. [12] He made a handsbreadth-sized rim around it, and he made a gold border around its rim. [13] He cast 4 gold rings for it, and he put the rings on the 4 corners that were on its 4 legs. [14] Next to the rim were the rings, for housing the bars used for carrying the table. [15] He made the acacia wood bars and overlaid them with gold to carry the table. [16] Then he made the vessels that were on the table—its bowls, its ladles, its libation jugs, and its jars with which to pour out libations—of pure gold.

[37:17] He made the pure gold lampstand; of hammered work he made the lampstand, its base and its stalk, its cups, its bulbs, and its petals were of one piece. [18] Six branches came out from its side, 3 branches from one side of the lampstand, and 3 branches from the other side of the lampstand. [19] Three almond blossom-shaped cups on one branch with a bulb and a petal, and 3 almond blossom-shaped cups on another branch with a bulb and a petal, and so on for the 6 branches that came out of the lampstand. [20] On the lampstand itself, there were 4 almond blossom-shaped cups, each with its bulb and petals, [21] a bulb under a pair of branches (of one piece with it), and a bulb under another pair of branches (of one piece with it), and a bulb under another pair of branches (of one piece with it)—for all 6 of the branches coming out of it. [22] Their bulbs and their branches were of one piece with it, all made of a single piece of hammered pure gold. [23] He then made the 7 lamps, its tongs, and its firepans of pure gold; [24] from a talent of pure gold he made it and its vessels.

[37:25] Then he made the acacia wood incense altar,[6] 1 cubit long and 1 cubit wide—square—and 2 cubits tall; its horns were of one piece

[6] The narrator's presentation of Bezalel's work here seems to be focused on having him create items of similar materials at the same time. First he worked with fabrics to create the curtains for the main structures themselves (the Dwelling Place and the covering over it), and in this chapter he makes the pure gold objects. All these objects are

with it. [26] He overlaid it with pure gold on its top, all around its sides, and its horns. He made a gold border around it. [27] He made 2 gold rings for it under its border on its 2 sides, on opposite sides, to house the bars used for carrying it. [28] He then made the acacia wood bars and overlaid them with gold. [29] Then he made the sacred anointing oil, the pure fragrant incense, made like a perfumer.

[38:1] He made the altar of burnt offering, out of acacia wood: 5 cubits long and 5 cubits wide—square—and 3 cubits tall. [2] He made its horns on its 4 corners; they were of one piece with it. Then he overlaid them with copper. [3] He made all the altar's vessels: the pots, the shovels, and the basins, the forks and the fire-pans. All the vessels he made of copper. [4] He made for the altar a grate of copper mesh under the ledge, from under it until its midpoint. [5] He cast 4 rings on the 4 corners of the copper grating, as housing for the bars. [6] Then he made the acacia wood bars and overlaid them with copper. [7] He put the bars into the rings on the side of the altar in order to carry it; with hollow boards he made it.

[38:8] He made the copper basin and its copper stand, from the mirrors of the women who served at the entrance to the Meeting Tent.[7] [9] Then he made the courtyard. On the southern side: 100 cubits of fine twisted-linen curtains for the courtyard, [10] their 20 pillars and their 20 copper receptacles, but the pillars' hooks and bands were silver. [11] For the northern side: 100 cubits, their 20 pillars and 20 copper receptacles, but the pillars' hooks and bands were silver. [12] For the western side: 50 cubits of curtains, their 10 pillars and 10 receptacles; the pillars' hooks and bands were silver. [13] For the eastern side, the front: 50 cubits. [14] The curtains: 15 cubits to one side, their 3 pillars and 3 receptacles, [15] and the same for the other side. On each side of the courtyard gate were 15 cubits of curtains, their 3 pillars and their 3 receptacles. [16] All the

---

those that will be closest to Yahweh when Yahweh takes up residence in the space. The furniture and curtains in this area will never be visible to ordinary Israelites, but through these descriptions they are getting a kind of "glimpse" into Yahweh's private chamber. In the next chapters, Bezalel and his team will move to the outer areas of the Meeting Tent complex—those that are visible to non-priests.

[7] This is the only mention in the story of women having a role at the Meeting Tent, and the exact nature of their role remains unclear.

courtyard curtains on all sides were of fine twisted linen. [17] The receptacles for the pillars were copper, and the pillars' hooks and bands were silver, the plating on their tops was silver and all the pillars of the courtyard were banded with silver.

[38:18] The screen for the gate of the courtyard was embroidered in blue, purple, and earthy red yarns and fine twisted-linen. It was 20 cubits long and its height—that is, width—was 5 cubits, like the courtyard's curtains. [19] They had 4 pillars and 4 copper receptacles, but their hooks were silver and the plating on their tops and their bands was silver. [20] All the tenons for all around the Dwelling Place and the courtyard were copper.

[38:21] These are the records of the Dwelling Place, the Dwelling Place of the *edut*, which were recorded at Moses's command, the work of the Levites under the leadership of Ithamar son of Aaron the priest.

[38:22] Bezalel son of Uri son of Hur from the tribe of Judah made everything that Yahweh had commanded Moses, [23] and with him was Oholiab son of Ahisamakh from the tribe of Dan, engraver, designer, and embroiderer in blue, purple, and earthy-red yarns and in fine linen.

[38:24] All the gold that was used for the labor, in all the labor for the sanctuary—the gifted gold: 29 talents and 730 shekels by the sanctuary weight. [25] The silver from those who were mustered in the community: 100 talents and 1,775 shekels by the sanctuary weight. [26] (A half-shekel per head, half a shekel by the sanctuary weight, for each person who passed through the muster from twenty years old and up: 603,550 men).

[38:27] The 100 talents of silver were for casting the sanctuary's receptacles and the receptacles for the curtain; 100 receptacles per 100 talents, a talent a receptacle. [28] Of the 1,775 shekels he made hooks for the pillars and plating for their tops and their bands. [29] The gifted copper: 70 talents and 2,400 shekels. [30] He made with it the receptacles for the entrance to the Meeting Tent, and the copper altar and its copper grate, and all the altar's utensils, [31] and the receptacles all around the courtyard and the receptacles of the courtyard's gate, and all the tenons for the Dwelling Place and all the tenons for around the court-yard. [39:1] From the blue, purple, and earthy-red yarns they made woven garments for serving in the sanctuary; they made Aaron's sacred garments as Yahweh commanded Moses. [2] They made the *ephod:* gold, blue, purple, and earthy-red yarns and fine twisted linen. [3] They hammered a sheet of gold and cut threads to work into the blue and into the purple and into the earthy-red yarns, as embroidery work. [4] They made attached shoulder pieces for it, joined on its two edges. [5] The embroidered band that was on it was of one piece with it, the same work as it: gold, blue, purple, and earthy-red yarns and fine twisted linen, as Yahweh commanded Moses. [6] They made the onyx stones enclosed in gold settings, engraved, like an engraved seal, with the names of the sons of Israel. [7] He set them on the shoulders of the *ephod* as memorial stones for the Israelites as Yahweh commanded Moses.

[39:8] He made the breastplate of embroidered work, like the work of the *ephod:* gold, blue, purple, and earthy-red yarns and fine twisted linen. [9] It was square; They made the breastplate doubled, a span in length and a span in its width, doubled. [10] They filled it with 4 rows of stone: a row of carnelian, topaz, and emerald—the first row.[8] [11] The second row: turquoise, sapphire, and a *yahalom* stone. [12] The third row: jacinth, agate, and amethyst. [13] The fourth row: beryl, onyx, and jasper. They were enclosed in their gold settings. [14] There were stones with the names of the sons of Israel—12, corresponding to their names; they were engraved each with its name, for the 12 tribes. [15] On the breastplate they made twisted corded chains of pure gold. [16] They made 2 gold settings and 2 gold rings. They put the 2 rings on the 2 ends of the breastplate, [17] and they put the 2 gold chains into the 2 rings on the ends of the breastplate. [18] The 2 ends of the 2 cords they put on the 2 settings and they put them on the shoulders of the *ephod,* at its front. [19] They made 2 gold rings and they put them on the 2 ends of the breastplate, on its inner edge which was next to the *ephod.* [20] They made 2 gold rings and they put them on the 2 shoulders of the *ephod,* on the lower part of its front next to its seam above the embroidered band of the

[8] The patterning of the language in this verse is somewhat reminiscent of the language in Genesis 1, where the activities of the day's creation are recounted and then concluded with the refrain "it was evening, it was morning—the first day."

ephod. [21] They bound the breastplate from its rings to the rings of the *ephod* with a blue cord, so that it was on the embroidered band of the *ephod,* and so that the breastplate would not detach from the *ephod* as Yahweh commanded Moses.

[39:22] They made a robe for the *ephod,* of woven work, entirely blue. [23] The opening of the robe was in its middle, like the opening of a coat of mail, with edging around its opening so that it would not tear. [24] They made the robe's hem with pomegranates of blue, purple, and earthy-red yarns, twisted. [25] They made pure gold bells and they put the bells in between the pomegranates all around the hem of the robe, between the pomegranates. [26] Bell and pomegranate, bell and pomegranate all around the hem of the robe for serving as Yahweh commanded Moses.

[39:27] They made a woven tunic of fine linen for Aaron and for his sons, [28] the fine-linen turban and the fine-linen headdresses, and the undergarments of fine twisted linen, [29] the sashes of fine twisted linen, blue, purple, and earthy-red yarns with embroidered work as Yahweh commanded Moses. [30] They made a pure gold blossom for the holy diadem and they wrote on an inscription, like a seal engraving: "holy to Yahweh." [31] They put it on a blue cord to put it on the turban above it, as Yahweh commanded Moses.

[39:32] All the work of the Dwelling Place of the Meeting Tent was complete. The Israelites did everything that Yahweh commanded Moses, so they did.

[39:33] They brought the Dwelling Place to Moses, to the tent, along with all its furniture:[9] its clasps, its boards, its bars, its pillars, and its receptacles, [34] the reddened ram-skin covering, and the dyed green-blue leather coverings, and the curtain for the screen, [35] the ark of the *edut,*

[9] This recitation of all the parts of the Meeting Tent that have been created follows a familiar pattern for this story: it starts with the interior structure (the Dwelling Place itself), then recounts the furniture placed closest to Yahweh in his private chamber (the inner sanctuary), moves outward to the outer sanctuary, and then moves outside the structure of the Dwelling Place itself to the courtyard of the Meeting Tent complex where the large altar for animal sacrifices is to be placed. This movement from inner chambers to outer courtyard traces a decreasing level of holiness in each stage.

its bars, and its cover, [36] the table and its utensils, and the display bread, [37] the pure lampstand, its lamps (the lamps assembled), its utensils, and the oil for lighting, [38] the gold altar, the anointing oil, and the fragrant incense, along with the screen for the entrance of the tent, [39] the copper altar and its copper grating, its bars, and its utensils, the basin and its stand, [40] the curtains for the courtyard, its pillars and its receptacles, and the screen for the gate of the courtyard, its cords and its tenons, and all the vessels for the ritual labor of the Dwelling Place, for the Meeting Tent, [41] the woven garments to serve in the sanctuary, the sacred garments for Aaron the priest, and the garments for his sons to serve as priests. [42] Just as Yahweh commanded Moses, so the Israelites did all the labor. [43] When Moses saw all the work that they had done—just as Yahweh commanded so they did—Moses blessed them.

[40:1] Yahweh spoke to Moses: [2] "On the first day of the first month, you will erect the Dwelling Place of the Meeting Tent. [3] Put the ark of the *edut* there, and screen off the ark with the curtain. [4] Bring in the table and set its settings, then bring in the lampstand and light its lamps. [5] Then put the gold altar for incense in front of the ark of the *edut* and put up the screen for the entrance to the Dwelling Place. [6] Put the burnt-offering altar in front of the entrance to the Dwelling Place of the Meeting Tent. [7] Put the basin between the Meeting Tent and the altar and put water in it. [8] Set up the courtyard all around and put up the screen for the gate of the courtyard. [9] Then take the anointing oil and anoint the Dwelling Place and everything that is in it and consecrate it so that it will be holy. [10] Then anoint the burnt-offering altar and all its utensils and consecrate that altar so that it will be the highest level of holiness. [11] Then anoint the basin and its stand and consecrate it.

[40:12] Then bring Aaron and his sons to the entrance of the Meeting Tent and wash them with water. [13] Clothe Aaron with the sacred garments, anoint him, and consecrate him to serve me as a priest. [14] Then his sons bring forward, clothe them with tunics, [15] and anoint them as you anointed their father, so that they will serve me as priests. Their anointing will create a perpetual priesthood for them, throughout their generations."

6

The Eight-Day Inauguration of Yahweh's Dwelling Place

_{Exodus 40:16} Moses did everything that Yahweh commanded him, so he did: [17] on the first day of the first month of the second year, he erected the Dwelling Place. [18] Moses erected the Dwelling Place; he set its receptacles and put down its boards, he set up its bars, and he erected its pillars. [19] He stretched the tent over the Dwelling Place and he set the cover of the tent above it, just as Yahweh commanded Moses. [20] He took and put the *edut* in the ark and he set the bars in the ark. He put the cover above the ark. [21] Then he brought the ark into the Dwelling Place and he set up the curtain for a screen, and he screened off the ark of the *edut*, as Yahweh commanded Moses. [22] He put the table in the Meeting Tent on the northern side of the Dwelling Place, outside the curtain, [23] and he set on it a serving of bread, in front of Yahweh, just as Yahweh commanded Moses.[1] [24] He put the lampstand in the Meeting Tent, opposite the table on the southern side of the Dwelling Place, [25] and he lit the lamps in front of Yahweh, just as Yahweh commanded Moses. [26] He set the gold altar in the Meeting Tent, in front of the curtain, [27] and he burned fragrant incense on it, just as Yahweh commanded Moses. [28] Then he set up the screen at the entrance to the Dwelling Place. [29] The burnt-offering altar he set at the entrance of the

---

[1] One of the interesting parts of this section of the narrative is that immediately after putting a piece of furniture into place, Moses puts it to use. In doing this, he is quite literally making an inviting and comfortable space for Yahweh—one that has food, light, and smells pleasant.

Dwelling Place of the Meeting tent, and he sent up[2] a whole burnt offering on it, along with a grain offering, just as Yahweh commanded Moses. [30] Then he put the basin between the Meeting Tent and the altar and he put water in it for washing. [31] Moses, Aaron, and his sons washed from it, both their hands and their feet; [32] whenever they entered the Meeting Tent, or whenever they made offerings on the altar, they would wash, just as Yahweh commanded Moses. [33] Then Moses erected the courtyard all around the Dwelling Place and the altar, and he put up the screen for the gate of the courtyard. When Moses had completed the physical labor, [34] a cloud covered the Meeting Tent and the presence of Yahweh filled the Dwelling Place. [35] Moses was not able to enter the Meeting Tent because the cloud was dwelling on it and the presence of Yahweh filled the Dwelling Place.

[40:36] (When the cloud would lift from the Dwelling Place, the Israelites would set out on all their travels, [37] but if the cloud did not lift, they would not set out until the day it lifted. [38] Yahweh's cloud was over the Dwelling Place by day, and fire was in it at night, visible to all the house of Israel in all their travels.)

Leviticus 1:1 He summoned Moses, and Yahweh spoke to him from the Meeting Tent:[3] [2] "Speak to the Israelites and say to them: 'Any one of you who would offer an offering to Yahweh—from domesticated animals, either from the herd or from the flock, you should offer your offering.

[1:3] 'If his offering is a whole burnt offering from the herd, he should offer an unblemished male. He should bring it to the entrance of the

---

[2] The word here in the Hebrew is not the typical word used for someone offering a sacrifice. Instead, it is from root that means to "go up" or to "ascend." The change in terminology here is quite likely intentional and points to the current physical location of Yahweh being at a distance from the Meeting Tent—probably in the heavens. Moses "sends up" this burnt offering as a kind of signal to Yahweh that his home is ready to inhabit.

[3] The timeline of the story continues uninterrupted from Moses's completion of the physical labor of building the Meeting Tent and its Dwelling Place. There is, however, a significant shift in the story here from the physical labor of constructing and assembling the various components of Yahweh's Meeting Tent to the ritual labor involved for its inauguration and ongoing maintenance.

Meeting Tent to be accepted on his behalf in front of Yahweh. [4] He should lay his hand on the head of the whole burnt offering so that it is accepted on his behalf, to effect purification on his behalf. [5] He should slaughter the herd animal in front of Yahweh.

[1:5] 'The sons of Aaron, the priests, should bring forward the blood and toss the blood all around the altar that is at the entrance to the Meeting Tent. [6] Then they should skin the whole burnt offering and butcher it. [7] The sons of Aaron the priest should put fire on the altar, and they should arrange wood on the fire. [8] The sons of Aaron, the priests, should arrange the butchered pieces, the head, and the fat on the wood that is on the fire that is on the altar. [9] But its intestines and its legs should be washed with water, and then the priest should turn all of it to smoke on the altar; it is a whole burnt offering, a food offering with a pleasing smell for Yahweh.[4]

[1:10] 'If his offering is from the flock, either from the sheep or from the goats, as a whole burnt offering, he should offer an unblemished male. [11] He should slaughter it on the northern side of the altar, in front of Yahweh.

[1:11] 'The sons of Aaron, the priests, should toss its blood all around the altar.[5] [12] It should be butchered, along with its head and its fat, and the priest should arrange them on the wood that is on the fire that is on the altar. [13] But the intestines and the legs he should wash with water.

[4] Many of the sacrificial offerings described in this section of the story are explicitly labeled as "food offerings" for Yahweh. This term (*isheh*) has traditionally been translated as "fire offerings," in part because of resistance to the idea that Yahweh would need or desire food. Noted Leviticus scholar Jacob Milgrom has argued convincingly that this term is best understood as "food offering." In several places in these ritual instructions, this term is used in apposition with the phrase *lehem adonai*, literally: Yahweh's food. There can be no doubt that the priestly narrative imagines a god who desires and perhaps requires food offerings.

[5] At this point in these instructions, we can see a common literary tendency of this author: to abbreviate subsequent iterations of similar instructions. The first case of the animal from the herd is spelled out in great detail, but this second case is abbreviated, and certain necessary steps are omitted from the description (such as Aaron's sons bringing the blood to the altar).

Then the priest should bring everything forward and turn it to smoke on the altar; it is a whole burnt offering, a food offering with a pleasing smell for Yahweh.

1:14 'If his offering for Yahweh is a bird,[6] for a whole burnt offering, he should bring either a turtledove or a pigeon as his offering. 15 The priest should bring it to the altar and pinch off its head. Then he should turn it to smoke on the altar, and its blood should be drained on the side wall of the altar. 16 He should remove its crop[7] and its feathers and throw it to the eastern side of the altar, to the ash heap. 17 Then he should split it with its wings, but not fully dividing it, and the priest should turn it to smoke on the altar on the wood that is on the fire. It is a whole burnt offering, a food offering with a pleasing smell for Yahweh.

2:1 'When someone wants to offer a grain offering to Yahweh, his offering should be of fine flour. He should pour oil on it and put frankincense on it. 2 Then he should bring it to the sons of Aaron, the priests, and he should take a handful of the fine flour and its oil along with its frankincense, and the priest should turn the memorial portion to smoke on the altar. It is a food offering with a pleasing odor for Yahweh. 3 The remainder of the grain offering will be for Aaron and for his sons. It is of the holiest level of Yahweh's food offerings.

2:4 'When you bring a grain offering baked in an oven: fine flour in unleavened cakes mixed with oil, or unleavened wafers spread with oil. 5 If your offering is a grain offering on a griddle: it should be fine flour mixed with oil, unleavened. 6 Break it into pieces and smear oil on it. It is a grain offering. 7 If your offering is a grain offering in a pan, you should make it of fine flour with oil. 8 Then you should bring the

---

[6] The bird offering is an interesting addition that the initial part of this chapter doesn't prepare for, as it is neither a herd nor a flock animal. Bird offerings would have been much less expensive than either of the other types of offerings.

[7] A bird's crop is a pouch in its neck that stores undigested foods (such as insects or worms). These types of animals are not fit for sacrifice on Yahweh's altar, so it makes sense that the priest would remove them prior to offering the rest of the bird.

grain offering that was made in these ways to Yahweh;[8] it should be brought to the priest and he should take it to the altar. 9 The priest should remove some of the grain offering, and turn its memorial portion to smoke on the altar as a food offering with a pleasing smell for Yahweh. 10 The remnants of the grain offering will be for Aaron and his sons. It is of the holiest level of Yahweh's food offerings. 11 Of all the grain offerings that you bring to Yahweh, none should be made with leaven! No leaven and no honey can be turned to smoke as a food offering for Yahweh. 12 As an offering of the first harvest, you can bring them to Yahweh, to the altar, but you will not send them up as a pleasing smell. 13 All your grain offerings you should salt with salt; do not cease from using the salt of your God's covenant[9] on your grain offering. On all your offerings, you must offer salt.

2:14 'If you bring a grain offering of the first fruits of harvest to Yahweh, you should bring new ears roasted in fire, coarse fresh grain, as your first fruits grain offering. 15 You should put oil on it and set frankincense on it. It is a grain offering. 16 The priest will turn a memorial portion of the grain and of the oil with its frankincense to smoke as a food offering for Yahweh.[10]

3:1 'If his offering is a sacrifice of well-being, if it is an offering from the herd, whether male or female, he should bring it in front of Yahweh

[8] This is the only type of sacrifice that is prepared away from the Meeting Tent. It presumes that the Israelites will do the work of cooking either in an oven, pan, or griddle— that is, in their own home kitchens—and then bring the result to offer to Yahweh.

[9] "The salt of your god's covenant" is a somewhat enigmatic phrase that scholars have struggled to explain. Salt is best known as a preservative and its use in all sacrifices (grain or animal) could be meant in a symbolic manner: the Israelites' continued offerings, with their required salt, is a way of signaling their commitment to the preservation of Yahweh's presence in their midst.

[10] It is worth pointing out here a pattern that has held for all the offerings so far: the individual Israelite who brings the offering is an active part of the sacrificial process. He is the one who prepares the grain, or in the case of the animal offerings, slaughters the animal. It is only at the point that the altar must be used that the sacrifice is turned over to the priests. This is because the altar is consecrated and considered holy; moreover, as is described in the instructions to build it, only those who have been consecrated (that is, the priests) are permitted to come into contact with it.

unblemished. [2] He should lay his hand on the head of the offering, and slaughter it at the entrance to the Meeting Tent. The sons of Aaron, the priests, should toss its blood all around the altar. [3] He should bring part of the sacrifice of well-being as a food offering for Yahweh: the fat that covers the intestines and all the fat that is around the intestines, [4] and the two kidneys and the fat that is on them, that is on the loins, and the lobe of the liver that he removes with the kidneys. [5] The sons of Aaron should turn it to smoke on the altar, on the whole burnt offering that is on the wood that is on the fire, as a food offering with a pleasing smell for Yahweh.

[3:6] 'If his offering is from the flock, as a sacrifice of well-being for Yahweh, he should offer a male or a female, unblemished. [7] If his offering is a sheep offering, he should bring it in front of Yahweh, [8] and lay his hand on his offering's head and slaughter it in front of the Meeting Tent. Aaron's sons should toss its blood all around the altar. [9] He should bring some of the sacrifice of well-being as a food offering for Yahweh: its fat, its unblemished broad tail—it should be removed next to its backbone—the fat that covers the intestines and all the fat that is around the intestines, [10] the two kidneys, and the fat that is on them that is next to the loins, and the lobe of the liver that he should remove with the kidneys. [11] The priest should turn it to smoke on the altar as food,[11] a food gift for Yahweh.

[3:12] 'If his offering is a goat, he should bring it in front of Yahweh [13] and lay his hand on its head and slaughter it in front of the Meeting Tent. Aaron's sons should toss its blood all around the altar. [14] He should bring some of his offering as a food gift for Yahweh: the fat that covers the intestines and all the fat that is around the intestines, [15] and the two kidneys and the fat that is on them, that is next to the loins, and the lobe of the liver that he will remove with the kidneys. [16] The priest should turn them to smoke on the altar as food, a food offering with a pleasing smell. All fat belongs to Yahweh. [17] It is a perpetual law throughout your generations, in all your settlements: you must not consume any fat or blood.'"

[11] This is the first time that a sacrifice is specifically labeled with the more common word for food (*lehem*).

4:1 Yahweh spoke to Moses: 2 "Tell the Israelites: 'When a person unintentionally acts wrongly with any of Yahweh's prohibitive commandments, and does any one of them,[12]

4:3 'If the anointed priest acts wrongly in a way that imparts guilt on the people, he should offer an unblemished bull of the herd to Yahweh for the wrong that he did, as a decontamination offering. 4 He should bring the bull to the entrance of the Meeting Tent, in front of Yahweh, lay his hand on the bull's head, and slaughter the bull in front of Yahweh. 5 The anointed priest should take some of the bull's blood[13] and bring it into the Meeting Tent. 6 Then the priest should dip his finger in the blood and sprinkle some of the blood seven times in front of Yahweh,[14] on the front of the sanctuary's curtain. 7 Then the priest should put some of the blood on the horns of the fragrant incense altar in front of Yahweh, which is inside the Meeting Tent, and the rest of the bull's blood he should pour out at the base of the burnt-offering altar that is at the

---

[12] This is the first time in the story that the possibility of the Israelites transgressing one of Yahweh's commands is raised. What is particularly interesting about this is that Yahweh hasn't really given any prohibitive commands that could be transgressed yet. Those will come later in the story, but this section is laying the groundwork for that. This whole chapter is focused on the unintentional error someone might make. Intentionality is important in this story. People are still held responsible for their errors and transgressions even if they are done unintentionally, but the cost for this type of transgression is lower.

[13] The blood of an animal sacrificed as a decontamination offering has a very specific use in this story: it is a kind of ritual detergent that is applied to various surfaces in the Meeting Tent and its courtyard. Unintentional sins are imagined as creating a kind of contamination that adheres to holy things (like the Meeting Tent and its furniture). The application of blood to these items is thought of as decontaminating them— hence the name of the sacrifice itself: a decontamination offering.

[14] One of the major differences between the four different types of decontamination offerings (one in each of the next four paragraphs) involves the question of where the priest puts the animal's blood. In this case and the next case of the whole community, the blood is brought into the Meeting Tent itself, and it is applied to various parts of the outer sanctuary. In the third and fourth cases, the blood stays outside the Meeting Tent in the courtyard and is only applied to that altar. The more deeply into the Meeting Tent the blood is applied, the more serious the transgression is. What we learn from this part of the story is that if the anointed priest or the community as a whole goes against Yahweh, their action has a greater effect on him and his Dwelling Place than if a leader or an ordinary individual does so.

entrance to the Meeting Tent. [8] He should remove all the fat of the bull of the decontamination offering: the fat covering the intestines and the fat that is all around the intestines, [9] the two kidneys and the fat that is on them, next to the loins; the lobe of the liver he should remove with the kidneys, [10] just as it was removed from the ox of the sacrifice of well-being. Then the priest should turn them to smoke on the burnt-offering altar. [11] But the bull's skin and all its flesh, along with its head, legs, intestines, and dung, [12] all the rest of the bull, he should bring outside the camp to a pure place, to the ash heap, and he should burn it on wood in a fire; it should be burned on the ash heap.

[4:13] 'If the entire Israelite community unintentionally errs and the error is not recognized by the community, and they do something that Yahweh prohibited causing them to incur guilt, [14] and then their error becomes apparent to them, the community should offer a bull of the herd as a decontamination offering. They should bring it before the Meeting Tent, [15] and the elders of the community should lay their hands on the bull's head in front of Yahweh, and the bull should be slaughtered in front of Yahweh. [16] Then the anointed priest should bring some of the bull's blood into the Meeting Tent, [17] and the priest should dip his finger in some of the blood and sprinkle it seven times in front of Yahweh, on the front of the curtain. [18] Then he should put some of the blood on the horns of the incense altar that is in front of Yahweh, which is inside the Meeting Tent, and the rest of the blood he should pour out at the base of the burnt-offering altar that is at the entrance to the Meeting Tent. [19] All the fat should be removed from it and turned to smoke on the altar. [20] He should do with the bull just as he did with the other bull for a decontamination offering, so he should do. In this way, the priest will effect purification on their behalf; then they will be forgiven.[15] [21] He should then take the bull outside the

[15] Personal forgiveness for an unintentional transgression against Yahweh can come only after Yahweh's Dwelling Place has been decontaminated from the contaminating effects of that transgression. To put it differently, there are two separate processes at play here: (1) the priest effecting purification of the Meeting Tent; and (2) Yahweh's forgiveness of the individual for their transgression. The second cannot happen without the first, in large part because if too much contamination builds in the Meeting Tent from unintentional sins, the Meeting Tent will no longer serve its function as a pure place that enables Yahweh to dwell among the Israelites.

camp and burn it just as he burned the first bull. It is the community's decontamination offering.

4:22 'If a leader errs and unintentionally does one of the things that Yahweh his God prohibited and incurs guilt, 23 when his error is made known to him, he should bring his offering of an unblemished male goat. 24 He should lay his hand on the goat's head and slaughter it in the place where the burnt offering is slaughtered in front of Yahweh. It is a decontamination offering. 25 The priest should take some of its blood with his finger and put it on the horns of the burnt-offering altar. The rest of the blood he should pour out at the base of the burnt-offering altar. 26 All its fat he should turn to smoke on the altar, just like the fat of the sacrifice of well-being. In this way, the priest will effect purification on his behalf for his error; then he will be forgiven.

4:27 'If an ordinary person unintentionally errs[16] by doing one of the things that Yahweh prohibited and incurs guilt, 28 when his error is made known to him, he should bring as his offering an unblemished female goat for the error he committed. 29 He should lay his hand on the head of the decontamination offering and slaughter the decontamination offering in the place of the burnt offering. 30 The priest should take some of its blood with his finger and put it on the horns of the burnt-offering altar. The rest of its blood, he should pour out at the base of the altar. 31 All its fats should be removed as the fats were removed from the sacrifice of well-being, and the priest should turn it to smoke on the altar for a pleasing aroma for Yahweh. The priest should effect purification on his behalf, and then he will be forgiven. 32 If the offering he brings as a decontamination offering is a sheep, he should bring an unblemished female. 33 He should lay his hand on the head of the decontamination offering and slaughter it as a decontamination offering in the place where the burnt offering is slaughtered. 34 Then the priest should take some of the decontamination offering's blood with his finger and put it on the horns of the burnt-offering altar. The rest of the blood he should pour out at the base of the altar.

[16] The success of the Meeting Tent and Yahweh's Dwelling Place within it relies on the participation of every single Israelite in its maintenance, not just the priests and leaders.

³⁵ All its fats should be removed, as the fats of the sheep of the well-being offering were removed. Then the priest should turn them to smoke on the altar, with Yahweh's food offerings. In this way, the priest will effect purification on his behalf for his error; then he will be forgiven.

⁵:¹ 'If a person errs when he has heard public testimony, and he could be a witness who has seen or has knowledge of the case, and he does not speak up, then he must bear his punishment; ² or if a person touches an impure object like the carcass of an impure wild animal,[17] or the carcass of an impure domestic animal, or the carcass of an impure insect or reptile, and it remains unknown to him, then he will be impure and incur guilt; ³ or if a person touches human impurity, any of the impurities that can cause impurity, and forgets about it though he should be aware, he is guilty; ⁴ or if a person swears a thoughtless oath, whether for bad or for good, for anything that a person might make a thoughtless oath, and he forgets about it though he should be aware—if he is guilty in any of these matters, ⁵ when he recognizes his guilt in any of these matters,[18] he should confess the error he has made, ⁶ and bring his guilt penalty to Yahweh for his error: a female from the flock, either a sheep or a goat, as a decontamination offering. Then the priest will effect purification on his behalf for his error.

⁵:⁷ 'But if he cannot afford a sheep,[19] then he should bring as his guilt penalty for his error two turtledoves or two pigeons for Yahweh, one as a decontamination offering and one as a burnt offering. ⁸ He should bring them to the priest, who should offer the first as a decontamination

[17] The category of "impure wild animal" here does not make much sense yet in the story as there has not been any distinction made between pure and impure animals. This designation is anticipating a later part of Yahweh's speech to Moses.

[18] The four cases offered here are all slightly more serious than the unintentional errors described in the previous chapter. In these cases, the individual acted knowingly (or knowingly failed to act) and simply ignored, or forgot about, or procrastinated in dealing with, the ritual consequences of their behavior.

[19] In this paragraph and the next paragraph, we get a clear look at the possible economic realities of many ordinary Israelites. For most, sacrificing a whole animal would have been well out of their reach. These next couple of paragraphs allow for equally efficacious, but less expensive, offerings.

offering, pinching off its head from its neck, but not entirely severing it. [9] He should sprinkle some of the decontamination offering's blood on the side wall of the altar, and the remainder of the blood he should drain at the base of the altar. It is a decontamination offering. [10] The second, he should offer as a burnt offering according to the regulation. In this way, the priest will effect purification on his behalf for his error; then he will be forgiven.

5:11 'If he cannot afford two turtledoves or two pigeons, he should bring as his offering for his error a tenth of an *ephah* of fine flour as a decontamination offering. He should not put oil or frankincense on it since it is a decontamination offering. [12] He should bring it to the priest, and the priest will take a handful from it as a memorial portion and turn it to smoke on the altar, with Yahweh's food offerings. It is a decontamination offering. [13] In this way, the priest will effect purification for whichever of these errors he committed; then he will be forgiven. Like the grain offering, the remainder will belong to the priest.'"

5:14 Yahweh spoke to Moses: [15] "When someone commits a sacrilegious act, erring unintentionally with respect to Yahweh's sacred objects, he should bring his guilt-penalty to Yahweh: an unblemished ram from the flock, convertible to silver according to the sanctuary shekel, as a guilt-offering. [16] For his error with respect to a sacred object, he should make restitution, and he should add a fifth to it and give it to the priest. The priest will effect purification on his behalf with the ram of the guilt offering, and then he will be forgiven.

5:17 "When a person errs and does something that Yahweh prohibited without knowing it, he has incurred guilt and will bear his punishment.[20] [18] He should bring an unblemished ram from the flock, or its monetary equivalent, as a guilt offering to the priest. Then the priest will effect purification on his behalf for the unintentional error that is

---

[20] There is a logical question to ask here: if the person does not know he has done something wrong, why would he know to bring an offering for it? The main difference between this and the cases described earlier in the chapter or in Leviticus 4 seems to be that the person never gains direct knowledge about how he erred, but he might instead be plagued with a vague feeling of guilt that he can't quite place.

unknown to him, and he will be forgiven. [19] It is a guilt offering; he has incurred guilt against Yahweh."

5:20 Yahweh spoke to Moses: [21] "When a person errs and commits a sacrilegious act against Yahweh by cheating his neighbor[21] with a deposit or a pledge, or by robbery, or by extorting his neighbor, [22] or by finding a lost object and lying about it, or by swearing falsely about any of the things a person does in error, [23] when he has erred and incurred guilt, he should return the stolen goods, or the money extorted, or the deposit he kept, or the lost object he found, [24] or anything else that he swore falsely about, he should repay the original amount and add a fifth to it. He should pay it as soon as he recognizes his guilt. [25] Then his guilt offering he should bring to the priest for Yahweh: an unblemished ram from the flock, or its monetary equivalent, for a guilt offering to the priest. [26] The priest will effect purification on his behalf in front of Yahweh and then he will be forgiven for whatever he did to incur guilt."

6:1 Yahweh spoke to Moses: [2] "Command Aaron and his sons:[22] 'This is the instruction for the burnt offering: The burnt offering itself should

[21] This part of Yahweh's instructions is noteworthy because it is one of the first places that Yahweh addresses relationships between Israelites, and not just between Israelites and himself. Cheating your neighbor in some way is placed on par with misusing or abusing Yahweh's sacred objects—in other words, it is one of the most severe crimes there is.

[22] This part of Yahweh's speech seems to be a bit repetitive on the surface. He goes back and starts describing each of the five types of sacrifice again. However, the differences between this part of the speech and what preceded it in Leviticus 1–5 are subtle and important. The secondary audience (the people Moses is supposed to relay Yahweh's message to) in Leviticus 1–5 is the Israelite community as a whole. Here, in Leviticus 6–7, it is solely the priests. The content has a bit to do with this, In Leviticus 1–5, the parts of the sacrificial process described were those that were (for the most part) public-facing— things a normal Israelite could see the priests doing or might witness aspects of. In this set of instructions in Leviticus 6–7, Yahweh picks up where he left off in Leviticus 1–5 and describes what the priests should do to finish up each sacrificial offering. The instructions here focus much more on the final stages of the process, and especially on the cleanup and disposal of non-sacrificial remains involved. This is something that happens out of the sight of the Israelites, but by virtue of its being included in this story, ordinary Israelites are getting a glimpse into the inner workings of their cult that they might otherwise not have gotten.

remain on the kindling on the altar all night long until morning; the altar's fire should remain burning. [3] The priest should wear his linen garment, and the linen underwear he should wear next to his skin. He should remove the ashes, those of the burnt offering on the altar, which the fire has consumed,[23] and he should put them next to the altar. [4] Then he should strip[24] his garments and put on new garments, and then take the ashes outside the camp to a pure place. [5] The fire on the altar should be kept burning on it; it should not be extinguished. The priest should burn wood on it every morning, arrange the burnt offering on it, and turn the fats of the sacrifice of well-being to smoke on it. [6] A continual fire[25] should be kept burning on the altar; it should not be extinguished.

[6:7] 'This is the instruction for the grain offering: Aaron's sons should bring it in front of Yahweh, to the front of the altar, [8] and remove a handful of the grain offering's fine flour and oil from it, along with any frankincense on the grain offering, and turn it to smoke on the altar as a pleasing smell, a memorial portion for Yahweh. [9] The remainder of it should be eaten by Aaron and his sons; it should be eaten unleavened in a sacred place; they should eat it in the courtyard of the Meeting Tent. [10] It should not be baked with leaven; I have given it as their portion from my food offerings. It is of the highest level of holiness, like the decontamination offering and the guilt offering. [11] Only Aaron's male children can eat it. It is a perpetual portion throughout your generations from Yahweh's food gifts; anyone who touches them must be holy.'"

[6:12] Yahweh spoke to Moses: [13] "This is the offering Aaron and his sons should offer to Yahweh when they are anointed: a tenth of an *ephah* of fine flour as a regular grain offering, half of it in the morning and half of it in the evening, [14] made on a griddle with oil. You should bring it

[23] Literally: eaten

[24] This is the same verb used earlier in the sacrificial instructions to describe skinning the animal before offering it on the altar.

[25] This statement is almost exactly parallel to the one in verse 5, but adds the term *tamid*, meaning regular or continual. The *tamid* is also a specific type of sacrificial offering (recall Exod 29:38–46) that makes up Yahweh's two daily meals, one in the morning and one in the evening. The introduction of the term *tamid* in this verse intensifies the command for a perpetual fire on the altar while also calling to mind that regular offering for Yahweh.

saturated and offer it as a baked grain offering in pieces as a pleasing smell for Yahweh. [15] The priest who is anointed after him from among his sons will prepare it. It is a perpetual portion for Yahweh. It should be burned entirely. [16] Every grain offering from a priest should be burned entirely; it should not be eaten."

[6:17] Yahweh spoke to Moses: [18] "Tell Aaron and his sons: 'This is the instruction for the decontamination offering. In the place where the burnt offering is slaughtered, the decontamination offering should be slaughtered, in front of Yahweh. It is of the holiest level. [19] The priest who offers the decontamination offering should eat it; it should be eaten in a holy place, in the courtyard of the Meeting Tent. [20] Anyone who touches its flesh must be holy, and if its blood is sprinkled on a garment, you must wash what has been stained in a holy place. [21] Any earthenware vessel used to boil it should be broken, and if it was boiled in a copper vessel, it should be scrubbed and rinsed with water. [22] Any male priest can eat it.[26] It is of the holiest level. [23] However, any decontamination offering whose blood has been brought into the Meeting Tent to effect purification in the sanctuary may not be eaten. It must be burned in fire.

[7:1] 'This is the instruction for the guilt offering; it is of the holiest level. [2] In the place where they slaughter the burnt offering, they should slaughter the guilt offering. They should toss its blood all around the altar, [3] and they should offer all its fat: the broadtail, the fat that covers the intestines, [4] the two kidneys and the fat on them, next to the loins, and the lobe of the liver, which should be removed with the kidneys. [5] The priest should turn them to smoke on the altar as a food offering for Yahweh. It is a guilt offering. [6] Every male priest may eat it, though it should be eaten in a holy place. It is of the holiest level.[27]

[7:7] 'The decontamination offering and the guilt offering are alike; they share a single instruction: it will belong to the priest who effects purifi-

[26] Here the referent is the meat of the decontamination offering, and not the blood-stained priestly garment.

[27] This refrain (more repetitive in Hebrew: *kodesh kodashim hu*) serves as a kind of inclusio, marking the opening and the closing of the instructions for the guilt offering in this passage.

cation with it. [8] The priest who offers someone's burnt offering can have the skin of the burnt offering he has offered. [9] Every grain offering that is baked in an oven, and everything that is made in a pan or on a griddle goes to the priest who offered it. [10] Every other grain offering, whether mixed with oil or dry, should belong equally to all Aaron's sons.

7:11 'This is the instruction for the sacrifice of well-being[28] that is offered to Yahweh. [12] If he offers it with thanksgiving, he should bring with the sacrifice of thanksgiving an unleavened cake mixed with oil, and unleavened wafers smeared with oil, and cakes made of fine flour, saturated in oil. [13] With cakes of leavened bread he should offer his offering of a thanksgiving sacrifice of well-being. [14] He should bring from it one of each kind of offering as a gift for Yahweh; it will belong to the priest who tosses the blood of the well-being offering. [15] But the flesh of the thanksgiving sacrifice of well-being should be eaten on the day it was offered; none of it should be left over until morning.

7:16 'If his offering is a vow or a freewill offering, his sacrifice should be eaten on the day he offers it, and on the next day anything left over from it should be eaten. [17] Any remaining meat from the sacrifice should be burned in fire on the third day. [18] But if any of the meat of his sacrifice of well-being is consumed on the third day, it will not be accepted. And as for the one who offered it, it is no longer considered his.[29] It is ritually unacceptable. The person who eats it will incur guilt because of it.

[28] This is the final type of sacrifice that is addressed in this section. Readers might notice that the order of instructions in Leviticus 6–7 does not follow the order in Leviticus 1–5. In part, this is because the instructions in Leviticus 6–7 start with the most simple offering (the burnt offering) and progress to the most complicated (the well-being offering). The well-being offering can be sacrificed for at least three different purposes, each with different rules, so this is saved for last in the instructions to the priests.

[29] There is a very specific legal concept related to property law that this story invokes with respect to portions of the sacrifice of well-being. The basic idea is that Yahweh is the owner of the sacrifice (as Yahweh owns all things given to him on the altar), and that he allows the person who offered it to make use of/eat certain parts of the animal, but only under a particular set of rules—namely, that he must only eat the meat on days one and two. If he violates those rules and consumes the meat on day three, he is in breach of the contract made with Yahweh; the meat of the animal is no longer his to use. This is one of the most serious crimes there can be in this story: the person is effectively stealing from Yahweh.

7:19 'Meat that touches anything impure should not be eaten. It should be burned in fire. As for other meat, anyone who is clean can eat the meat. 20 A person who eats the meat from a sacrifice of well-being for Yahweh while he is impure, that person will be cut off from their people. 21 A person who touches anything impure, whether human impurity or animal impurity or any impure insect or reptile, and then eats meat from a sacrifice of well-being for Yahweh, that person will be cut off from their people.'"

7:22 Yahweh spoke to Moses: 23 "Speak to the Israelites:[30] 'You should not eat any fat from an ox or a sheep or a goat. 24 The fat of an animal that died or the fat of an animal killed by wild animals may be used for any labor, but you should never eat it. 25 If anyone eats the fat of a domesticated animal that could be offered as a food offering for Yahweh, the person who ate it will be cut off from their people. 26 You should not consume any blood, whether from a bird or a domesticated animal, in any of your settlements. 27 Anyone who eats any blood, that person will be cut off from their people.'"

7:28 Yahweh spoke to Moses: 29 "Speak to the Israelites: 'Anyone who offers his sacrifice of well-being to Yahweh, he must bring his offering as a sacrifice of well-being to Yahweh. 30 His hands must bring Yahweh's food offering. The fat along with the breast he should present: the breast to be elevated in front of Yahweh as an elevation offering. 31 The priest should turn the fat to smoke on the altar, and the breast will belong to Aaron and his sons. 32 The right thigh of your sacrifices of well-being you should give to the priest as a gift. 33 The right thigh will belong to whichever of Aaron's sons offered the blood of the well-being offering and the fats, as an allotted portion. 34 I have taken[31] the breast of the elevation offering and the thigh that is gifted from the Israelites' sacrifices of well-being and I have given them to Aaron the priest and to his sons as a perpetual portion from the Israelites.

[30] Here the secondary addressee changes again and these instructions are meant for the entire community, not just the priests.

[31] This is one of the few times that Yahweh switches to first-person discourse in his speeches. These moments are almost always moments of emphasis, usually with long-term implications.

[35] This is Aaron's consecrated portion and the consecrated portion of his sons from Yahweh's food offerings once they have been offered[32] to serve Yahweh as priests. [36] These things Yahweh commanded to be given to them once he anointed them, as a perpetual portion from the Israelites, throughout their generations.'"

[7:37] This is the instruction for the burnt offering, the grain offering, the decontamination offering, the guilt offering, the ordination offering, and the sacrifice of well-being [38] that Yahweh commanded Moses on Mount Sinai, when he commanded the Israelites to bring their offerings to Yahweh in the wilderness of Sinai.

[8:1] Yahweh spoke to Moses: [2] "Take Aaron and his sons, the garments, the anointing oil, the bull for the decontamination offering, the two rams, and the basket of unleavened bread, [3] and gather the whole community at the entrance to the Meeting Tent."[33]

[8:4] Moses did just as Yahweh commanded. When the community gathered at the entrance to the Meeting Tent, [5] Moses said to the community: "This is what Yahweh commanded to be done."

[8:6] Moses brought forward Aaron and his sons and washed them with water. [7] He put the tunic on him, and bound him up with the sash, dressed him in the robe, and put the *ephod* on him. Then he bound him with the decorated band of the *ephod* and tied[34] the *ephod* to him with it. [8] Then he put on him the breastplate and put the *urim* and the *tummim* in the breastplate. [9] He set the turban on his head and put the golden blossom, the holy diadem, on the front of the turban just as Yahweh commanded Moses. [10] Then Moses took the anointing oil and

[32] Perhaps unexpectedly, the verb used here to describe the ordination of Aaron and his sons is the same verb used to describe the offering of sacrifices on the altar.

[33] This first set of Yahweh's instructions lists the people or objects that will be used in the subsequent ritual in order of their use with one exception—the community. Though listed last, the community is the first group brought to the Meeting Tent in order to witness the inauguration of the priests.

[34] The Hebrew for this verb is from the same root as the noun *ephod*, creating a threefold repetition of the root *ephod* in this sentence and giving that particular garment, unique to the high priest, more of an emphasis.

anointed the Dwelling Place and everything in it, consecrating them. [11] He sprinkled some of it on the altar seven times,[35] and anointed the altar with its vessels and the basin and its stand to consecrate them. [12] Then Moses poured some of the anointing oil on Aaron's head, anointing him in order to consecrate him. [13] Then Moses brought forward Aaron's sons and clothed them with tunics and bound them up with sashes, and bound their headdresses for them, just as Yahweh commanded Moses.

[8:14] He led forward the bull for the decontamination offering, and Aaron and his sons laid their hands on the head of the bull of the decontamination offering, [15] and it was slaughtered. Moses then took the blood and put it all around the horns of the altar with his finger; he decontaminated the altar. The rest of the blood he poured out at the base of the altar. He consecrated it by effecting purification on it. [16] Then he took all the fat that was on the intestines and the lobe of the liver, along with the two kidneys and their fat, and Moses turned them to smoke on the altar. [17] The bull, its skin, its flesh, and its dung were burned in fire outside the camp, just as Yahweh commanded Moses.

[8:18] Then he offered the ram for a burnt offering. Aaron and his sons laid their hands on the ram's head, [19] and it was slaughtered. Moses then tossed the blood all around the altar. [20] The ram was butchered, and Moses turned the head, the pieces, and the fat to smoke. [21] Then he washed the intestines and the legs with water, and Moses turned the rest of the ram to smoke on the altar. It was a burnt offering with a pleasing smell, a food offering for Yahweh, just as Yahweh commanded Moses.

[8:22] He brought forward the second ram, the ordination ram, and Aaron and his sons laid their hands on the ram's head, [23] and it was slaughtered. Then Moses took some of the blood and put it on Aaron's right

---

[35] This refers to the altar of burnt-offering that is outside the Dwelling Place, in the courtyard of the Meeting Tent. On the first day of this seven-day ritual, it is anointed seven times compared with the Dwelling Place being anointed once. This is in part what will make the burnt-offering altar an object of the holiest degree: more applications of the anointing oil mean a higher degree of sanctity. This principle will hold when it comes to the anointing of the priests themselves.

earlobe, on the thumb of his right hand, and on the big toe of his right foot. [24] Then he brought forward Aaron's sons, and Moses put some of the blood on their right earlobes, on the thumb of their right hands, and on the big toe of their right feet. Then Moses tossed the blood all around the altar. [25] He took the fat: the broadtail, all the fat on the intestines, the lobe of the liver, the two kidneys and their fat, and the right thigh. [26] From the basket of unleavened bread that was in front of Yahweh, he took one unleavened cake, one cake of oiled bread, and one wafer and he put them on top of the fats and on top of the right thigh. [27] He then put all this in the hands of Aaron and his sons,[36] and they elevated them as an elevation offering in front of Yahweh. [28] Moses then took them from their hands and turned them to smoke on the altar with the burnt offering. They were an ordination offering with a pleasing smell; Yahweh's food offering. [29] Moses took the breast and elevated it as an elevation offering in front of Yahweh; from the ordination ram, this was Moses's portion,[37] just as Yahweh commanded Moses.

[8:30] Then Moses took some of the anointing oil and some of the blood that was on the altar and he sprinkled it on Aaron and on his garments, on his sons and on his sons' garments; he consecrated Aaron and his garments along with his sons and his sons' garments.[38]

[36] The Hebrew idiom in the priestly narrative for ordination is literally translated as "to fill the hands of." It might well come from this moment in the story, where critical portions of the ordination sacrifice are put into the soon-to-be priests' hands for them to present to Yahweh.

[37] According to the instructions given by Yahweh in Leviticus 7:28–36, the breast and the right thigh are specially marked portions of the sacrificial animal. The right thigh is designated specifically for the person "from among Aaron's sons" who tosses the blood of the offering on the altar. In this case, none of Aaron's sons have done this; only Moses has. The right thigh, then, is burned on the altar and given to Yahweh. The breast is a different matter. This, too, is designated as a portion for Aaron the priest or his sons as a payment for their ritual labor, but it can belong to them only *after* they are ordained as priests (7:35). In this scene in the story, Aaron and his sons are not yet priests. Moses, however, is acting as a priest, even though he is not actually a priest, and so the breast becomes his payment for the ritual labor in this one instance. He will never again have access to priestly portions of the sacrifice. This is one of the ways that the story highlights the unique nature of this ritual and the liminal status of both Moses and Aaron, as well as the latter's sons.

[38] Just as the burnt-offering altar is anointed seven times (compared to the incense altar's single anointing; see 8:10–11), here Aaron is anointed for a second time, whereas

[31] Moses said to Aaron and his sons: "Boil the meat at the entrance to the Meeting Tent and eat it there along with the bread that is in the ordination basket, as I commanded; Aaron and his sons should eat it.[39] [32] Whatever is left over from the meat and bread should be burned in fire.

[8:33] You should not leave the entrance to the Meeting Tent for seven days (until your ordination is complete) because your ordination takes seven days. [34] As it was done today, Yahweh commanded doing in order to effect purification on your behalf. [35] You will remain at the entrance to the Meeting Tent for seven days and nights; you will perform Yahweh's guard duty, lest you die, as I have been commanded.'"[40] [36] Aaron and his sons did everything that Yahweh commanded through Moses.

[9:1] On the eighth day,[41] Moses summoned Aaron, his sons, and the Israelite elders. [2] He said to Aaron: "Take for yourself a calf from the herd for a decontamination offering and a ram for a burnt offering, both unblemished, and bring them in front of Yahweh. [3] To the Israelites, say: 'Take a male goat as a decontamination offering, and a calf and a lamb, both a year old, unblemished, for a burnt offering, [4] and an ox and a ram for well-being offerings to sacrifice in front of Yahweh, along with a grain offering mixed with oil. Today Yahweh will appear to you!'"[42]

---

his sons are anointed for the first time. This extra degree of anointing for Aaron distinguishes him as being of a higher level of holiness than his sons. This (along with his distinctive garments, which are also doubly anointed) is what makes him a "high priest."

[39] The portion of meat here is not the breast (which belongs to Moses), but the rest of the meat of the ram that has not been burned on the altar.

[40] This "as I have been commanded" phrase marks a nice inclusio with the same phrase (a single passive form of the verb in Hebrew) in v. 31, and thus marks off the completion of Moses's instructions to Aaron and his sons for the next seven days.

[41] Here the narrator has accelerated the passage of time and skipped right to the end of the priests' ordination process on the eighth day. The only notice of the passage of the previous seven days is in the final verse of chapter 8.

[42] This day is the culmination of all the work the Israelites have put in over the last year at the base of Mount Sinai to build the various parts of the Meeting Tent. Yahweh is finally about to permanently take up residence in his new home.

⁹˸⁵ They brought the things Moses commended to the entrance of the Meeting Tent, and the whole community came forward and stood in front of Yahweh. ⁶ Then Moses said, "This is what Yahweh commanded you to do so that Yahweh's presence would appear to you." ⁷ Moses said to Aaron: "Approach the altar and sacrifice your decontamination offering and your burnt offering, effecting purification on your behalf and on behalf of the people. Then sacrifice the people's offering to effect purification on their behalf, as Yahweh commanded."

⁹˸⁸ Aaron approached the altar and slaughtered his calf for his decontamination offering. ⁹ Aaron's sons brought its blood to him and he dipped his finger in the blood and put it on the horns of the altar. The rest of the blood he poured out at the base of the altar. ¹⁰ The fat and the kidneys, and the lobe of the liver of the decontamination offering he turned to smoke on the altar, just as Yahweh commanded Moses. ¹¹ But the meat and the skin he burned in a fire outside the camp.

⁹˸¹² Then he slaughtered the burnt offering. Aaron's sons gave him the blood and he tossed it all around the altar. ¹³ They gave the burnt offering to him in pieces, with its head, and he turned them to smoke on the altar. ¹⁴ Then he washed the intestines and the legs and turned those to smoke on top of the burnt offering on the altar.

⁹˸¹⁵ Then he brought forward the people's offering: he took the goat for the people's decontamination offering and he slaughtered it and offered it as a decontamination offering like the first one. ¹⁶ Then he brought forward the burnt offering and sacrificed it according to regulation. ¹⁷ Then he brought forward the grain offering and filled his hand with some of it and turned it to smoke on the altar. (This was in addition to the morning burnt offering.) ¹⁸ Then he slaughtered the ox and the ram—the people's sacrifices of well-being. Aaron's sons brought him the blood and he tossed it all around the altar. ¹⁹ The fats from the ox and the ram—the broad tail, those covering the intestines, the kidneys, and the lobe of the liver—²⁰ they put these fats on the breasts and turned the fats to smoke on the altar. ²¹ The breasts and the right thigh Aaron elevated as an elevation offering in front of Yahweh, just as Moses commanded.

9:22 Then Aaron lifted his hands toward the people, and he blessed them. When he came down from sacrificing the decontamination offering, the burnt offering, and the well-being offering, 23 Moses and Aaron entered the Meeting Tent.[43] They came out and blessed the people. Then the presence of Yahweh appeared to all the people. 24 Fire burst out from in front of Yahweh and consumed the burnt offering and the fats on the altar. All the people saw this, and they joyfully shouted and prostrated themselves.[44]

10:1 But Aaron's sons Nadav and Avihu each took his own fire pan and put coals on it and then set incense on it. They brought in front of Yahweh an unauthorized fire that he had not instructed them. 2 Fire burst out from in front of Yahweh and consumed them.[45] They died in front of Yahweh. 3 Moses said to Aaron: "This is what Yahweh said: 'By those near to me, I will be sanctified, but before all the people I will be present.'"[46] Aaron was silent.

10:4 Moses summoned Misha'el and Elzaphan, the sons of Uzzi'el, Aaron's uncle. He said to them: "Come forward and carry your relatives away from the front of the sanctuary to somewhere outside the camp." 5 They came forward and carried them by their tunics outside the camp, just as Moses directed. 6 Moses said to Aaron, and to Eleazar and Ithamar, his sons: "Your heads you should not uncover, and your garments you should not tear or else you will die, and fury strike the entire community. Your family, the entire house of Israel, may mourn the burning that Yahweh has done. 7 But you should not leave the

[43] This is the first time that Aaron is able to enter Yahweh's Dwelling Place, and it is an indication that he is now fully ordained as high priest.

[44] Literally: "they fell on their faces."

[45] There is a conscious parallel here with the divine fireball in 9:24: as the first divine fireball consumed the legitimately offered sacrifices, this second divine fireball consumes those who attempt to offer illegitimate sacrifices.

[46] This is something of an enigmatic statement, but it seems to suggest that while the priests are the ones who serve Yahweh, Yahweh's presence requires the physical presence of the Israelites as well.

entrance to the Meeting Tent,[47] or else you will die because Yahweh's anointing oil is on you."[48] They did as Moses said.

10:8 Yahweh spoke to Aaron:[49] 9 "Whenever you enter the Meeting Tent, you and your sons should not drink wine or strong drink, or else you will die. This is a perpetual law throughout your generations. 10 You must be able to distinguish between the holy and the profane, between the impure and the pure, 11 and to instruct the Israelites in all the rules that Yahweh has given to them through Moses."

10:12 Moses said to Aaron, Eleazar, and Ithamar, his remaining sons: "Take the remaining grain offering from Yahweh's food gifts and eat it unleavened next to the altar. It is of the holiest level. 13 You should eat it in a sacred place, as it is your portion and your sons' portion from Yahweh's food gifts; so I was commanded. 14 The breast of the elevation offering and the gifted thigh you should eat in a pure place, you and your sons and daughters with you, as they are given as your portion and your sons' portion from the Israelites' sacrifices of well-being. 15 The gifted thigh and the breast of the elevation offering, together with the fat of the food offerings, they must bring to elevate as an elevation offering in front of Yahweh. It is a perpetual portion for you and your sons, as Yahweh commanded."

10:16 But then Moses inquired about the goat of the decontamination offering and he discovered that it had been burned. He became furious with Eleazar and Ithamar, the remaining sons of Aaron. 17 "Why didn't you eat the decontamination offering in a sacred place? It is of the

[47] This prohibition from leaving the area of the Meeting Tent echoes the same prohibition in Leviticus 8:33, when the soon-to-be priests are instructed not to leave the complex for seven days.

[48] This is one of the first indications in the story that the priests are expected to behave in a manner different from that of ordinary Israelites now that they have been consecrated.

[49] This is the first time in the story that Yahweh speaks directly to Aaron, and it is an important shift. Aaron is now granted direct access to Yahweh's ritual instructions, and he no longer needs Moses to mediate for him. The content of Yahweh's speech is a kind of high-level priestly job description.

holiest level! It was given to you to remove the guilt of the community, to effect purification on their behalf in front of Yahweh. [18] See—its blood was not brought inside the sanctuary. You should have eaten it in a sacred place as I commanded!"

[10:19] Aaron said to Moses, "See[50]—today they have offered their decontamination offerings and their burnt offerings in front of Yahweh. Then these things happened to me. If I had consumed the decontamination offering, would it have been right in Yahweh's eyes? [20] Moses listened and he agreed.[51]

[11:1] Yahweh spoke to Moses and to Aaron, saying to them, [2] "Speak to the Israelites: 'These are the animals that you can eat from any of the land animals on the earth: [3] any animal with divided hoofs, with a hoof split by a cleft, and that chews the cud—you can eat it. [4] However, these you cannot eat, even though they chew the cud or have divided hoofs: the camel, as it chews its cud, but does not have divided hoofs; it is impure for you. [5] The rock badger, as it chews the cud, but the hoof is not divided; it is impure for you. [6] The hare, as it chews the cud, but its hoof is not divided; it is impure for you. [7] The pig, as it has divided hoofs and has a hoof split with a cleft, it does not chew the cud; it is impure for you. [8] You cannot eat their meat or touch their carcasses; they are impure for you.

[11:9] 'These things you can eat from everything in the water: anything in the water that has fins and scales, whether in the seas or in the rivers, you can eat them. [10] Anything in the seas or in the rivers that does not have fins and scales, any reptiles in the water or any other living creatures that are in the water—they are repugnant[52] for you. [11] They will be repugnant for you; you cannot eat their meat, and their carcasses

[50] Here Aaron's discourse mirrors that of Moses and it has the effect of a kind of mocking mimicry as he rejects Moses's accusation and defends his sons.

[51] Moses accepts not only Aaron's argument but also his authority to make decisions about ritual matters. It is fitting, then, that Aaron is given the last word in this argument, and that just as Aaron was struck silent by Moses's words earlier in this chapter (10:3), Moses is now struck silent by Aaron's.

[52] In the Hebrew, there is something of an alliterative wordplay here, the word for reptiles (or, perhaps more broadly, swarming creatures) is *sheretz,* and these creatures are labeled as *sheketz* (repugnant).

you should consider repugnant. [12] Everything in the water that does not have fins and scales, it is repugnant for you.

[11:13] 'These are the repugnant creatures from the birds. They should not be eaten; they are repugnant: the eagle, the bearded vulture, and the black vulture, [14] the kite, and falcons of every kind, [15] ravens of every kind, [16] and the ostrich, the nighthawk, the seagull, and any kind of hawk, [17] the little owl, the fisher owl, and the screech owl, [18] the white owl, the pelican, and the vulture, [19] the stork, all kinds of heron, the hoopoe, and the bat. [20] All the winged insects[53] that walk on four legs—they are repugnant for you. [21] However, these winged insects that walk on all four legs you can eat: those that have knees above their feet in order to use them to leap on the ground. [22] From that category you can eat: locusts of all kinds, all kinds of bald locust, all kinds of cricket, and all kinds of grasshopper. [23] But any other winged insects that have four feet, they are repugnant for you.

[11:24] 'You will become impure by these things;[54] anyone who touches their carcasses will become impure until evening. [25] Anyone who carries their carcasses must wash their clothing and be impure until evening.

[11:26] 'Any land animal that has a divided hoof, but does not have a cleft in its hoofs, or who does not chew the cud—they are impure for you; anyone who touches them will become impure. [27] All animals that walk on their paws, among the animals that walk on four legs—they are impure for you; anyone who touches their carcasses will be impure until evening. [28] Anyone who carries their carcass must wash their clothes and be impure until evening; they are impure for you.

[11:29] 'These are impure for you from among the animals that swarm on land: the weasel, the mouse, and lizards of all kinds, [30] the gecko, the land

[53] The term for "insect" here is the same as the term for "reptile" earlier—it essentially means creeping or swarming creature and takes on a specific category when modifiers are added to it (like "winged" or "in the water").

[54] There is a shift in focus here from the consumption of animals to external contact with them.

crocodile, the lizard, the sand lizard, and the chameleon. [31] These are impure for you among all the swarming creatures; anyone who touches them when they are dead will be impure until evening. [32] Anything that one of them falls onto when dead will be impure, whether it is a wooden vessel or a garment, or an animal skin, or a sack, any object that can be used for any kind of labor; it should be put in water and be impure until evening. Then it will be pure. [33] If any of them falls into an earthenware vessel, everything in it will be impure, and you should break the vessel. [34] Any edible food that water has come into contact with will be impure. Any drinkable liquid in the vessel will be impure. [35] Anything that some part of the carcass falls on will be impure, the oven or the stove should be broken to pieces; they are impure, and they will be impure for you. [36] However, a spring or a cistern that holds water will be pure, but whoever touches the carcass in it will be impure. [37] If any part of the carcass falls on the seeds meant for sowing, it is pure, [38] but if water is put on the seed and any part of the carcass falls on it, it is impure for you.

[11:39] 'If any animal that is edible for you dies, anyone who touches its carcass will be impure until evening. [40] Anyone who eats its carcass must wash their clothes and be impure until evening. Anyone who carries its carcass must wash their clothes and be impure until evening.

[11:41] 'All land-based swarming creatures are repugnant; they cannot be eaten. [42] Anything that moves on its belly, or anything that walks on four legs, or anything that has many feet, from any of the land-based swarming creatures: you cannot eat them because they are repugnant. [43] You cannot make yourselves repugnant with any swarming creature; you cannot make yourselves impure with them and become impure. [44] I am Yahweh your God. You must sanctify yourselves and be holy because I am holy. Do not make yourselves impure with any swarming creature that moves on the earth. [45] I am Yahweh who brought you up from the land of Egypt to be your God. You will be holy because I am holy.'"

[11:46] These are the instructions for the land animals, the birds, and every living creature that moves in the water, and every creature that swarms on land, [47] to distinguish between the impure and the pure, between edible creatures and inedible creatures.

¹²:¹ Yahweh spoke to Moses: ² "Say to the Israelites: 'If a woman conceives and gives birth to a male, she will be impure for seven days; like at the time of her menstrual impurity, she will be impure. ³ On the eighth day, the flesh of his foreskin should be circumcised. ⁴ For 33 days, she will be in a state of blood purification. She cannot touch any sacred object or enter the sanctuary until the days of her purification are complete.

¹²:⁵ 'If she gives birth to a female, she will be impure for two weeks, like with her menstrual impurity. Then for 66 days she will be in a state of blood purification.

¹²:⁶ 'When the time of her blood purification for either a son or daughter is complete, she should bring a year-old lamb as a burnt offering, and a pigeon or a turtledove as a decontamination offering to the entrance of the Meeting Tent, to the priest. ⁷ He should offer it in front of Yahweh to effect purification on her behalf; then she will be pure from her blood flow. This is the instruction for one who bears a child, whether male or female.

¹²:⁸ 'If she cannot afford a sheep, she can take two turtledoves or two pigeons, one as a burnt offering and one as a decontamination offering. The priest should effect purification on her behalf and she will be pure.'"

¹³:¹ Yahweh spoke to Moses and Aaron: ² "When a person has on his skin a swelling, a rash, or a discoloration, and it becomes a type of skin affliction on the skin of his body, he should be brought to Aaron the priest or to one of his sons the priests. ³ The priest should look at the skin affliction. If the hair in the afflicted area has turned white or if the afflicted area appears deeper than the rest of his skin, it is a skin disease. After the priest has looked at him, he will declare him impure.[55]

[55] The purity and impurity described in this chapter and in chs. 13–15 is purely ritual in nature. "Pure" means that the person is able to live and work in the Israelite camp and attend to ritual matters at the Meeting Tent—for example, bringing offerings. As was made clear in the case of childbirth, an "impure" person is not able to enter the sanctuary or to come into contact with sacred objects. Similarly, if the impurity

¹³:⁴ 'But if it is a white discoloration on his skin, and it does not appear deeper than the rest of his skin, and the hair has not turned white, then the priest should quarantine the afflicted person for seven days. ⁵ The priest should look at him on the seventh day. If he sees that the affliction appears the same and that the skin affliction has not progressed, the priest should quarantine him for another seven days. ⁶ The priest should look at him again on the seventh day. If the affliction has faded and has not spread on the skin, then the priest should declare him pure. It is a rash. He should wash his clothing and then he will be pure. ⁷ But if the rash spreads on the skin after he showed it to the priest in order to be pronounced pure, he must present himself to the priest again. ⁸ The priest should look at it. If the rash has spread on the skin, the priest will declare him impure. It is a skin disease.

¹³:⁹ 'When a person contracts a skin disease, he should be brought to the priest. ¹⁰ The priest should look at it. If there is a white swollen area on the skin that has turned the hair white, and there is a section of raw skin in the swelling, ¹¹ it is a chronic skin disease on his body's skin. The priest should declare him impure; he should not quarantine him because he is impure. ¹² If the disease spreads on the skin and the disease covers all the skin of the afflicted person from his head to his feet, as far as the priest can see, ¹³ the priest should look at him. If the skin disease covers all his skin, then he should pronounce him pure from the disease. All of it has turned white; he is pure. ¹⁴ If raw skin appears on it, he will be impure. ¹⁵ The priest should look at the raw flesh and declare him impure. Raw flesh is impure; it is a skin disease. ¹⁶ If the raw flesh again turns white, he should come to the priest. ¹⁷ The priest should look at him, and if the affliction has turned white, the priest should declare the afflicted person pure. He is pure.

¹³:¹⁸ 'When there is an inflammation on the skin of someone's body and it heals, ¹⁹ and in the place of the inflammation there is a white swollen

---

is of a specific kind, like the one discussed in chapters 13–14, the possibility of contaminating the sanctuary with the impurity is too great and so the afflicted individual must move to a place farther away from the sanctuary while he remains afflicted. There is no moral judgment in these chapters, but rather ritual pronouncements that address the person's status vis-à-vis the newly build Meeting Tent.

spot or a reddish-white discoloration, it should be shown to the priest.
[20] The priest should look at it. If it appears deeper than the rest of the
skin, or its hair has turned white, the priest should declare him impure.
It is a skin disease that has broken out in an inflammation. [21] But if the
priest sees it and there is no white hair in it, it is not lower than the rest
of his skin, and it has faded, the priest should quarantine him for seven
days. [22] If it spreads on the skin, the priest should declare him impure.
It is skin disease. [23] If the discoloration stays in one place and has not
spread, it is a scar from the inflammation. The priest should declare
him pure.

[13:24] 'When the body has a burn on its skin and the raw skin of the burn
becomes a reddish-white or white discoloration, [25] the priest should
look at it. If the hair in the discoloration has turned white and it looks
deeper than the skin, it is a skin disease. It has broken out in the burn,
and the priest should declare him impure. It is a skin disease. [26] If the
priest looks at it and the hair in the discoloration is not white and it is
not lower than the rest of his skin, and it has faded, the priest should
quarantine him for seven days. [27] The priest should look at him on the
seventh day. If it has spread on the skin, then the priest should declare
him impure. It is a skin disease. [28] If the discoloration has stayed in one
place and has not spread on his skin, and it has faded, then it is swelling from the burn. The priest should declare him pure because it is a
scar from the burn.

[13:29] 'If a man or a woman has an affliction on the head or in a beard,
[30] the priest should look at the affliction. If it appears to be deeper than
the rest of the skin and there is thin yellow hair in it, the priest should
declare that person impure. It is a scab; it is a skin disease of the head
or beard. [31] If the priest looks at the scab affliction, and it does not
appear deeper than the skin and there is no black hair in it, the priest
should quarantine the scab-afflicted person for seven days. [32] The
priest should look at the afflicted person on the seventh day. If the scab
has not spread, and if there is no yellow hair in it, and if the scab does
not appear to be lower than the skin, [33] they should shave themselves,
but not shave the scab. The priest should quarantine the afflicted person for another seven days. [34] The priest should look at the afflicted
person on the seventh day. If the scab has not spread on the skin and

it does not appear deeper than the skin, then the priest should declare that person pure. They should wash their clothing and they will be pure. [35] If the scab has spread on the skin after they have been declared pure, [36] the priest should look at them. If the scab has spread on the skin, the priest does not need to look for a yellow hair. That person is impure. [37] If the scab's appearance is unchanged and a black hair has sprouted in it, the scab is healed. That person is pure. The priest should declare them pure.

[13:38] 'If a man or a woman has spots on the skin on their body, white spots, [39] The priest should look, and if the spots on their body's skin are a faded white, it is a rash that has broken out on the skin. It is pure.

[13:40] 'If someone's head becomes smooth, he is bald, but he is pure. [41] If his head becomes smooth at the front near the forehead, he is bald, but he is pure. [42] But if a reddish-white discoloration appears in the bald spot, it is a skin disease breaking out on his bald head or bald forehead. [43] The priest should look at it. If the swollen affliction is reddish-white on his bald head or on his bald forehead, and it appears like a skin disease of the body, [44] the man has a skin disease. He is impure. The priest should pronounce him impure; he has a skin disease on his head.

[13:45] 'As for the person who is afflicted with a skin disease, his clothes should be torn, and his head should be uncovered; he should cover his upper lip and shout: 'impure! impure!' [46] As long as the disease is on him, he will be impure. He is impure. He should live alone; his dwelling should be outside the camp.

[13:47] 'When fabric has a disease-like affliction on it, whether it is a wool or linen garment, [48] in the warp or woof of the linen or wool, or in leather or anything made of leather, [49] if the affliction in the fabric is greenish or reddish, or in leather, or in the warp or woof, or in anything made of leather, it is a disease. It should be shown to the priest. [50] The priest should look at the disease, and he should put the diseased object in quarantine for seven days. [51] He should look at the diseased object on the seventh day. If the disease has spread on the fabric or in the warp or in the woof or on the leather, whatever the use of the leather, the disease is a malignant disease. It is impure. [52] The fabric that contains the disease, in the warp or the woof, either wool or linen or anything made of leather, should be burned. It is a malignant disease; it should be burned in fire. [53] If the priest looks and the disease has not spread in the fabric, in warp or woof or anything of leather, [54] the priest should then command that they wash the diseased object, and then quarantine it for another seven days. [55] The priest should look at the diseased fabric after it has been washed. If the disease has not changed color, and the disease has not spread, it is impure. You should burn it in fire, whether the diseased spot is on the inside or outside. [56] If the priest looks and the diseased spot has faded after it has been washed, he should tear it out from the fabric or from the leather, or from the warp or woof. [57] If it appears again on the fabric, in the warp or woof, or on anything of leather, it is spreading. You should burn the diseased object in fire. [58] If you wash the fabric, or the warp or the woof, or anything of leather and the disease disappears from it, you should wash it again and it will be pure." [59] This is the instruction for disease in fabric of wool or linen, in warp or in woof, or in anything of leather to determine if it is pure or impure.'"

[14:1] Yahweh spoke to Moses: [2] "This is the instruction for the person afflicted with skin disease when he becomes pure: He should be brought to the priest; [3] the priest should go outside the camp and the priest should look at him. If the skin disease has healed for the afflicted person, [4] the priest should order for the person who is to be purified: two pure live birds, cedarwood, red yarn, and hyssop to be brought. [5] The priest should order one of the birds slaughtered over an earthenware vessel with fresh water in it. [6] He should take the living bird, along with the cedarwood, red yarn, and hyssop, and dip them (together with the live bird) in the blood of the bird slaughtered over the fresh water. [7] He should then sprinkle the person who is to be purified from skin disease seven times and purify him. Then he should set free the live bird into the open field.

[14:8] "The person being purified should wash his garments and shave all his hair, then wash in water and he will become pure. Afterward, he can return to the camp, but he must live outside his tent for seven days. [9] On the seventh day, he must shave off all the hair, on his head, his beard, and his eyebrows. When he has shaved all his hair, he should wash his clothes and then wash his body in water. Then he will be pure. ¹⁰ On the eighth day, he should take two unblemished male lambs, one year-old unblemished female lamb, three-tenths of a measure of fine flour for a grain offering mixed with oil, and one *log* of oil. ¹¹ The priest who is enacting purification should stand the person being purified along with these objects in front of Yahweh at the entrance to the Meeting Tent. ¹² The priest should take one male lamb and offer it as a guilt offering with a *log* of oil. He should elevate them as an elevation offering in front of Yahweh. ¹³ The lamb should be slaughtered in the place where the decontamination offering and the burnt offering are slaughtered, in a holy place, because the guilt offering is like the decontamination offering in that it belongs to the priest. It is of the holiest level. ¹⁴ The priest should take some of the blood of the guilt offering, and the priest should put it on the right earlobe of the person being purified, and on the thumb of his right hand, and the big toe of his right foot.[56] ¹⁵ The priest should take some of the *log* of oil and pour it into the palm of his own left hand. ¹⁶ The priest should then dip his right finger in some of the oil that is in his left hand, and sprinkle some of the oil with his finger seven times in front of Yahweh. ¹⁷ The priest should put some of the remaining oil in his hand on the right earlobe of the person being purified, and on his right thumb, and on the big toe of his right foot, along with the blood of the guilt offering. ¹⁸ The priest should put the remainder of the oil in his hand on the head of the person being purified. The priest will effect purification on his behalf in front of Yahweh. ¹⁹ Then the priest should sacrifice the decontamination offering, and effect purification on behalf of the person being purified from his impurity. After this, he[57] should slaughter the burnt offering, ²⁰ and the priest should burn the burnt offering along with the grain offering on the altar. The priest will effect purification on his behalf, and then he will be pure.

¹⁴:²¹ "If the person is poor, and he cannot afford this, he should take one male lamb for a guilt offering, to be elevated to effect purification on

[56] This is reminiscent of the ordination procedure for the priests in Leviticus 8 and is the only other time in this story that blood from a sacrificial animal is directly applied to a human being.

[57] That is, the person being purified.

his behalf, and a one-tenth measure of fine flour mixed with oil as a grain offering, and a *log* of oil, ²² and two turtledoves or two pigeons, depending on what he can afford; one should be for a decontamination offering, and one for a burnt offering. ²³ He should bring them to the priest on the eighth day of his purification process, to the entrance of the Meeting Tent in front of Yahweh. ²⁴ The priest should take the lamb for the guilt offering and the *log* of oil and elevate them as an elevation offering in front of Yahweh. ²⁵ The lamb should be slaughtered as a guilt offering and the priest should take some of the blood of the guilt offering and put it on the right earlobe of the person being purified, and on his right thumb, and on the big toe of his right foot. ²⁶ The priest should pour some of the oil into his own left hand, ²⁷ and the priest should sprinkle some of the oil that is in his left hand with his right finger seven times in front of Yahweh. ²⁸ Then the priest should put some of the oil in his hand on the right earlobe, right thumb, and right big toe of the person being purified, in the same places as the blood of the guilt offering. ²⁹ The priest should put the remaining oil in his hand on the head of the person being purified, to effect purification on his behalf in front of Yahweh. ³⁰ He should then sacrifice one of the turtledoves or pigeons (whichever he can afford), ³¹one as a decontamination offering, and the other as a burnt offering, along with the grain offering. The priest will effect purification in front of Yahweh on behalf of the person being purified. ³² This is the instruction for a person afflicted with skin disease who cannot afford what is needed for his purification."

¹⁴:³³ Yahweh spoke to Moses and Aaron: ³⁴ "When you enter the land of Canaan that I am giving you as a holding, and I put a disease-affliction in a house in the land of your holding, ³⁵ the owner of the house should tell the priest: 'It seems a disease has appeared in my house.' ³⁶ The priest should order the house be emptied before the priest comes to look at the disease, so that nothing inside the house can be declared impure.[58] After this, the priest should enter and look at the house. ³⁷ The priest

[58] What is particularly interesting about this law is that proximity to the disease does not automatically make something impure. It becomes impure only *after* the priest declares the disease itself to be impure. Therefore, if the owner removes all their stuff from the house before this declaration, they are preventing those objects from possibly having to be destroyed as well.

should look at the disease, and if the disease in the walls of the house is greenish or reddish and appears deeper than the wall, [38] the priest should go out to the entrance of the house and quarantine the house for seven days. [39] The priest should return on the seventh day and look at it. If the disease has spread in the walls of the house, [40] the priest should order that they remove the stones with the disease on them and throw them outside the city in an impure place. [41] The house should be scraped down, all around the inside, and the plaster that is scraped off should be poured out in an impure place outside the city. [42] They should take other stones and replace those stones with them and take other dust and plaster the house.

[14:43] "If the disease breaks out again in the house after the stones have been replaced and after the house has been scraped and replastered, [44] the priest should come and look at it. If the disease has spread in the house, it is a malignant disease in the house. It is impure. [45] The house should be torn down, its stones and its wood, and all the plaster of the house, and it should be taken to an impure place outside the city. [46] Whoever enters the house while it is quarantined will be impure until evening. [47] Whoever sleeps in the house must wash his clothes, and whoever eats in the house must wash his clothes.

[14:48] "If the priest comes and looks at it, and the disease has not spread in the house after the house was replastered, the priest should declare the house to be pure because the disease has been healed. [49] He should take (for decontaminating the house) two birds, cedarwood, red yarn, and hyssop. [50] One of the birds should be slaughtered over an earthenware vessel filled with fresh water. [51] He should take the cedarwood, and the hyssop and the red yarn, with the live bird, and dip them in the blood of the slaughtered bird and the fresh water, and he should sprinkle the house seven times. [52] The house will be decontaminated with the blood of the bird and with the fresh water, and the live bird, the cedarwood, the hyssop, and the red yarn. [53] Then he should set free the live bird outside the city, into an open field. He will effect purification on behalf of the house, and it will be pure."

[14:54] These are the instructions for all diseases: for scabs, [55] for diseased fabric and houses, [56] for swellings, for rashes, and for discolorations,

[57] to determine when they are impure and when they are pure. This is the instruction for diseases.

[15:1] Yahweh spoke to Moses and Aaron: [2] "Speak to the Israelites and say to them: 'When any man has a discharge from his genitals, his discharge renders him impure.

[15:3] 'This is what causes impurity with respect to his discharge: if his genitals flow with a discharge or if his genitals are sealed from discharging, it is impure for him. [4] Any bedding that the man with the discharge slept on will be impure, and any objects that he sat on will be impure. [5] Anyone who touches his bedding should wash their clothes and bathe in water; they will be impure until evening. [6] Anyone who sits on an object that the person with the discharge sat on should wash their clothes and bathe in water; they will be impure until evening. [7] Anyone who touches the body of the person with a discharge should wash their clothes and bathe in water; they will be impure until evening. [8] If a person with a discharge spits on a pure person, the pure person should wash their clothes and bathe in water; they will be impure until evening. [9] Any saddle that the person with a discharge has used for riding will be impure. [10] Anyone who touches anything that was underneath him will be impure until evening. Anyone who carries these things must wash their clothes and bathe in water; they will be impure until evening. [11] Anyone who the person with a discharge touches without having rinsed his hands with water must wash his clothes and bathe in water; they will be impure until evening. [12] Any earthen vessel that the person with a discharge touches must be broken; any wooden vessel must be rinsed with water.

[15:13] 'When a man with a discharge becomes pure of that discharge, he should count off seven days for his purification. Then he should wash his clothes and bathe his body in fresh water. Then he will be pure. [14] On the eighth day, he should take two turtledoves or two pigeons and come in front of Yahweh, at the entrance to the Meeting Tent, and give them to the priest. [15] The priest should sacrifice one of them as a decontamination offering, and the other as a burnt offering; the priest will effect purification in front of Yahweh on his behalf for his discharge.

15:16 'When a man has a seminal emission, he should bathe his entire body in water; he will be impure until evening. 17 Any fabric or leather that the semen lands on should be washed with water; it will be impure until evening. 18 If a man has sex with a woman and emits semen, they should bathe in water; they will be impure until evening.

15:19 'When a woman has a discharge, and her discharge is blood from her genitals, for seven days she will be in a state of menstrual impurity. Anyone who touches her will be impure until evening. 20 Anything that she lies on during her menstrual impurity will be impure. Anything that she sits on will be impure. 21 Anyone who touches her bedding should wash their clothes and bathe in water; they will be impure until evening. 22 Anyone who touches any object she sat on should wash their clothes and bathe in water; they will be impure until evening. 23 Whether it is bedding or an object she sat on, when he touches it, he will be impure until evening. 24 If a man has sex with her, her menstrual impurity is transmitted to him; he will be impure for seven days and any bedding that he lies on will be impure.

15:25 'When a woman has a discharge of blood for many days, but it is not the time of her menstrual impurity, or if she has a discharge in addition to her menstruation, she will be impure for the duration of the discharge, she will be impure like during the time of her menstrual impurity. 26 Any bedding that she lies on during her discharge is like the bedding during her menstrual impurity; everything that she sits on will be impure, as with her menstrual impurity. 27 Anyone who touches these things will be impure; they should wash their clothes and bathe in water; they will be impure until evening. 28 When she becomes pure from her discharge, she should count off seven days, and after this she will be pure. 29 On the eighth day, she should take two turtledoves or two pigeons and bring them to the priest at the entrance to the Meeting Tent. 30 The priest should sacrifice one as a decontamination offering and the other as a burnt offering; the priest will effect purification in front of Yahweh on her behalf for her impure discharge.

15:31 'You should separate the Israelites from their impurities, so that they do not die because of their impurities when they render my sanctuary impure in their midst. 32 These are the instructions for discharges: for the person who has a seminal emission and is rendered impure by it, [33] and for someone who is menstruating, or who has a discharge (either male or female), and for a man who has sex with an impure woman.'"

[16:1] Yahweh spoke to Moses after the death of two of Aaron's sons when they approached Yahweh and then died.[59] [2] Yahweh spoke to Moses: 'Tell your brother Aaron that he cannot enter the sanctuary inside the curtain, in front of the cover that is on the ark, in just any manner, or else he could die, because I appear in a cloud over the cover. [3] In this way Aaron may enter the sanctuary: with a bull of the herd for a decontamination offering and a ram for a burnt offering. [4] He should dress in his sacred linen tunic, and wear linen underwear next to his skin; he should be bound with a linen sash and wrapped with a linen headdress; these are the sacred garments. He should bathe his body in water and then put them on.

[16:5] 'He should take two male goats for decontamination offerings and one ram for a burnt offering from the Israelite community. [6] Then Aaron should bring his bull for a decontamination offering, to effect purification on his behalf and on behalf of his household. [7] He should take the two goats and stand them in front of Yahweh at the entrance to the Meeting Tent. [8] Aaron should then put lots on the two goats, one lot for Yahweh and the other lot for Azazel. [9] Then Aaron should bring forward the goat with the lot for Yahweh and sacrifice it as a decontamination offering. [10] The goat with the lot for Azazel should be stood, alive, in front of Yahweh to effect purification with it in order to send it into the wilderness for Azazel. [11] Then Aaron should offer his bull for a decontamination offering in order to effect purification on his behalf an on behalf of his household. He should slaughter the bull of his decontamination offering, [12] and take a firepan full of burning coals from on top of the altar that is in front of Yahweh, along with two handfuls of finely ground fragrant incense and bring them inside the curtain. [13] Then he should put the incense on the coals in front of Yahweh so that a cloud of

[59] In this verse, the narrator reorients the reader to the timeline in the story after a long and technical speech by Yahweh. We are still on the eighth day, the same day Nadav and Avihu died.

incense covers the cover that is on the *edut*, so that he does not die.
[14] Then he should take some of the blood of the bull and sprinkle it with
his finger on the front of the cover, and in front of the cover he should
also sprinkle some of the blood seven times with his finger.

[16:15] 'Then the people's goat for a decontamination offering should be
slaughtered, and its blood brought inside the curtain. He should do the
same with its blood as he did with the bull's blood and sprinkle it on
the cover and in front of the cover. [16] So he should effect purification
for the sanctuary from the Israelites' impurities and from their transgressions, as well as all their sins. Then he should do this for the Meeting Tent, which dwells with them in the midst of their impurities. [17] No
one may be inside the Meeting Tent when he enters to effect purification for the sanctuary until he comes out and effects purification on
his behalf, on behalf of his household, and on behalf of the whole Israelite community. [18] He should go out to the altar that is in front of
Yahweh and effect purification on it: he should take some of the bull's
blood and some of the goat's blood and put all around the horns of the
altar. [19] Then he should sprinkle some of the blood on it with his finger
seven times. He should purify it and consecrate it from the Israelites'
impurities. [20] When he is done purifying the sanctuary and the Meeting Tent and the altar, he should bring forward the living goat. [21] Aaron
should lay his two hands on the living goat's head, and confess over it
all the Israelites' iniquities, all their transgressions, and all their sins.
He should put them on the goat's head and send it with a designated
man into the wilderness. [22] The goat will carry all their iniquities into
a desolate region; he should send the goat into the wilderness.

[16:23] 'Aaron should enter the Meeting Tent and strip the linen garments
he was wearing when he entered the sanctuary. He should leave them
there. [24] Then he should bathe his body in water in a sacred place and
put on his garments. He should go out and offer his burnt offering and
the people's burnt offering in order to effect purification on his behalf
and on the people's behalf. [25] He should turn the fat of the decontamination offering to smoke on the altar.

[16:26] 'The one who sent the goat to Azazel must wash his garments and
bathe his body in water; after this he may reenter the camp.

[16:27] 'The bull of the decontamination offering and the goat of the decontamination offering whose blood was brought in to purify the sanctuary should be brought outside the camp and burned in fire: their skins, their meat, and their dung. [28] The person who burns them should wash his clothing and bathe his body in water; after this he may reenter the camp.

[16:29] 'This is a perpetual law for you: in the seventh month, on the tenth day of the month, you should humble yourselves and do no labor, neither the citizen nor the foreigner who lives among you. [30] On this day, purification will be effected on your behalf, to purify you from all your sins; you will become pure in front of Yahweh. [31] It is a complete cessation for you; you should humble yourselves. This will be a perpetual law: [32] the anointed priest who has been ordained to serve as a priest in place of his father will effect purification. He should wear the linen garments and the sacred garments. [33] He should effect purification of the inner sanctuary; of the Meeting Tent and of the altar he should effect purification; and for the priests and all the people he should effect purification. [34] This will be a perpetual law for you, to effect purification on behalf of the Israelites from all their sins once a year.'" Moses did as Yahweh commanded.[60]

[17:1] Yahweh spoke to Moses: [2] "Speak to Aaron and his sons, and to all the Israelites and say to them: 'This is what Yahweh commanded: [3] Any Israelite who would slaughter an ox, a sheep, or a goat in the camp, or who would slaughter outside the camp, [4] and does not bring it to the entrance of the Meeting Tent as a gift for Yahweh, in front of Yahweh's Dwelling Place, its blood should be understood as belonging to that man;[61] he has

---

[60] Yahweh's command at the beginning of this chapter (v. 2) was for Moses to tell Aaron these instructions, which is precisely what this verse refers to him doing. There is no indication in the text that Aaron carries out this purification ritual at this point in the story. It, like all the laws about purity and purification that have proceeded it, should be understood as instructions meant for a future occasion. It is also worth noting that in the story's timeline, we are currently on the eighth day of the first month and that this ritual is prescribed for the tenth day of the seventh month, nearly six months in the future.

[61] The problem with this is that all blood (like fats from the sacrificial offerings) belongs by right to Yahweh, not to human beings. The individual who does not bring his slaughtered animal to Yahweh's altar is thought of as keeping the blood for himself, and thus as stealing something from Yahweh.

shed blood. That man will be cut off from the midst of his people. [5] This is so that the Israelites will bring their sacrifices that they have been sacrificing in the open, that they bring them to Yahweh at the entrance of the Meeting Tent, to the priest. They will sacrifice the well-being offerings to Yahweh, [6] so that the priest can toss the blood on Yahweh's altar at the entrance to the Meeting Tent and turn the fat to smoke as a pleasing aroma for Yahweh, [7] and so that they will never again slaughter their sacrifices for the idols who they have been lusting after. This will be a perpetual law for them throughout their generations.'

[17:8] Say to them: 'Any Israelite or foreigner who is living in their midst who would offer a burnt offering or a sacrifice, [9] and who does not bring it to the entrance of the Meeting Tent to offer it to Yahweh, that man will be cut off from his people.

[17:10] 'As for any Israelite or foreigner who is living in their midst who consumes any blood: I will set my face against the person who eats the blood; I will cut that person off from among their people [11] because the animating force of all flesh is in its blood; I have given it to you on the altar for purification on your behalf. It is the blood, with its animating force, that will effect purification. [12] Therefore, I have said to the Israelites: "no person among you should consume blood, neither should a foreigner living in your midst consume blood."

[17:13] 'As for any Israelite or foreigner who lives among them who would hunt a game animal or a bird that can be eaten, he should pour out its blood and cover it with dirt [14] because the animating force of all flesh is in its blood. Therefore, I said to the Israelites, "you should not eat the blood of any flesh because the animating force of all flesh is its blood. Anyone who eats of it will be cut off."

[17:15] 'As for any person, whether citizen or foreigner, who eats an animal found dead or torn apart: he should wash his clothes, bathe in water, and remain impure until evening. Then he will be pure. [16] If he does not wash his clothes or bathe his body, he will bear his guilt.'"

[18:1] Yahweh spoke to Moses: [2] "Speak to the Israelites and say to them: 'I am Yahweh your God. [3] You should not act as they do in the land of

Egypt, where you lived, and you should not act like those in the land of Canaan where I am bringing you. Do not follow their laws. [4] Rather, you should follow my rules and you should obey and enact my laws. I am Yahweh your God. [5] You should obey my laws and my rules; the person who follows them will live. I am Yahweh.

18:6 'No one should come near one of their own relatives to expose nudity.[62] I am Yahweh. [7] You should not expose your father's nudity (that is, your mother's nudity).[63] She is your mother; you should not uncover her nudity. [8] Do not expose the nudity of your father's wife; it is your father's by right.[64] [9] Do not expose the nudity of your sister, either your father's daughter or your mother's daughter, whether she is born inside or outside the household. [10] Do not expose the nudity of your son's daughter or your daughter's daughter, because they are your responsibility.[65] [11] Do not expose the nudity of the daughter of your father's wife who was born into your father's household; she is your sister. [12] Do not expose the nudity of your father's sister; she is your father's relative. [13] Do not expose the nudity of your sister's mother because she is your mother's relative. [14] Do not encroach on the rights[66] of your father's brother; do not go near his wife. She is your aunt. [15] Do not expose the nudity of your daughter in law; she is your son's wife. Do not expose her nudity. [16] Do not expose the nudity of your brother's wife; it is your brother's by right.

[62] This is a literal translation of the Hebrew, but the concept here is a bit more complicated than simply indecent or incestuous exposure. "Exposing nudity" refers to a woman's genitals and a man's rights to them. To put it differently, uncovering a man's nudity is something of a technical term that designates someone encroaching on his sexual rights to his wife. Uncovering a woman's nudity is much more literal: it is to engage in illicit sexual activity with her. In all cases, the charge of exposing nudity in this context is about the relationship between parties, and about one person infringing on someone else's rights.

[63] The second half of this sentence redefines the "father's nudity" as the mother's genitals, which are understood as belonging to the father.

[64] Literally: it is your father's nakedness.

[65] Literally: they are your nakedness. Here the man addressed is assumed to be the head of the extended household, and, as such, any women or girls are his responsibility until they marry and leave his household. In this case, their bodies are also his property, but not quite in the same way as his wife's body is his property.

[66] Literally: do not expose the nakedness of your father's brother.

18:17 'Do not expose the nudity of a mother and her daughter. Do not marry her son's daughter or her daughter's daughter to expose their nudity. They are relatives; it is depravity. 18 Do not marry a woman in addition to her sister, creating a rivalry and exposing her nudity during her sister's lifetime. 19 Do not come near a woman during her menstrual impurity to expose her nudity. 20 Do not have sexual intercourse with your relative's wife, rendering yourself impure with her. 21 Do not give any of your children to be sacrificed to Molech; do not defile the name of your God. I am Yahweh. 22 Do not lie with a male as one lies with a woman; it is an abomination. 23 Do not have sexual intercourse with any animal and render yourself impure with it. No woman should stand in front of an animal to mate with it; it is a perversion.

18:24 'Do not render yourselves impure in any of these ways, because in all these ways the nations I am expelling before you have rendered themselves impure. 25 The land became impure, and I punished it for its crime; the land vomited out its inhabitants. 26 But you must obey my laws and my rules. Do not do any of these abominable things—neither the citizen nor the foreigner who lives among you. 27 The people who were in the land before you did all these abominable things, and the land was rendered impure. 28 Do not let the land vomit you out because you rendered it impure, just as it vomited out the nation that was there before you. 29 Anyone who does one of these abominable things will be cut off from their people. 30 You must obey my injunction not to do any of the abominable practices that were done before you. Do not render yourselves impure with them. I am Yahweh your God.'"

19:1 Yahweh spoke to Moses: 2 "Speak to the entire Israelite community and say to them: 'You must be holy because I, Yahweh your God, am holy. 3 You each must respect your mother and father; you must observe my sabbaths. I am Yahweh your God. 4 Do not turn to idols; do not cast molten gods for yourselves. I am Yahweh your God. 5 When you sacrifice a sacrifice of well-being to Yahweh, sacrifice it so that it is accepted on your behalf. 6 It must be eaten on the day you sacrifice it or on the next day. Anything that remains until the third day must be burned in fire. 7 If it is eaten on the third day, it is ritually unacceptable; it will not be accepted. 8 The person who eats it will bear his guilt because he has defiled Yahweh's sacred object. That person will be cut off from his people.

¹⁹:⁹ 'When you harvest the harvest of your land, do not harvest to the very ends of your field, and do not glean the gleanings of your harvest. ¹⁰ Do not completely pick your vineyard, and do not glean your vineyard's fallen grapes. You should leave them for the poor and for the foreigner. I am Yahweh your God. ¹¹ Do not steal, do not deceive, and do not lie to one another. ¹² Do not make a false oath in my name, defiling the name of your God. I am Yahweh. ¹³ Do not oppress your neighbor, and do not commit robbery. Do not keep a worker's wages overnight. ¹⁴ Do not insult a deaf person or put an obstacle in front of a blind person. You must respect your God. I am Yahweh.

¹⁹:¹⁵ 'Do not render an unfair verdict. Do not favor the poor or honor the rich. Judge your neighbor fairly. ¹⁶ Do not walk around slandering your people. Do not profit from the blood of your neighbor. I am Yahweh. ¹⁷ Do not internally bear hate for your family; you can reprimand your relative, but do not incur guilt because of him. ¹⁸ Do not take revenge or keep a grudge against any of your people but love your neighbor as yourself. I am Yahweh.

¹⁹:¹⁹ 'You must obey my laws. Do not allow your animals to mate with a different kind. Do not plant your field with two kinds of seed. Do not wear a garment made from two kinds of material.[67] ²⁰ If a man has sexual intercourse with a woman, but she is a slave who has been designated for another man and she has not been redeemed or granted her freedom, there should be an inquiry. They should not be killed because she was not freed. ²¹ He should bring a guilt offering to Yahweh, to the entrance of the Meeting Tent: a ram for the guilt offering. ²² The priest should effect purification on his behalf in front of Yahweh with the ram of the guilt offering for the error he committed. Then he will be forgiven for the error he committed.

[67] In this story, texts made from more than one kind of material (typically wool and linen blends) are reserved for the priests and the textiles used in the Dwelling Place. There is a similar prohibition on lay Israelites using the same blend of incense used in the sanctuary (see Exod 30:33).

^{19:23} 'When you enter the land and plant any tree for food, you should treat its fruit as forbidden. For three years it will be forbidden for you; it must not be eaten. ²⁴ In the fourth year all its fruit should be set aside as a celebratory offering for Yahweh. ²⁵ In the fifth year, you may eat its fruit, so that its harvest will increase for you. I am Yahweh your God.

^{19:26} 'You should not eat anything with its blood. You should not practice divination, and you should not practice witchcraft. ²⁷ You should not round off the hair on the sides of your head, and you should not remove the sides of your beard. ²⁸ You should not make cuts on your body for the dead, and you should not put any tattoo on yourselves. I am Yahweh. ²⁹ Do not defile your daughter by making her a prostitute, or else the land will become like a prostitute and filled with depravity. ³⁰ You must keep my sabbaths and respect my sanctuary. I am Yahweh. ³¹ Do not turn to necromancers; do not inquire of ghosts, becoming impure by them. I am Yahweh your God. ³² You should rise for those with gray hair and honor the elderly. You must fear your God. I am Yahweh.

^{19:33} 'When a foreigner lives with you in your land, you must not oppress him. ³⁴ The foreigner who lives with you will be like a citizen among you. You must love him as yourself because you were foreigners in the land of Egypt. I am Yahweh your God.

^{19:35} 'Do not cheat with measurements of length, weight, or capacity. ³⁶ You must have an honest scale, honest weights, an honest *ephah*, and an honest *hin*. I am Yahweh your God who brought you out from the land of Egypt. ³⁷ You must obey all my laws and my rules and enact them. I am Yahweh.'"

^{20:1} Yahweh spoke to Moses: ² "Say to the Israelites: 'Any person, whether Israelite or a foreigner living with the Israelites who gives any of his children to Molech should be put to death; the people of the land should stone him. ³ I will set my face against that person and I will cut him off from his people because he gave his child to Molech, rendering my sanctuary impure and defiling my sacred name. ⁴ If the people of the land close their eyes to that man when he gives his child to Molech and do not put him to death, ⁵ I will set my face against that person and his family and I will cut him off—and all those who follow

him in lusting after Molech—from his people. ⁶ If any person turns to a necromancer or to ghosts to lust after them, I will set my face against that person and cut him off from his people. ⁷ You must sanctify yourselves and be holy because I am Yahweh your God. ⁸ You must obey my laws and enact them. I am Yahweh who sanctifies you.

²⁰:⁹ 'If anyone curses his father or mother, he should be put to death. He has cursed his father or mother; his blood is on his own hands.[68] ¹⁰ If a man commits adultery with his neighbor's wife, both the man and the woman should be put to death. ¹¹ If a man has sex with his father's wife, he has usurped his father's right.[69] They should be put to death; their blood is on their own hands. ¹² If a man has sex with his daughter-in-law, both of them should be put to death. They have committed a perversion and their blood is on their own hands. ¹³ If a man has sex with a male as with a woman, they both have committed an abominable act. They should be put to death; their blood is on their own hands. ¹⁴ If a man marries a woman and her mother, it is depravity. They should all be burned in fire. There should be no depravity in your midst. ¹⁵ If a man has sex with an animal, he should be put to death and you should kill the animal.[70] ¹⁶ If a woman approaches an animal to mate with it, you should kill the woman[71] and the animal; they should be put to death; their blood is on their own hands.

²⁰:¹⁷ 'If a man marries his sister, his father's daughter or his mother's daughter, and he exposes her nudity and she exposes his nudity, it is a disgrace. They should be cut off in the sight of their people. He has

---

[68] The literal translation here is: his blood is upon him. Some translators have rendered "blood" as "bloodguilt." In either case, the idea being expressed here is that the individual who committed this act is responsible for his own death. This corresponds nicely with the English idiom "his blood is on his own hands," and so that is how I have chosen to translate this idiomatic Hebrew phrase.

[69] Literally: he has exposed his father's nudity. The sense here is the same as in chapter 18.

[70] It is worth noting here that the passive form of the verb is used for the death penalty punishment for human beings whereas the active form of the verb "to kill" is used for animals.

[71] Here the active form of the verb for the death penalty is also applied to the woman who behaves like an animal.

exposed the nudity of his sister and will incur guilt. [18] If a man has sex with a menstruating woman, he has exposed her nudity; he has made her flow visible, and she has exposed her blood flow. Both of them should be cut off from their people. [19] You should not expose the nudity of your mother's sister or of your father's sister because that is to expose one's own flesh.[72] They will incur guilt. [20] If a man has sex with his aunt, he has usurped his uncle's right.[73] They will incur guilt and they will die childless. [21] If a man marries his brother's wife, it is a form of impurity. He has usurped his brother's right;[74] they will be childless.

[20:22] 'You must obey my laws and my regulations and enact them, otherwise the land that I am bringing you to settle in will vomit you out. [23] Do not follow the laws of the nation that I am expelling before you because they did these things and I loathed them. [24] Now I have said to you: you will possess their land; I will give it to you to possess, a land flowing with milk and honey. I am Yahweh your God who separated you from other people. [25] You must separate the pure animals from the impure, the impure birds from the pure. You must not make yourselves detestable with animals or birds or with anything that moves on land that I have separated as impure for you. [26] You must be holy because I, Yahweh, am holy, and I have separated you from the other people to be mine. [27] Any man or woman who is a necromancer or communicates with ghosts should be put to death; they must be stoned. Their blood is on their own hands.'"

[21:1] Yahweh spoke to Moses: "Speak to the priests, Aaron's sons, and say to them: 'No one should render themselves impure for a dead person in his family, [2] except if it is his immediate relative: his mother, his father, his son, his daughter, his brother, [3] or his unwed sister, who is considered his immediate family because she is not married. He may render himself impure for her. [4] He may not render himself impure among his extended family and defile himself. [5] They must not shave any bald spots on their heads or shave off the edges of their beards. They must not make gashes in their skin. [6] They must be holy for their God; they

---

[72] Flesh here carries the double meaning of physical body and close relative.
[73] Literally: he has exposed his uncle's nudity.
[74] Literally: he has exposed his brother's nudity.

must not defile the name of their god because they are the ones who offer Yahweh's food offerings, their God's food. They must be holy.

21:7 'They cannot marry a prostitute or a woman who has been defiled. They cannot marry a woman who is divorced from her husband because they are holy to their God. 8 You must treat them as holy because they offer your God's food; they will be holy to you because I, Yahweh, who consecrate them, am holy. 9 If a priest's daughter defiles herself with prostitution, she defiles her father. She must be burned in fire.

21:10 'The priest who is in charge of the other priests, who had anointing oil poured on his head and who was ordained to wear the garments, cannot uncover his head or tear his garments. 11 He cannot enter a place where there is a dead body; he cannot render himself impure for his father or his mother.[75] 12 He cannot leave the sanctuary and thus defile the sanctuary of his God because he has been set apart by the anointing oil of his God. I am Yahweh. 13 He must marry a woman who has not been wed before;[76] 14 a widow, a divorced woman, or a woman defiled by prostitution—he cannot marry any of these. He can marry only an unmarried woman from his own extended family 15 so that he does not defile his descendants among his family. I am Yahweh who consecrated him.'"

21:16 Yahweh spoke to Moses: 17 "Say to Aaron: 'None of your descendants throughout the generations who has a blemish can approach to offer his God's food. 18 No one who has a blemish can make an offering: a man who is blind, or who has a limp, or who is disfigured or deformed, 19 or a man who has a broken foot or a broken hand, 20 or

[75] This differs sharply from the instructions for ordinary priests at the beginning of this chapter. The high priest is held to a stricter standard for a fairly simple reason: when someone is rendered impure by a dead body, they are unable to enter the sanctuary are for seven days. This is inconvenient for an ordinary priest, but there are many ordinary priests, and the others are able to continue the necessary work. There is only one high priest, however, and if he is rendered impure, there is no one who can take over his work in the sanctuary.

[76] Literally: an adolescent woman. Sometimes this is translated as a young virgin, but it is not entirely clear that the word *betulah* in Hebrew means a virgin.

one with a crooked back, or a dwarf, or one with a defect in his eye, or a scar, or a scab, or crushed testicles. [21] No descendent of Aaron the priest who has a blemish may approach and offer Yahweh's food; because he has a blemish, he cannot approach to offer his God's food. [22] He can eat his God's food, whether it is of the highest level of holiness or simply holy. [23] However, he cannot go behind the curtain, or approach the altar because he has a blemish. He must not defile my sacred places because I, Yahweh, have consecrated them.'" [24] Moses told this to Aaron, to his sons, and to all the Israelites.

[22:1] Yahweh spoke to Moses: [2] "Tell Aaron and his sons that they should separate themselves from the Israelites' sacred offerings, so that they do not defile my holy name, which they have sanctified to me. I am Yahweh. [3] Say to them: 'Throughout your generations, if any one of your descendants comes near the sacrificial portions that the Israelites consecrate to Yahweh while he is impure, that person will be cut off from me. I am Yahweh. [4] Any of Aaron's descendants who have skin disease or a discharge cannot eat the sacrificial portions until he is pure. If someone touches a dead body or has a seminal emission, [5] or if he touches any swarming creature that would render him impure, or any human being who would render him impure—whatever his impurity is, [6] the person who touches it will be impure until evening and cannot eat of the sacrificial portions until he has bathed his body in water. [7] When the sun sets, he will be pure. Afterwards, he can eat the sacrificial portions because it is his food. [8] He cannot eat an animal that has died or one that has been killed by other animals, rendering him impure. I am Yahweh. [9] They must obey my injunction so they do not commit an error and die because of it. They will have defiled it: I am Yahweh who consecrates them.

[22:10] 'No ordinary person can eat of the sacrificial portions.[77] No immigrant laborer or hired laborer of a priest's can eat of the sacrificial portions. [11] But, if the priest has purchased someone, he can eat it.

[77] This paragraph obliquely explains how far the priests' sanctified status is imagined as extending. As Yahweh explained in one of his earlier speeches, only people who are considered to have a "holy" status are allowed to eat of the sacred offerings. In this case, that status seems to extend to permanent members of a priest's household.

Those who are born into his house may also eat his food. [12] If a priest's daughter marries an ordinary person, she cannot eat the sacred gifts. [13] If a priest's daughter is widowed or divorced, does not have any children, and she returns to her father's household like before she was married, then she can eat her father's food. However, any ordinary person cannot eat it. [14] If a person unintentionally eats a sacrificial portion, he must add one-fifth to its value and give that to the priest for the sacred offering. [15] But they must not desanctify the sacrificial portions of the Israelites which they have elevated for Yahweh [16] and thereby cause them to incur guilt by eating their sacrificial portions. I am Yahweh who sanctifies them.'"

[22:17] Yahweh spoke to Moses: [18] "Speak to Aaron, to his sons, and to all the Israelites and say to them: 'When any Israelite or foreigner who lives among the Israelites brings his burnt offering as a freewill or votive offering to Yahweh, [19] it must be an unblemished male from the cattle, sheep, or goats for it to be accepted. [20] You cannot offer anything that has a blemish on it because it will not be accepted on your behalf.

[22:21] 'When someone offers a sacrifice of well-being to Yahweh, for the fulfillment of a vow or as a freewill offering, it should be an unblemished animal from the herd or from the flock; to be accepted it must not have any blemish on it. [22] Any animal that is blind, injured, maimed, has an open sore, a scab, or a scar cannot be offered to Yahweh. You cannot put any of them on the altar as a food gift for Yahweh. [23] However, you can offer an ox or a sheep with a limb that is either too long or too short as a freewill offering, but it will not be accepted for a vow. [24] You cannot offer an animal to Yahweh with its testicles bruised, crushed, torn, or removed. You should not do these things in your land, [25] and you should not accept any animals like this from foreigners to offer as food for your God because they are mutilated and have a blemish on them. They will not be accepted on your behalf.'"

[22:26] Yahweh spoke to Moses: [27] "When an ox, sheep, or goat is born, it must stay with its mother for seven days. On the eighth day and after, it will be acceptable as a gift of a food offering for Yahweh. [28] However, an ox or sheep cannot be slaughtered on the same day as its offspring. [29] When you sacrifice a sacrifice of thanksgiving to Yahweh, sacrifice it in a way that it will be accepted on your behalf. ³⁰ It must be eaten on the same day; nothing can be left over until morning. I am Yahweh.

^{22:31} "You must obey my commandments and enact them. I am Yahweh. ³² Do not defile my sacred name, so that I can be sanctified in the midst of the Israelites. I am Yahweh who sanctifies you, ³³ who brought you out from the land of Egypt to be your God. I am Yahweh."

^{23:1} Yahweh spoke to Moses: ² "Speak to the Israelites and say to them: 'These are Yahweh's appointed times that you must declare. These are declarations of holy times;[78] they are my appointed times.

^{23:3} 'For six days, you may do labor, but on the seventh day there must be a sabbath of complete cessation; it is declared holy. You cannot do any labor; it is a sabbath for Yahweh in all your settlements.

^{23:4} 'These are Yahweh's appointed times, declarations of holy times that you must declare at their appointed times. ⁵ In the first month in the evening of the fourteenth day of the month, it is Yahweh's passover. ⁶ On the fifteenth day of that month, it is Yahweh's festival of unleavened bread. For seven days, you must eat unleavened bread. ⁷ On the first day, it will be declared a holy time for you; you cannot do any form of labor. ⁸ You should offer food gifts to Yahweh for seven days. The seventh day will be a declared holy time; you cannot do any form of work.'"

^{23:9} Yahweh spoke to Moses: ¹⁰ "Speak to the Israelites and say to them: 'When you enter the land that I am giving to you, and you harvest its harvest, you must bring the first sheaf of your harvest to the priest. ¹¹ He will elevate the sheaf in front of Yahweh to be accepted on your behalf; the priest should elevate it the day after the sabbath. ¹² On the day that you elevate the sheaf, you should offer an unblemished year-

---

[78] Just as the priests are responsible for distinguishing between things that are pure and impure, they are also responsible for distinguishing between the holy and the ordinary (see Lev 10:10–11). In order for something to be considered impure, the priest must first declare it to be so (see Lev 14:36). The same is true with marking off holy times: they must be declared as holy; they are not inherently so.

old male lamb as a burnt offering for Yahweh. [13] Its grain offering should be two-tenths of a measure of fine flour mixed with oil, as a food gift for Yahweh with a pleasing smell. Its libation should be a quarter of a *hin* of wine. [14] You should not eat any bread, roasted grain, or fresh grain until the exact day that you bring your God's gift. This is a perpetual law throughout your generations in all your settlements.

[23:15] 'You should count from the day after the sabbath, from the day you bring your sheaf as an elevation offering, seven weeks. They must be complete: [16] you must count until the day after the seventh week, 50 days. Then you should bring a new grain offering to Yahweh. [17] From all your settlements, you should bring two loaves of bread as an elevation offering; they should be made from two-tenths of a measure of fine flour, baked with leaven, as a first-fruits offering for Yahweh. [18] You should offer seven one-year-old unblemished lambs, one bull from the herd, and two rams with the bread. They will be a burnt offering for Yahweh, along with their grain offerings and their libations, a food gift with a pleasing smell for Yahweh. [19] You should also offer one male goat as a decontamination offering and two one-year-old lambs as a sacrifice of well-being. [20] The priest will elevate them (the two lambs) along with the first-fruits bread as an elevation offering in front of Yahweh. They will be holy to Yahweh, for the priest. [21] On that same day you should make a declaration; it will be a declaration of a holy time for you. You cannot do any form of work. It is a perpetual law in all your settlements throughout your generations.

[23:22] 'When you harvest your land's harvest, do not harvest to the very edges of your field, or gather the gleanings of your harvest. You must leave them for the poor and the foreigner. I am Yahweh your God.'"

[23:23] Yahweh spoke to Moses: [24] "Speak to the Israelites: 'In the seventh month, on the first day of the month, you will have a complete cessation, a declared holy day marked with horn blasts. [25] You cannot do any form of labor, and you must bring a food gift to Yahweh.'"

[23:26] Yahweh spoke to Moses: [27] "However, the tenth day of this seventh month is the day of purification. It is a declared holy time for you. You must humble yourselves and bring a food gift for Yahweh. [28] You cannot do any labor on that day because it is a day of purification to effect purification on your behalf in front of Yahweh your God. [29] If a person does not humble themselves on that day, they will be cut off from their people. [30] Anyone who does work on that day, I will destroy that person from the midst of their people. [31] You cannot do any labor. This is a perpetual law throughout your generations in all your settlements. [32] It is a sabbath of complete cessation for you. You must humble yourselves. On the evening of ninth day of the month, from evening until evening, you must practice cessation on your sabbath."

[23:33] Yahweh spoke to Moses: [34] "Say to the Israelites: 'On the fifteenth day of this seventh month, there is a festival of booths for Yahweh for seven days. [35] It is a declared holy time on the first day. You cannot do any form of labor. [36] For seven days, you should bring food gifts to Yahweh. On the eighth day, there will be a declared holy time for you, and you should bring a food gift for Yahweh. It is a time for assembly; you cannot do any form of work.

[23:37] 'These are Yahweh's appointed times that you should declare. They are declared holy times for bringing food gifts to Yahweh, burnt offerings and grain offerings, sacrifices and libations, each on its appropriate day, [38] in addition to Yahweh's sabbaths, in addition to all your gifts, in addition to all your vow offerings, and in addition to all your freewill offerings that you give to Yahweh.

[23:39] 'However, on the fifteenth day of the seventh month, when you have gathered the land's harvest, you should celebrate a festival for Yahweh for seven days. It is a complete cessation on the first day, and a complete cessation on the seventh day. [40] On the first day, you should take the fruit of splendid trees, branches of palm trees, branches of leafy trees, and willows of the brook and you should celebrate in front of Yahweh your God for seven days. [41] You should celebrate a festival for Yahweh for seven days in the year. This is a perpetual law throughout your generations: in the seventh month you should celebrate it. [42] You should dwell in booths for seven days; all Israelite citizens should dwell in booths [43] in order that your future generations know that I caused the Israelites to dwell in booths when I brought them out of the land of Egypt. I am Yahweh your God.'"

²³⁴⁴ Moses declared Yahweh's appointed times to the Israelites.

²⁴⁴¹ Yahweh spoke to Moses: ² "Command the Israelites to bring you pure, beaten olive oil for lighting, to light the lamps regularly. ³ Aaron should set them up outside the curtain of the *edut* in the Meeting Tent from evening until morning, in front of Yahweh regularly. This is a perpetual law throughout your generations. ⁴ He should set up the lamps on the pure lampstand in front of Yahweh regularly. ⁵ You should take fine flour and bake it into twelve loaves, two-tenths of a measure for each loaf. ⁶ You should put them in two rows, six per row, on the pure table in front of Yahweh. ⁷ Then you should put pure frankincense with each row; it is a memorial portion for the bread, a food gift for Yahweh. ⁸ Every sabbath day, he should regularly arrange them in front of Yahweh; it is a perpetual commitment from the Israelites. ⁹ It belongs to Aaron and to his sons, and they must eat it in a sacred place because it is of the highest level of holiness from Yahweh's food gifts, a perpetual portion."

²⁴⁴¹⁰ Now, a man with an Israelite mother and an Egyptian father came out into the midst of the Israelites. There was a fight in the camp between the Israelite woman's son and another Israelite. ¹¹ The Israelite woman's son exlaimed the name and cursed.[79] They brought him to Moses. (His mother's name was Shlomit, daughter of Divri, of the tribe of Dan.) ¹² They detained him until it was clear to them what Yahweh would decide. ¹³ Yahweh spoke to Moses: ¹⁴ "Take the one who cursed outside the camp and let everyone who heard him lay their hands on his head.[80] Let the entire community stone him. ¹⁵ To the Israelites, say this: 'Anyone who curses his God will incur his sin. ¹⁶ If he exclaims the name of Yahweh, he should be put to death. The entire community should stone him, whether he is a foreigner or a citizen. If he exclaims the name, he should be put to death. ¹⁷ If a person kills a human being,

[79] Here the name is presumably the divine name Yahweh.
[80] This hand-laying ritual is a curious detail particularly because it parallels ones that occur in the instructions for sacrificial offerings, as well as the one performed by Aaron on the day of purification. The fact that it is carried out only by those who heard the man curse suggests that it serves as a way of transferring any guilt they contracted by hearing the curse back to the individual who pronounced it.

he should be put to death. [18] Someone who kills an animal must make restitution for it: a life for a life. [19] If a person puts a blemish on another person, as he did so should be done to him: [20] break for break, eye for eye, tooth for tooth. The blemish he put on another should be put on him. [21] Someone who kills an animal should make restitution for it. Someone who kills a person should be put to death. [22] You will have one rule for foreigners and citizens. I am Yahweh your God.'" [23] Moses spoke to the Israelites and they took the one who cursed outside the camp and they stoned him. The Israelites did as Yahweh commanded Moses.

[25:1] Yahweh spoke to Moses at Mount Sinai: [2] "Speak to the Israelites and say to them: 'When you enter the land that I am giving to you, the land should observe a cessation, Yahweh's sabbath. [3] For six years, you can plant your field and for six years you can prune your vineyard and gather their crops, [4] but in the seventh year, the land should have a complete cessation, Yahweh's sabbath. You should not plant your field and you should not prune your vineyard. [5] You should not harvest the aftergrowth of your harvest and you should not gather the untrimmed grapes. It is a year of complete cessation for the land. [6] However, the land will produce food for you in its sabbath: for you, and for your male and female slaves, and for your hired and immigrant laborers who live with you, [7] and for your cattle and the animals on your land. All its crops will be for food.

[25:8] 'You must count off seven weeks of years (seven times seven years), so that the duration of seven weeks of years equals 49 years. [9] Then you should have the horn sounded loudly on the tenth day of the seventh month, the day of purification, you should have the horn sounded throughout your land. [10] You should sanctify the fiftieth year: you should declare restoration throughout the land for all its inhabitants. It will be a jubilee for you: each person should return to his allotted holding; each should return to his family. [11] The fiftieth year will be a jubilee year for you; you should not plant, and you should not harvest the aftergrowth, and you should not gather the untrimmed vines [12] because it is a jubilee. It is holy for you, you can eat only from what the field produces.

[25:13] 'In this jubilee year, each person should return to his allotted holding. [14] When you sell something to your neighbor, or buy something from your neighbor, you should not cheat each other. [15] When buying from your neighbor, you should do so based on the number of years until the jubilee; when he sells to you, it should be based on the number of crop years remaining. [16] If there are more years, you should increase his price, and if there are fewer years, you should decrease his price because what is sold is the number of harvests. [17] You should not cheat each other; fear your God. I am Yahweh your God.

[25:18] 'You must observe my laws, obey my rules and enact them so that you can live securely on the land. [19] The land will give its fruit, and you will eat your fill and live securely on it. [20] If you ask, "what will we eat in the seventh year if we cannot plant or gather our crops?" [21] then I command my blessing for you in the sixth year, that it will produce a crop to last three years. [22] When you plant in the eighth year, you will be eating of the old crop; until the ninth year's crops come in, you will be eating of the old crop.

[25:23] 'The land should not be permanently sold because the land belongs to me. You are foreigners and tenants with me. [24] While all the land is your allotted holding, you must give the redemption for the land. [25] If one of your relatives becomes poor and must sell some of his allotted holding, then his nearest redeemer must come to him and redeem what his relative has sold. [26] If a man has no redeemer, but he prospers and finds enough for its redemption, [27] then he should calculate the years since the sale and refund the difference to the person he sold it to. Then he should return to his allotted holding. [28] If he is too poor to recover it, what he sold will remain in the possession of the purchaser until the jubilee year; in the jubilee year it will be released, and he will return to his allotted holding.

[25:29] 'If a man sells a dwelling house in a walled city, it can be redeemed in the first year of its sale; its redemption period is one year. [30] If it is not redeemed in the first year, then the house in the walled city will transfer to the purchaser, throughout his generations; it cannot be released in the jubilee. [31] However, houses in villages that do not have walls around them are considered as open land; they can be redeemed and they will be released in the jubilee. [32] As for the Levites' cities: the Levites will always be able to redeem the houses in the cities of their allotted holdings. [33] Places that can be redeemed from the Levites, houses sold in a city in their allotted holding, can be released in the jubilee. The houses in the Levites' cities are their allotted holding among the Israelites. [34] However, the open land around their cities cannot be sold because it is their permanent allotted portion.

[25:35] 'If one of your relatives becomes poor and is dependent on you, you must support him like a foreigner who lives with you. [36] Do not take advance interest or profit from him; fear your God. Let your relative live with you. [37] Do not lend him money with advance interest or give him food for a profit. [38] I am Yahweh your God who brought you out of the land of Egypt to give you the land of Canaan, to be your God.

[25:39] 'If your relative who is dependent on you is so poor that he sells himself to you, you cannot make him serve as a slave. [40] He will be like an immigrant laborer or a hired laborer with you; he will serve you only until the jubilee. [41] Then he and his children will be free from your authority and he will return to his family and return to his ancestral allotted holding. [42] They are my slaves whom I brought out from the land of Egypt. They may not be sold as a slave. [43] You cannot rule over them ruthlessly; fear your God. [44] As for male and female slaves that you own, you must buy these male and female slaves from the nations that are around you. [45] You can also buy them from the children of resident foreigners among you and from their families that are among you that were born in your land. They will become your property.[81] [46] You can keep them as a possession for your children after you to inherit as perpetual property. These you can treat as slaves, but your Israelite relatives—no one can rule ruthlessly over each other.

[25:47] 'If a resident foreigner among you has prospered and your relative has become poor and sells himself to the resident foreigner, or to some part of the foreigner's family, [48] after he has been sold, he can be redeemed. One of his relatives should redeem him, [49] or his uncle or

[81] The word for property here is the same word in Hebrew as the word for "allotted portion." The idea here is that foreign slaves can be passed down throughout generations of families just like portions of ancestral land.

his uncle's son should redeem him, or anyone in his family who is related to him should redeem him, or if he prospers, he can redeem himself. [50] He should calculate the amount from the year he sold himself until the jubilee year with his purchaser; the price of his sale will be applied to the number of years, as if it is for the term of a hired laborer with him. [51] If there are many remaining years, he will pay for his redemption in proportion to the purchase price. [52] If there are few years remaining until the jubilee year, he will calculate it: he will make a payment for his redemption based on his years. [53] He will be like a laborer hired by the year; he should not rule over him ruthlessly in your presence. [54] If he has not been redeemed in any of these ways, then he and his children will be released in the jubilee year. [55] The Israelites are slaves to me. They are my slaves whom I brought out from the land of Egypt. I am Yahweh your God.

[26:1] 'You cannot make idols for yourselves, or erect statues or pillars, or put stone figures in your land to worship. I am Yahweh your God. [2] You must keep my sabbaths and respect my sanctuary. I am Yahweh. [3] If you follow my laws, obey my commandments, and enact them; [4] I will provide your rains in their proper season, so that the land produces its crops, and the trees of the field will produce their fruit. [5] Your threshing will overtake the vintage and the vintage will overtake the planting; you will eat your bread until you are full, and you will dwell safely on your land. [6] I will give peace throughout the land, and you will lie down untroubled. I will remove[82] wild animals from the land, and no sword will pass through your land. [7] You will chase your enemies and they will fall by the sword in front of you. [8] Five of you will chase one hundred, and one hundred of you will chase ten thousand; your enemies will fall by the sword in front of you. [9] I will turn to you and I will make you fertile and cause you to increase greatly. I will establish my covenant with you. [10] You will eat old grain that has been stored, and you will remove the old in favor of the new. [11] I will put my Dwelling Place in your midst, and I will not loathe you. [12] I will go about in your midst; I will be your God and you will be my people. [13] I am Yahweh your God who brought you out from the land of Egypt, away from

---

[82] Literally: cause to cease. The verb here is the same as the one used to describe the cessation associated with the sabbath.

being their slaves. I shattered the bars of your yoke and I enabled you to walk upright.

26:14 'However, if you do not obey me and you do not enact all these commandments, 15 if you reject my laws and loathe my rules, and you do not enact all my commandments, thus breaking my covenant, 16 then I will do this to you: I will visit terror on you, consumption and fever that make the eyes close and the body languish; you will plant your seed fruitlessly and your enemies will eat it. 17 I will set my face against you. You will be struck down in front of your enemies; those who hate you will pursue you and you will flee even though no one pursues you.[83]

26:18 'If you still do not obey me, I will continue to rebuke you sevenfold for your errors: 19 I will break your proud strength, and I will make your skies like iron and your land like copper 20 so that your strength is completely useless. Your land will not produce its crops and your trees will not produce their fruits. 21 If you continue in hostility with me, and are not willing to obey me, I will continue wounding you sevenfold for your errors. 22 I will send wild animals against you and they will kill your children and destroy your livestock; they will reduce your population and your roads will be desolate. 23 If these things do not instruct you for me, and you continue in hostility against me, 24 then I will continue in hostility against you. I will strike you sevenfold for your errors. 25 I will bring a sword against you to wreak vengeance for the covenant, and if you gather yourselves into your cities, then I will send a plague into your midst and you will be given into enemy hands. 26 When I break your staff of bread, ten women will bake your bread in one oven; they will ration your bread by weight, and even though you eat, you will not be full.

[83] It is particularly striking to read this section of Yahweh's speech while thinking about his promise after the flood (Gen 9) that he would never again destroy the entirety of humanity by means of a flood. There are many, many modes of destruction described in this and the following sections, but not one of them has to do with flood, drowning, or even dying of thirst. Yahweh keeps his promises in this story, even if he manages to find creative ways around some of them.

26:27 'If despite this, you do not obey me and you continue in hostility against me, 28 I will continue in wrathful hostility against you. I will punish you sevenfold for your errors. 29 You will eat the flesh of your sons; the flesh of your daughters you will eat. 30 I will destroy your cultic high places and I will cut down your incense altars. I will put your corpses on top of the corpses of your idols. I will loathe you. 31 I will utterly destroy your cities, and I will make your sanctuaries desolate. I will not enjoy your pleasing smells. 32 I will make the land desolate so that your enemies who settle in it will be appalled. 33 I will scatter you among the nations and I will unsheathe a sword after you. Your land will be desolate, and your cities will be in ruins.

26:34 'Then the land will restore its sabbath years while it remains desolate, while you are in the land of your enemies. Then the land will rest and enjoy its sabbath years. 35 While it remains desolate, it will observe the cessation that it did not have in the sabbath years you were dwelling in it. 36 And those of you who survive—I will bring them a faintness of heart in the land of their enemies. The sound of a windswept leaf will chase them, and they will flee as if fleeing from a sword; they will fall even though no one pursues them. 37 They will stumble over each other as if they were faced with a sword, but no one pursues them. You will not be able to stand in front of your enemies. 38 You will be destroyed among the nations, and the land of your enemies will consume you. 39 And those of you who survive will decay in the land of your enemies because of their guilt. Even more so, they will decay because of the guilt of their ancestors. 40 They will confess their guilt and the guilt of their ancestors, that they acted treacherously against me and that they continued in hostility against me, 41 such that I continued in hostility against them, and I brought them into the land of their enemies. Then, if their stubborn[84] hearts are humbled and they make amends for their guilt, 42 then I will remember my covenant with Jacob; my covenant with Isaac and my covenant with Abraham I will remember; I will remember the land. 43 The land will be deserted because of them, restoring its sabbath years in its desolation from them. They must make amends for their guilt in order that—indeed because—they have rejected my rules and loathed my laws. 44 Yet for

[84] Literally: uncircumcised.

all that, when they are in the land of their enemies, I will not reject them and I will not loathe them to the point of completely destroying them, breaking my covenant with them. I am Yahweh their god. ⁴⁵ I will remember the covenant with their ancestors for their sakes, that I brought them out of the land of Egypt in the sight of the nations to be their god. I am Yahweh.'"

²⁶:⁴⁶ These are the laws, the rules, and the instructions that Yahweh established between himself and the Israelites through Moses at Mount Sinai.

²⁷:¹ Yahweh spoke to Moses: ² "Speak to the Israelites and say to them: 'When someone makes an explicit vow to Yahweh for the equivalent of a human being, ³ the equivalent for a male is: from 20 to 60 years old, the equivalent is 50 shekels of silver according to the sanctuary shekel. ⁴ If it is a female, the equivalent is 30 shekels. ⁵ If the person is 5 to 20 years old, the equivalent for a male is 20 shekels and 10 shekels for a female. ⁶ If the person is one month up to 5 years old, the equivalent for a male is 5 shekels of silver, and 3 shekels of silver for a female. ⁷ If the person is 60 years old or older, if it is a male, the equivalent is 15 shekels, 10 shekels for a female. ⁸ If someone cannot afford the equivalent, he should be presented to the priest and the priest will assess him. The priest will assess him according to what the person making the vow can afford.

²⁷:⁹ 'If the vow concerns an animal that can be brought as an offering for Yahweh, anything that can be given to Yahweh will be holy. ¹⁰ He cannot exchange or substitute another for it, either good for bad or bad for good. If someone does substitute one animal for another, then the thing that was vowed and its substitute are both holy. ¹¹ If it concerns any impure animal that cannot be brought as an offering for Yahweh, the animal should be presented to the priest, ¹² and the priest will assess it, whether good or bad; it will go according to the priest's assessment. ¹³ If he wants to redeem it, he must add one-fifth to its assessment.

²⁷:¹⁴ 'If someone consecrates their house to Yahweh, the priest should assess it. Whether it is good or bad, whatever the priest assesses will

stand. [15] If the person who has consecrated his house wants to redeem it, he must add one-fifth of its assessed value to it, then it will be his. [16] If anyone consecrates some of the land from his allotted portion to Yahweh, its assessment will be according to its seed requirements: fifty shekels of silver per *homer* of barley seed. [17] If he consecrates his land in the jubilee year, the assessment stands. [18] If he consecrates his land after the jubilee, the priest should calculate the value according to the years remaining until the next jubilee year and its assessment will be reduced. [19] If the person who consecrated the land wants to redeem it, he must add one-fifth to the assessed value, and it will transfer to him. [20] If he does not redeem the land and the land is sold to someone else, it is no longer redeemable. [21] When the land is released in the jubilee, it will be holy to Yahweh, like dedicated land; it becomes the priests' allotted holding. [22] If he consecrates land that he has purchased to Yahweh, land that is not part of his allotted holding, [23] then the priest must calculate the proportional assessment for him until the jubilee year. He must pay the assessment on that day as a sacred gift to Yahweh. [24] In the jubilee year, the land will return to him from the person who bought it, the one whose allotted holding the land is. [25] All assessments should be according to sanctuary weight; a shekel is 20 *gerahs*.

[27:26] 'However, a firstborn animal—which, as a firstborn, is Yahweh's—cannot be consecrated by anyone. Whether it is an ox or a sheep, it is Yahweh's. [27] If it is one of the impure animals, it can be ransomed with its assessment plus one-fifth its value. If it is not ransomed, it should be sold at its assessment. [28] Nothing that a person owns that has been dedicated to Yahweh, whether it is a human or an animal or his allotted holding, can be sold or ransomed. Everything that is dedicated is of the highest level of holiness to Yahweh. [29] No human being who has been dedicated can be ransomed; they must be put to death. [30] All tithes from the land, whether seed from the ground or fruit from the trees belong to Yahweh. They are holy to Yahweh. [31] If anyone wants to redeem his tithes, he must add one-fifth to them. [32] All tithes of the herd or of the flock—every tenth thing that passes under the shepherd's staff—will be holy to Yahweh. [33] He cannot look at whether it is good or bad or make a substitution for it. If he does make a substitution for it, then both it and its substitute will be holy; it cannot be redeemed.'"

27:34 These are the commands that Yahweh gave Moses for the Israelites at Mount Sinai.

Numbers 1:1 Yahweh spoke to Moses in the wilderness of Sinai, at the Meeting Tent, on the first day of the second month of the second year after they departed from the land of Egypt: 2 "Take a census of the entire Israelite community according to the families of their ancestral houses, counting the names of each individual male[85] 3 from the age of twenty and up, all those in Israel who can go to war. You and Aaron should muster them, unit by unit. 4 There will be a man from each tribe with you, each one a head of his ancestral house. 5 These are the names of the men who will assist you: From Reuben, Elizur son of Shedei'ur; 6 from Simeon, Shelumi'el son of Zurishaddai; 7 From Judah: Nahshon son of Amminadav; 8 from Issachar, Netanel son of Zu'ar; 9 From Zebulun, Eli'av son of Helon; 10 From Joseph's sons, from Ephraim, Elishama son of Ammihud, from Manasseh, Gamali'el son of Pedazur; 11 from Benjamin, Avidan son of Gideoni, 12 from Dan, Ahi'ezer son of Ammishaddai; 13 from Asher, Pagi'el son of Ochran; 14 from Gad, Eliasaph son of Deu'el; 15 from Naphtali, Ahira son of Enan. 16 These are the ones designated from the community, leaders of their ancestral tribes, they are the heads of Israel's divisions."

1:17 Moses and Aaron took these men that had been designated by name, 18 and they gathered the entire community on the first day of the second month. They registered themselves according to the families of

[85] At this point in the story, the narrator jumps forward about three weeks in the timeline, from the eighth day of the first month to the first day of the second month. The story will return to the eighth day of the first month in Numbers 7. But first, we are given an extensive list of the different Israelite tribes, their respective numbers and their physical location in the Israelite camp vis-à-vis the Meeting Tent. In some ways, this prolepsis in the story serves as a way to bridge the knowledge gap between the reader and the characters in the story. The characters in the story would be aware of the relative sizes of their families and where they live, but this information is not accessible to the reader unless it is explicitly shared, as it is through these census lists and descriptions of marching orders. At the end of Numbers 4, the readers will have as clear of a mental picture of the arrangement of the camp and the size of the Israelites as if they were characters in the story themselves. This allows for a different perspective to emerge for the reader with respect to the events in Numbers 7 (with the return to the eighth day of the first month) and following.

their ancestral houses, counting the names of those twenty years and older, individually. [19] As Yahweh had commanded Moses, so he mustered them in the wilderness of Sinai.

[1:20] These are the Reubenites, the firstborn of Israel, the registration of the families of their ancestral houses, counted by name individually, all the males from the age of twenty and up who could go to war: [21] those mustered from the tribe of Reuben: 46,500.

[1:22] From the Simeonites, the registration of the families of their ancestral houses, their muster counted by name individually, all the males from the age of twenty and up who could go to war: [23] those mustered from the tribe of Simeon: 59,300.

[1:24] From the Gadites, the registration of the families of their ancestral houses, counted by name, from the age of twenty and up who could go to war: [25] those mustered from the tribe of Gad: 45,650.

[1:26] From the Judahites, the registration of the families of their ancestral houses, counted by name, from the age of twenty and up who could go to war: [27] those mustered from the tribe of Judah: 74,600.

[1:28] From the Issacharites, the registration of the families of their ancestral houses, counted by name, from the age of twenty and up who could go to war: [29] those mustered from the tribe of Issachar: 54,400.

[1:30] From the Zebulunites, the registration of the families of their ancestral houses, counted by name, from the age of twenty and up who could go to war: [31] those mustered from the tribe of Zebulun: 57,400.

[1:32] From the Josephites—from the Ephraimites, the registration of the families of their ancestral houses, counted by name, from the age of twenty and up who could go to war: [33] those mustered from the tribe of Ephraim: 40,500; [34] from the Manassites, the registration of the families of their ancestral houses, counted by name, from the age of twenty and up who could go to war: [35] those mustered from the tribe of Manasseh: 32,200.

[1:36] From the Benjaminites, the registration of the families of their ancestral houses, counted by name, from the age of twenty and up who could go to war: [37] those mustered from the tribe of Benjamin: 35,400.

[1:38] From the Danites, the registration of the families of their ancestral houses, counted by name, from the age of twenty and up who could go to war: [39] those mustered from the tribe of Dan: 62,700.

[1:40] From the Asherites, the registration of the families of their ancestral houses, counted by name, from the age of twenty and up who could go to war: [41] those mustered from the tribe of Asher: 41,500.

[1:42] From the Naphtalites, the registration of the families of their ancestral houses, counted by name, from the age of twenty and up who could go to war: [43] those mustered from the tribe of Naphtali: 53,400.

[1:44] These are the musters that Aaron, Moses, and the twelve leaders of the Israelites (one man per ancestral house) recorded. [45] All the Israelites who were mustered by their ancestral houses, all those in Israel over the age of twenty who could go to war, [46] the total mustered was 603,550.

[1:47] However, the Levites were not mustered with them according to their ancestral tribe. [48] Yahweh had spoken to Moses: [49] "An exception—the tribe of Levi should not be mustered; they should not be included in the Israelites' census. [50] You should station[86] the Levites at the Dwelling Place of the *edut*, with its vessels and all its various components. They will carry the Dwelling Place and all its parts; they will tend to it and they will set up camp around the Dwelling Place. [51] Whenever the Dwelling Place needs to depart, the Levites will disassemble it; whenever the Dwelling Place needs to set up camp, the Levites will erect it. Any ordinary person who approaches it will be put to death. [52] The Israelites will set up camp according to their camps, each with its standard according to their division. [53] But the Levites will set up camp around the Dwelling Place of the *edut*, so that there is no fury

[86] This is the same Hebrew word that is used for mustering elsewhere in this chapter.

against the community of Israelites. The Levites should guard the Dwelling Place of the *edut*." [54] The Israelites did just as Yahweh had commanded Moses, so they did.

[2:1] Yahweh spoke to Moses and Aaron: [2] "The Israelites should set up camp, each with their standard, with banners for their ancestral houses; they should set up camp around the Meeting Tent.

[2:3] "Camped in front, to the east side, is the standard of the camp of Judah according to its division. The leader of the Judahites is Nahshon son of Amminadav. [4] His division, as mustered: 74,600. [5] Camped next to him is the tribe of Issachar. The leader of the Issacharites is Netanel son of Zu'ar. [6] His division, as mustered: 54,400. [7] Then the tribe of Zeubulun. The leader of the Zebulunites is Eli'av son of Helon. [8] His division, as mustered: 57,400. [9] The total muster for the Judahite camp: 186,400 by their divisions. They will march first.

[2:10] Camped to the south, the standard of the camp of Reuben, according to their divisions. The leader of the Reubenites is Elizur son of Shede'ur. [11] His division, as mustered: 46,500. [12] Camped next to him is the tribe of Simeon. The leader of the Simeonites is Shelumi'el son of Zurishaddai. [13] His division, as mustered: 59,300. [14] Then the tribe of Gad. The leader of the Gadites is Eliasaph son of Reu'el. [15] His division, as mustered: 45,650. [16] The total muster for the Reubenite camp: 151,450 by their divisions. They will march second.

[2:17] The Meeting Tent, and the Levite camp, will set out in the middle of the other camps; as they set up camp, so should they march, each in position with their units.

[2:18] Camped to the west is the standard of Ephraim, according to their divisions. The leader of the Ephraimites is Elishama son of Ammihud. [19] His division, as mustered: 40,500. [20] Next to him is the camp of Manasseh. The leader of the Manassites is Gamali'el son of Pedazur. [21] His division, as mustered: 32,200. [22] Then the tribe of Benjamin. The leader of the Benjaminites is Avidan son of Gideoni. [23] His division, as mustered: 35,400. [24] The total muster for the Ephramite camp: 108,100 by their divisions. They will march third.

^{2:25} Camped to the north is the standard of Dan, according to their divisions. The leader of the Danites is Ahiʻezer son of Ammishaddai. ²⁶ His division, as mustered: 62,700. ²⁷ Camped next to him is the tribe of Asher. The leader of the Asherites is Pagiʻel son of Ochran. ²⁸ His division, as mustered: 41,500. ²⁹ Then the tribe of Naphtali. The leader of the Naphtalites is Ahira son of Enan. ³⁰ His division, as mustered: 53,400. ³¹ The total muster for the Danite camp: 157,600. They will march last according to their units."

^{2:32} These are the musters of the Israelites, according to their ancestral houses. The total muster, by divisions: 603,550. ³³ The Levites were not mustered with the Israelites, as Yahweh commanded Moses. ³⁴ The Israelites did as Yahweh had commanded Moses; in this way, they set up camp according to their standards, and in this way they set out, each in the family of his ancestral house.

^{3:1} These are the descendants of Aaron and Moses when Yahweh spoke to Moses at Mount Sinai. ² These are the names of Aaron's sons: the firstborn Nadav, Avihu, Eleazar, and Ithamar. ³ These are the names of Aaron's sons, the anointed priests, who were ordained to serve as priests. ⁴ However, Nadav and Avihu died in front of Yahweh when they offered an unauthorized fire in front of Yahweh in the wilderness of Sinai. They had no sons. Therefore, Eleazar and Ithamar served as priests with their father Aaron.

^{3:5} Yahweh spoke to Moses: ⁶ "Bring forward the tribe of Levi and stand them in front of Aaron the priest so that they can serve him. ⁷ They will do the guard duty for the whole community in front of the Meeting Tent, performing the work of the Dwelling Place. ⁸ They will guard all the furnishings of the Meeting Tent on behalf of the Israelites, performing the work of the Dwelling Place. ⁹ You should assign the Levites to Aaron and his sons; they are wholly given over to him from the Israelites. ¹⁰ However, you should muster Aaron and his sons; they are responsible for their priestly work and any ordinary person who encroaches on it should be put to death."

^{3:11} Yahweh spoke to Moses: ¹² "I hereby take the Levites from the among the Israelites in place of all the firstborn, those who open the

womb of the Israelites; the Levites are mine. [13] Every firstborn is mine! When I struck down the firstborn in the land of Egypt, I consecrated every firstborn Israelite to me, whether human or animal. They are mine. I am Yahweh."

[3:14] Yahweh spoke to Moses in the wilderness of Sinai: [15] "Muster[87] the Levites according to their ancestral houses and by their families; every male who is one month old or older you should muster." [16] Moses mustered them at Yahweh's request, as he was commanded. [17] These are the sons of Levi, by their names: Gershon, Kehat, and Merari. [18] These are the names of the sons of Gershon, by their families: Livni and Shimi. [19] The sons of Kehat by their families: Amram, Yitzhar, Hevron, and Uzzi'el. [20] The sons of Merari by their families: Mahli and Mushi.

These are the families of the Levites, according to their ancestral houses:

[3:21] To Gershon: the family of the Livnites and the family of the Shimites. These are the Gershonite families. [22] Their muster, counting males from the age of one month and up; their muster: 7,500. [23] The Gershonite families would set up camp behind the Dwelling Place, to the west. [24] The leader of the ancestral house of the Gershonites: Eliasaph son of La'el. [25] The job of the Gershonites in the Meeting Tent: the Dwelling Place, the tent, its covering, the screen at the entrance to the Meeting Tent, [26] the courtyard curtains, the screen at the entrance to the courtyard that goes around the Dwelling Place and the altar, and its cords—everything associated with the ritual work for these things.

[3:27] To Kehat: the family of the Amramites, the family of the Yitzharites, the family of the Hevronites, and the family of the Uzzi'elites. These are the Kehatite families. [28] Counting all the males from the age of one month and up: 8,600 guarding the sanctuary. [29] The Kehatite families set up camp on the southern side of the Dwelling Place. [30] The leader of the ancestral house of the Kehatites: Elizafan son of Uzzi'el. [31] Their job: the ark, the table, the lampstand, the altars, and all the sacred

[87] In this case the Levites are being mustered for sanctuary service, and not for war.

vessels used with them, and the screen—everything associated with the ritual work for these things.

3:32 The head of the Levite leaders was Eleazar son of Aaron the priest, overseeing all those guarding the sanctuary.

3:33 To Merari: the family of the Mahlites and the family of the Mushites; these are the Merarite families. 34 Their muster, counting males one month and up: 6,200. 35 The leader of the ancestral house of the Merarites: Zuri'el son of Abihail. They set up camp on the northern side of the Dwelling Place. 36 The Merarites' assigned job: the boards of the Dwelling Place and its bars, pillars, and receptacles, along with all its furnishings—everything associated with the ritual work for these things, 37 and the courtyard pillars all around and their receptacles, pegs, and cords.

3:38 Those setting up camp in front of the Dwelling Place, to the east in front of the Meeting Tent, were Moses, and Aaron and his sons, guarding the sanctuary on behalf of the Israelites; any ordinary person who encroached on it would be put to death. 39 The total number of Levites mustered, that Moses and Aaron mustered at Yahweh's command, according to their families, all males from the age of one month and up: 22,000.

3:40 Yahweh said to Moses: "Muster every firstborn male Israelite, from the age of one month and up; count their names. 41 Then take the Levites for me (I am Yahweh) in place of each firstborn Israelite, and the Levites' cattle in place of the firstborn of the Israelites' cattle." 42 Moses mustered all the firstborn Israelites as Yahweh commanded him. 43 All the firstborn males counted, from the age of one month and up: 22,273.

3:44 Yahweh spoke to Moses: 45 "Take the Levites in place of the firstborn Israelites, and the Levites' cattle in place of their cattle. The Levites will be mine; I am Yahweh. 46 As for the redemption of the 273 firstborn Israelites beyond the number of Levites, 47 take five shekels per head; you should take it according to the sanctuary shekel, 20 *gerahs* to the shekel, 48 and give the money to Aaron and his sons as the redemption price for the extra people." 49 So Moses took the redemption money from those people who were left over after those redeemed by the Levites. [50] He took the money from the firstborn Israelites, a total of 1,365 sanctuary shekels. [51] Then Moses gave the redemption money to Aaron and his sons as Yahweh said, just as Yahweh commanded Moses.

[4:1] Yahweh spoke to Moses and Aaron: [2] "Take a census of the Kehatites apart from the other Levites, according to the families of their ancestral houses, [3] from the age of 30 up to 50, all who qualify to do the work for the Meeting Tent. [4] This is the labor for the Kehatites in the Meeting Tent: those objects of the highest level of holiness.

[4:5] "When the camp is to depart, Aaron and his sons should enter and take down the curtain and cover the ark of the *edut* with it. [6] They should put a cover of dyed green-blue leather over it and spread a piece of blue fabric over it; then they will put the bars in it. [7] Over the display table, they should spread a blue cloth and put the bowls, ladles, jugs, and libation jars on it; the regular display bread should also be on top. [8] Then they should spread an earthy-red cloth over it and cover that with a piece of dyed green-blue leather. Then they should put its bars in it. [9] They should take a blue cloth and cover the lampstand for the light and its lamps, its tongs, its firepans, and all the vessels for oil that are used to maintain it. [10] Then they should put it and all its furnishings into a dyed green-blue leather covering and put that on a carrying frame.

[4:11] "Next, they should spread a blue cloth over the gold altar and cover that with a piece of leather dyed blue-green and put its bars in it. [12] They should take all the ritual vessels that are used with it in the sanctuary and put them into a blue cloth, and then cover them with leather dyed blue-green. They should then put it on a carrying frame.

[4:13] "Then they should remove the ashes from the altar and spread a purple cloth over it. [14] They should put all its vessels used for the activity there on top of it: the firepans, the forks, the shovels, and the basins—all the altar's utensils. They should spread a piece of dyed green-blue leather over it and then put the poles in it.

[4:15] "When Aaron and his sons have finished covering the sanctuary and all the sanctuary's furnishings, whenever the camp departs, only after that should the Kehatites enter to carry them. This is so they do not touch the sacred objects and die. These are the things in the Meeting Tent that are to be carried by the Kehatites. [16] Eleazar, son of Aaron the priest, will be responsible for the lamp's oil, the fragrant incense, and the regular grain offering, along with the anointing oil. He also has ultimate responsibility for the entire Dwelling Place and everything in it, the sanctuary and its furnishings."

[4:17] Yahweh spoke to Moses and Aaron: [18] "Do not allow the Kehatite families to be cut off from the Levites. [19] You must do this with them so that they do not die when they approach the holiest objects: Aaron and his sons should enter and assign each man his work and his objects to carry. [20] They cannot enter to watch the enclosing[88] of the sacred objects, otherwise they could die."

[4:21] Yahweh spoke to Moses: [22] "Take a census of the Gershonites also, according to their ancestral houses and families. [23] From the age of 30 to 50, you should muster them—all who qualify to do the work for the Meeting Tent. [24] This is the labor for the Gershonites and their carrying duties: [25] They will carry the curtains of the Dwelling Place and the Meeting Tent with its covering, the dyed green-blue leather covering that is over it, and the screen that is at the entrance to the Meeting Tent, [26] the courtyard's curtains, the screen at the entrance to the courtyard gate around the Dwelling Place and altar, their cords, and all the things necessary for their use. [27] All the Gershonites' labor and carrying duties should be done at the instruction of Aaron and his sons; you should set them to supervise all the carrying work. [28] This is the job of the Gershonite family in the Meeting Tent; their duties are under the supervision of Ithamar son of Aaron the priest.

[4:29] "The Merarites: you should muster all their families according to their ancestral houses; [30] from the ages of 30 up to 50 you should muster them—all who qualify to do work for the Meeting Tent. [31] This is their carrying labor, for their labor in the Meeting Tent: the boards of the Dwelling Place and its bars, pillars, and receptacles, [32] the courtyard's pillars and their receptacles, cords, and pegs, along with all the

[88] Literally: the swallowing.

furnishings and things related to their use. You should record by name the objects that they are responsible for carrying. ³³ This is the work for the Merarite families, for their service in the Meeting Tent under the supervision of Ithamar son of Aaron the priest."

⁴:³⁴ So Moses and Aaron and the leaders of the community mustered the Kehatites, by their families and according to their ancestral houses, ³⁵ from the ages of 30 up to 50, all who qualified to work in the Meeting Tent. ³⁶ Those mustered according to their families: 2,750. ³⁷ These were those mustered in the Kehatite family, all who could work in the Meeting Tent, whom Moses and Aaron mustered at Yahweh's command through Moses. ³⁸ The muster of the Gershonites according to their families and their ancestral houses, ³⁹ from the age of 30 up to 50 who qualified to do work in the Meeting Tent, ⁴⁰ those mustered in their families and by their ancestral clan: 2,630. ⁴⁰ These were those mustered in the Gershonite family, all who could work in the Meeting Tent whom Moses and Aaron mustered at Yahweh's command. ⁴² The muster of the Merarites, according to their families and their ancestral houses, ⁴³ from the age of 30 up to 50, all who were qualified to work in the Meeting Tent. ⁴⁴ Those mustered according to their families: 3,200. ⁴⁵ These were those mustered in the Merarite family, who Moses and Aaron mustered at the command of Yahweh through Moses.

⁴:⁴⁶ All those who were mustered, those Moses, Aaron, and the leaders of the community mustered among the Levites, by their families and ancestral houses, ⁴⁷ from the age of 30 up to 50, all who qualified to work in and to carry the Meeting Tent, ⁴⁸ all those mustered: 8,580. ⁴⁹ According to Yahweh's command, through Moses, each one of them was appointed to their specific job and their objects to carry; each was mustered as Yahweh commanded Moses.

⁵:¹ Yahweh spoke to Moses: ² "Command the Israelites to send anyone out of the camp who has a skin disease or a discharge outside or anyone who has been rendered impure by a corpse. ³ Whether they are male or female, send them outside the camp; send them out so that they do not render their camp impure, where I dwell in the midst of them." ⁴ The Israelites did so: they sent them outside the camp as Yahweh commanded to Moses; so the Israelites did.

⁵:⁵ Yahweh spoke to Moses: ⁶ "Speak to the Israelites: 'Any man or woman who commits a wrong against another person, transgressing against Yahweh, and that person recognizes their guilt, ⁷ they should confess the wrong that they did and make restitution for the wrong adding one-fifth to it. They should give it to the person they wronged. ⁸ If the wronged person has no next of kin to receive the restitution for the wrong, the restitution for the wrong will belong to Yahweh for the priest; this is in addition to the ram of purification with which purification will be made on his behalf. ⁹ Any gift among the sacred offerings that the Israelites bring to the priest will become his. ¹⁰ Each priest should have his sacred offerings; anything that someone gives to the priest will become his.'"

⁵:¹¹ Yahweh spoke to Moses: ¹² "Speak to the Israelites and say to them: 'If any man's wife is unfaithful and commits a transgression against him: ¹³ if a man has sex with her, but it is kept secret from her husband, and she has hidden that she has made herself impure, and there is no witness against her because she was not caught—¹⁴ if a feeling of jealousy comes over him and he is jealous of his wife who has rendered herself impure; or if a feeling of jealously comes over him and he is jealous about his wife even though she has not rendered herself impure, ¹⁵ the man should bring his wife to the priest. He should bring an offering on her behalf: one-tenth of an *ephah* of barley flour. No oil should be poured on it and no frankincense should be put on it. It is a grain offering for jealousy, a memorial grain offering, which recalls the wrongdoing. ¹⁶ The priest should bring her forward and stand her in front of Yahweh. ¹⁷ The priest should take sacred water in an earthenware vessel. Then he should take some of the dirt that is on the floor of the Dwelling Place and put it in the water.

⁵:¹⁸ 'When the priest has made the woman stand in front of Yahweh, he should uncover her head and put the memorial grain offering in her hands; it is a grain offering of jealousy. The bitter water of cursing[89] should be in the priest's hands. ¹⁹ The priest should make her take an oath. He should say to her: "If no man has had sex with you, if you have not been unfaithful in impurity while under your husband's authority,

[89] The Hebrew term here is highly alliterative, a feature that evokes a spell or curse given this context (*may ha-marim ha-meararim*).

be unharmed from these bitter waters of cursing. [20] But if you have been unfaithful while under your husband's authority, and if you have rendered yourself impure, if a man who is not your husband has had sex with you," [21] (the priest should then have the woman swear the curse oath, and the priest should go on to say to the woman) "May Yahweh make you a curse and an oath among your people, when Yahweh causes your uterus[90] to fall and your womb to swell. [22] May this water of cursing enter your stomach and cause your belly to swell and your uterus to fall." Then the woman should say "amen, amen."

[5:23] 'The priest should write these curses on a scroll and then rub them off into the bitter water. [24] He should make the woman drink the bitter water of cursing so that the cursed waters enter her and bring about bitter pain. [25] The priest should take the grain offering of jealousy from the woman's hand and elevate the grain offering in front of Yahweh. Then he should bring it to the altar. [26] The priest should take a handful of the grain offering as a memorial portion of it and burn that on the altar. Finally, he should have the woman drink the water. [27] When he has made her drink the water, if she has rendered herself impure by transgressing against her husband, the bitter water will enter her and cause her pain; then her belly will swell, and her uterus will fall. The woman will become a curse among her people. [28] But if the woman has not rendered herself impure and she is in fact pure, then she will be unharmed and she will be able to conceive.'"

[5:29] This is the instruction for jealousy, when a woman has been unfaithful while under her husband's authority and has rendered herself impure, [30] or when a feeling of jealousy comes over a man and he is jealous of his wife: he will stand the woman in front of Yahweh and the priest will carry out these instructions for her. [31] The man will be free from guilt, but the woman will bear her guilt.

[6:1] Yahweh spoke to Moses: [2] "Speak to the Israelites and say to them: 'Any man or woman who makes an explicit vow, the nazirite vow,[91] to set themselves apart for Yahweh, [3] should separate themselves from wine and strong drink; they should not drink wine vinegar or any

---

[90] Literally: thigh, though this is almost certainly euphemistic.
[91] Literally: on his head.

other intoxicating vinegar, and they should not drink any grape juice or eat any grapes, whether fresh or dried. ⁴ For the duration of his nazirite vow, he should not eat anything that is produced by a grapevine, even seeds or skin. ⁵ For the duration of his nazirite vow, a razor should not pass over his head; until his term as Yahweh's nazirite is fulfilled, it is considered sacred; the hair of his head should be left alone to grow. ⁶ For the duration of him being set apart for Yahweh, he should not enter a place where there is a dead body. ⁷ Even if it is his father or his mother, his brother or his sister who dies, he should not render himself impure for them because his consecration to his God is visible. ⁸ For the duration of his nazirite vow, he is consecrated to Yahweh.

⁶:⁹ 'If a person dies near him suddenly and his consecrated head is rendered impure, he should shave his head on the day that he is pure; he should shave it on the seventh day. ¹⁰ On the eighth day, he should bring two turtledoves or two pigeons to the priest, to the entrance of the Meeting Tent. ¹¹ The priest should offer one of them as a decontamination offering and one of them as a burnt offering. He will effect purification on his behalf from the error concerning the corpse. Then, on that same day, he will consecrate his head ¹² and set apart for Yahweh his term as a nazirite. Then he should bring a year-old male lamb as a guilt offering. The previous term will be voided because his consecration was rendered impure.

⁶:¹³ 'This is the instruction for the nazirite:[92] On the day that his term as a nazirite has been fulfilled, he should be brought to the entrance of the Meeting Tent. ¹⁴ He should bring his offering for Yahweh: an unblemished year-old male lamb as a burnt offering, and an unblemished year-old female lamb as a decontamination offering, and an unblemished ram

[92] The Hebrew root underlying this word (*nzr*) means consecration (or sometimes crown). A Nazirite is literally "the consecrated one." In this case, the most visible symbol of the person's temporary consecration to Yahweh (as opposed to a priest's permanent consecration) is that their hair cannot be cut during the term of their vow. At several points in these instructions for the nazirite, there is a discussion of "his consecrated head." The idea of a consecrated head echoes the ritual in Leviticus 8 of pouring the anointing oil over Aaron's head, but there is no oil involved in this case. Here the consecration is in the individual's self-dedication to Yahweh for a period of time, visibly marked by their long hair, which is cut and offered on the altar alongside sacrifices at the end of the term of their vow.

as a well-being offering, [15] along with a basket of unleavened cakes made of fine flour with oil mixed in, and unleavened wafers smeared with oil, plus their accompanying grain offerings and libations. [16] The priest should bring them in front of Yahweh, and he should sacrifice his decontamination offering and his burnt offering. [17] The ram he should offer as a sacrifice of well-being to Yahweh along with the basket of unleavened bread. The priest should then offer the grain offering and the libation offering. [18] Next, the nazirite should shave his consecrated head at the entrance to the Meeting Tent and take the consecrated hair from his head and put it on the fire that is under the sacrifice of well-being. [19] The priest should take the shoulder of the ram that has been boiled, one unleavened cake from the basket, and one unleavened wafer and put them in the nazirite's hands after he has shaved his consecrated head. [20] Then the priest should elevate them as an elevation offering in front of Yahweh; it is a sacred offering for the priest, along with the breast of the elevation offering and the gifted thigh. After this, the nazirite can drink wine. [21] This is the instruction for the nazirite who takes a vow; his offering for Yahweh should accompany his consecration, in addition to anything else that he can afford. According to the vow that he takes, so he should offer, according to the instruction for his consecration.'"

[6:22] Yahweh spoke to Moses: [23] "Speak to Aaron and to his sons: 'In this way you should bless the Israelites. Say to them: [24] "May Yahweh bless you and guard you! [25] May Yahweh make his presence shine[93] for you and deal graciously with you! [26] May Yahweh show you favor and give you peace!' So they will set my name alongside the Israelites, and I will bless them."'"

[7:1] On the day Moses finished setting up the Meeting Tent, he anointed it and sanctified it along with all its vessels as well as the altar and its vessels. When he had anointed and sanctified them,[94] [2] the leaders of

---

[93] Recall that in Exodus 34, Moses's face shines with a kind of blinding radiance whenever he comes out from speaking with Yahweh. Here the phrase is literally "May Yahweh make his face shine," which echoes that scene from earlier in the story. The blessing here is for Yahweh's presence, his radiance, to continue to be visible to the people, meaning that he will continue to dwell in their midst.

[94] The day the altar of the altar's anointing should probably be understood as the day that the altar's anointing was completed, that is, the eighth day of the first month.

the Israelites, the heads of their ancestral houses, drew near (these are the leaders of the tribes, those in charge of the musters), [3] and they brought their offering in front of Yahweh: 6 sturdy wagons and 12 oxen, a cart for every 2 leaders and an ox for each leader. When they had brought them in front of the Dwelling Place, [4] Yahweh said to Moses: [5] "Take these from them so that they can be used for the labor of the Meeting Tent and give them to the Levites according to their duties."[95] [6] So Moses took the carts and the oxen and he gave them to the Levites.[96] [7] He gave 2 carts and 4 oxen to the Gershonites for their work, [8] and 4 carts and 8 oxen to the Merarites for their work, under the supervision of Ithamar son of Aaron the priest. [9] But he did not give anything to the Kehatites because their work was with the holiest objects, and they would carry them on their shoulders.

[7:10] The leaders also brought gifts for the dedication of the altar on the day of its anointing. The leaders brought their gifts in front of the altar. [11] Yahweh said to Moses: "Let one leader per day bring forward their gift for the dedication of the altar."

[7:12] The one who presented his gift on the first day was Nahshon son of Amminadav, from the tribe of Judah. [13] His gift: 1 silver bowl weighing 130 shekels, 1 silver basin[97] weighing 70 shekels according to the sanctuary shekel, both of them filled with fine flour mixed with oil for a grain offering, [14] 1 gold ladle[98] weighing 10 shekels filled with incense, [15] 1 bull from the herd, 1 ram, and 1 one-year-old male lamb for a burnt

[95] This instruction presumes knowledge that the Levites are responsible for carrying the disassembled Meeting Tent, and that these carts will help them do that.

[96] This means that the events in this chapter are likely happening simultaneously with the events following the inauguration of the Meeting Tent in Leviticus 9–10. Indeed, there is one part of the story in Leviticus 10, when Yahweh speaks to Aaron alone, in which Moses and the Israelite leaders are entirely absent from the plot, even though they are described as being present. It is in this chapter that we start to see the activity that might have been taking place at the entrance to the Meeting Tent while Yahweh was speaking to Aaron inside the Tent.

[97] Given its Hebrew root (*mzrq*), this is almost certainly a vessel designed to hold the blood that is tossed (*zrq*) on the altar.

[98] The literal translation of this term refers to the palm of one's hand, implying the cupped shape that a priest uses to scoop out parts of an offering—hence "ladle."

offering, [16] 1 male goat for a decontamination offering, [17] and for a sacrifice of well-being: 2 oxen, 5 rams, 5 male goats, 5 one-year-old male lambs. This was the gift from Nahshon son of Amminadav.

[7:18] On the second day, Netanel son of Zu'ar, from the tribe of Issachar, came forward. [19] He brought his gift: 1 silver bowl weighing 130 shekels, 1 silver basin weighing 70 shekels according to the sanctuary shekel, both of them filled with fine flour mixed with oil for a grain offering, [20] 1 gold ladle weighing 10 shekels filled with incense, [21] 1 bull from the herd, 1 ram, and 1 one-year-old male lamb for a burnt offering, [22] 1 male goat for a decontamination offering, [23] and for a sacrifice of well-being: 2 oxen, 5 rams, 5 male goats, 5 one-year-old male lambs. This was the gift from Netanel son of Zu'ar.[99]

[7:24] On the third day: the leader of the Zeubulunites, Eli'av son of Helon.[100] [25] His gift: 1 silver bowl weighing 130 shekels, 1 silver basin weighing 70 shekels according to the sanctuary shekel, both of them filled with fine flour mixed with oil for a grain offering, [20] 1 gold ladle weighing 10 shekels filled with incense, [21] 1 bull from the herd, 1 ram, and 1 one-year-old male lamb for a burnt offering, [22] 1 male goat for a decontamination offering, [23] and for a sacrifice of well-being: 2 oxen, 5 rams, 5 male goats, 5 one-year-old male lambs. This was the gift from Eli'av son of Helon.

[7:30] On the fourth day: the leader of the Reubenites, Elizur son of Shede'ur. [31] His gift: 1 silver bowl weighing 130 shekels, 1 silver basin weighing 70 shekels according to the sanctuary shekel, both of them filled with fine flour mixed with oil for a grain offering, [20] 1 gold ladle weighing 10

[99] Readers might notice that the gifts of Nahshon and Netanel are identical. This will also be the case for the gifts from the subsequent ten leaders. This is particularly noteworthy because the census lists in the previous chapters highlighted the disparity in the sizes of these tribes. The tribe of Judah (Nahshon's tribe) is the largest with 74,600 men of fighting age. The tribe of Manasseh (Gamaliel's tribe, which offers its gift on the eighth day) is the smallest with only 32,200 men of fighting age. Yet despite the fact that Judah is more than twice the size of Manasseh, their gifts are identical. This suggests that the twelve Israelite tribes are equally responsible for the maintenance of Yahweh's Dwelling Place.

[100] The order that the tribes present their gifts in is following the order that they are supposed to march in according to Yahweh's instructions in Numbers 2.

shekels filled with incense, [21] 1 bull from the herd, 1 ram, and 1 one-year-old male lamb for a burnt offering, [22] 1 male goat for a decontamination offering, [23] and for a sacrifice of well-being: 2 oxen, 5 rams, 5 male goats, 5 one-year-old male lambs. This was the gift from Elizur son of Shede'ur.

[7:36] On the fifth day: the leader of the Simeonites, Shelumi'el son of Zurishaddai. [37] His gift: 1 silver bowl weighing 130 shekels, 1 silver basin weighing 70 shekels according to the sanctuary shekel, both of them filled with fine flour mixed with oil for a grain offering, [20] 1 gold ladle weighing 10 shekels filled with incense, [21] 1 bull from the herd, 1 ram, and 1 one-year-old male lamb for a burnt offering, [22] 1 male goat for a decontamination offering, [23] and for a sacrifice of well-being: 2 oxen, 5 rams, 5 male goats, 5 one-year-old male lambs. This was the gift from Shelumi'el son of Zurishaddai.

[7:42] On the sixth day: the leader of the Gadites, Eliasaph son of Deu'el. [43] His gift: 1 silver bowl weighing 130 shekels, 1 silver basin weighing 70 shekels according to the sanctuary shekel, both of them filled with fine flour mixed with oil for a grain offering, [20] 1 gold ladle weighing 10 shekels filled with incense, [21] 1 bull from the herd, 1 ram, and 1 one-year-old male lamb for a burnt offering, [22] 1 male goat for a decontamination offering, [23] and for a sacrifice of well-being: 2 oxen, 5 rams, 5 male goats, 5 one-year-old male lambs.. This was the gift from Eliasaph son of Deu'el.

[7:48] On the seventh day: the leader of the Ephraimites, Elishama son of Ammihud. [49] His gift: 1 silver bowl weighing 130 shekels, 1 silver basin weighing 70 shekels according to the sanctuary shekel, both of them filled with fine flour mixed with oil for a grain offering, [20] 1 gold ladle weighing 10 shekels filled with incense, [21] 1 bull from the herd, 1 ram, and 1 one-year-old male lamb for a burnt offering, [22] 1 male goat for a decontamination offering, [23] and for a sacrifice of well-being: 2 oxen, 5 rams, 5 male goats, 5 one-year-old male lambs. This was the gift from Elishama son of Ammihud.

[7:54] On the eighth day: the leader of the Manassites, Gamali'el son of Pedazur. [55] His gift: 1 silver bowl weighing 130 shekels, 1 silver basin weighing 70 shekels according to the sanctuary shekel, both of them filled with fine flour mixed with oil for a grain offering, [20] 1 gold ladle weighing 10 shekels filled with incense, [21] 1 bull from the herd, 1 ram, and 1 one-year-old male lamb for a burnt offering, [22] 1 male goat for a decontamination offering, [23] and for a sacrifice of well-being: 2 oxen, 5 rams, 5 male goats, 5 one-year-old male lambs. This was the gift from Gamali'el son of Pedazur.

[7:60] On the ninth day: the leader of the Benjaminites, Avidan son of Gideoni. [61] His gift: 1 silver bowl weighing 130 shekels, 1 silver basin weighing 70 shekels according to the sanctuary shekel, both of them filled with fine flour mixed with oil for a grain offering, [20] 1 gold ladle weighing 10 shekels filled with incense, [21] 1 bull from the herd, 1 ram, and 1 one-year-old male lamb for a burnt offering, [22] 1 male goat for a decontamination offering, [23] and for a sacrifice of well-being: 2 oxen, 5 rams, 5 male goats, 5 one-year-old male lambs. This was the gift from Avidan son of Gideoni.

[7:66] On the tenth day: the leader of the Danites, Ahi'ezer son of Ammishaddai. [67] His gift: 1 silver bowl weighing 130 shekels, 1 silver basin weighing 70 shekels according to the sanctuary shekel, both of them filled with fine flour mixed with oil for a grain offering, [20] 1 gold ladle weighing 10 shekels filled with incense, [21] 1 bull from the herd, 1 ram, and 1 one-year-old male lamb for a burnt offering, [22] 1 male goat for a decontamination offering, [23] and for a sacrifice of well-being: 2 oxen, 5 rams, 5 male goats, 5 one-year-old male lambs. This was the gift from Ahi'ezer son of Ammishaddai.

[7:72] On the eleventh day: the leader of the Asherites, Pagi'el son of Ochran. [73] His gift: 1 silver bowl weighing 130 shekels, 1 silver basin weighing 70 shekels according to the sanctuary shekel, both of them filled with fine flour mixed with oil for a grain offering, [20] 1 gold ladle weighing 10 shekels filled with incense, [21] 1 bull from the herd, 1 ram, and 1 one-year-old male lamb for a burnt offering, [22] 1 male goat for a decontamination offering, [23] and for a sacrifice of well-being: 2 oxen, 5 rams, 5 male goats, 5 one-year-old male lambs. This was the gift from Pagi'el son of Ochran.

[7:78] On the twelfth day: the leader of the Naphtalites, Ahira son of Enan. [79] His gift: 1 silver bowl weighing 130 shekels, 1 silver basin weighing 70 shekels according to the sanctuary shekel, both of them filled with fine flour mixed with oil for a grain offering, ²⁰ 1 gold ladle weighing 10 shekels filled with incense, ²¹ 1 bull from the herd, 1 ram, and 1 one-year-old male lamb for a burnt offering, ²² 1 male goat for a decontamination offering, ²³ and for a sacrifice of well-being: 2 oxen, 5 rams, 5 male goats, 5 one-year-old male lambs. This was the gift from Ahira son of Enan.

⁷:⁸⁴ This was the gift for the dedication of the altar from the Israelite leaders on the day it was anointed: twelve silver bowls, 12 silver basins, 12 gold ladles. ⁸⁵ 130 shekels of silver per bowl, 70 per basin. The total silver for the vessels: 2,400 shekels by the sanctuary shekel. ⁸⁶ The 12 gold ladles filled with incense: 10 shekels per ladle by the sanctuary shekel for a total of 120 for the gold ladles. ⁸⁷ The total for the herd animals for burnt offerings: twelve bulls, 12 rams, 12 one-year-old male lambs, along with their grain offerings and 12 male goats for decontamination offerings. ⁸⁸ The total of the herd animals for sacrifices of well-being: twenty-four bulls, plus 60 rams, 60 male goats, and 60 one-year-old lambs. This was the gift for the dedication of the altar after it had been anointed.

⁷:⁸⁹ Now, whenever Moses would enter the Meeting Tent to speak with him, he would hear the voice speaking to him from above the cover that was on the ark of the *edut*, between the two *keruvim*. He spoke to him. ⁸:¹ Yahweh said to Moses, "Speak to Aaron and say to him: 'Whenever you light the lamps, the seven lamps should give off light in front of the lampstand.'" ³ Aaron did this: he lit the lamps at the front of the lampstand, as Yahweh had commanded Moses. ⁴ This is how the lampstand was made: from hammered gold, hammered from its base to its petals; according to the pattern that Yahweh showed Moses, so he made the lampstand.

⁸:⁵ Yahweh spoke to Moses: ⁶ "Take the Levites from among the Israelites and make them pure. ⁷ This is what you should do to purify them: sprinkle the waters of purification on them, have them run a razor over their entire body, and wash their clothes, thus purifying themselves. ⁸ Then take a bull of the herd and its grain offering of fine flour mixed with oil. Take a second bull from the herd as a decontamination

offering. [9] Bring the Levites in front of the Meeting Tent and assemble the entire Israelite community.[101] [10] You should bring the Levites in front of Yahweh and the Israelites should lay their hands on the Levites.[102] [11] Then Aaron should present[103] the Levites as an elevation offering from the Israelites in front of Yahweh so that they can do Yahweh's work.

8:12 "The Levites should then lay their hands on the heads of the bulls, and one should be offered as a decontamination offering and one as a burnt offering to Yahweh, to effect purification on behalf of the Levites. [13] You should stand the Levites in front of Aaron and his sons, and you should present them as an elevation offering to Yahweh. [14] You should set apart the Levites from the rest of the Israelites; the Levites will belong to me. [15] After this, the Levites will be able to enter to work in the Meeting Tent, once you have purified them and presented them as an elevation offering. [16] They are officially dedicated to me from among the Israelites; I have taken them for myself in place of those who open the womb, the firstborn, of the Israelites. [17] Every firstborn of the Israelites, whether human or animal, is mine. When I struck down all the firstborns in the land of Egypt, I consecrated them for myself. [18] But I have taken the Levites in place of all the Israelite firstborn, [19] and I have given the Levites to Aaron and his sons as a gift from the Israelites, to do the work for the Israelites in the Meeting Tent and to effect purification on behalf of the Israelites so that there will not be a plague on the Israelites for encroaching on the sanctuary."

[101] This ritual of purifying the Levites has a number of parallels with the ordination of the priests in Leviticus 8, especially this command to gather the whole Israelite community to watch the event. One significant difference, however, is that the Levites are never sanctified/consecrated the way that the priests are; they are only purified and then designated as belonging to the priests. The form of the ritual itself communicates a hierarchy in which the priests occupy the highest level, closest to Yahweh, and the Levites occupy the space below the priests, yet closer to Yahweh and his Dwelling Place than an ordinary Israelite.

[102] Throughout this ritual the Levites will be in the position of a sacrificial offering. Typically, in this story it is the animal that is subjected to the hand-laying ritual, or that is elevated before Yahweh. Here the Levites take on that role.

[103] Literally: elevate, though in this case it is clear that Aaron cannot lift and present the Levites as he would a breast or right thigh of a sacrificial offering.

8:20 Moses, Aaron, and the entire Israelite community did this with the Levites; according to everything that Yahweh commanded Moses about the Levites, so the Israelites did for them: 21 The Levites decontaminated themselves and washed their clothes. Aaron presented them as an elevation offering in front of Yahweh, and then Aaron effected purification on their behalf so that they would be pure. 22 After this, the Levites could enter to perform their work in the Meeting Tent, in front of Aaron and his sons. As Yahweh had commanded Moses concerning the Levites, so they did.

8:23 Yahweh spoke to Moses: 24 "This is for the Levites: from the age of 25 and up, they can enter the service[104] of the Meeting Tent. 25 At the age of 50, they should retire from service; they should no longer serve. 26 They can help their family in the Meeting Tent by guarding it, but they cannot perform any labor. This is what you should do with the Levites when assigning their tasks."

9:1 Yahweh spoke to Moses in the wilderness of Sinai, in the first month of the second year after they departed from the land of Egypt: 2 "Let the Israelites sacrifice the passover offering at its appointed time. 3 You should sacrifice it on the fourteenth day of this month at twilight, at its appointed time. You should sacrifice it according to all its laws and all its rules."

9:4 Moses told the Israelites to sacrifice the passover offering, 5 and they sacrificed the passover offering in the first month on the fourteenth day of the month at twilight in the wilderness of Sinai. Just as Yahweh had commanded Moses, so the Israelites did. 6 But there were some people who had been rendered impure by a corpse and they could not sacrifice the passover offering on that day. They approached Moses and Aaron that day, 7 and these people said to them: "We are impure because of a corpse. Why must we be prevented from bringing Yah-

---

[104] The term used here in Hebrew is often used in military contexts. In this case, it is equating the Levites' work in transporting the Meeting Tent (when the camp is on the move) with the actual military service the other Israelite tribes have been mustered to perform. Rather than age 20 and up with the tribes, it is age 25 and up for the Levites.

weh's offering at its appointed time with the rest of the Israelites?"[105] 8 Moses said to them: "Wait here while I go hear what Yahweh commands concerning your situation."

9:9 Yahweh said to Moses: 10 "Speak to the Israelites: 'Anyone who is rendered impure by a corpse or who is far away on a journey, whether it is you or one of your descendants, should sacrifice Yahweh's passover. 11 They should sacrifice it in the second month on the fourteenth day of the month, at twilight; they should eat it along with unleavened bread and bitter herbs, 12 and they should not leave any of it over until morning. They should not break a bone in it. They should sacrifice it according to the law of the passover offering. 13 However, in the case of a man who is pure or is not on a journey who refrains from sacrificing the passover offering, that person will be cut off from his people because he did not bring Yahweh's offering at its appointed time. That man will incur guilt. 14 If a foreigner lives with you and wants to sacrifice the passover offering to Yahweh, he must sacrifice it according to the laws and rules of the passover offering. You should have one law for the foreigner and the citizen in the land.'"

9:15 On the day that the Dwelling Place was erected, a cloud had covered the Dwelling Place and the tent of the *edut*. In the evening it remained over the Dwelling Place, looking like a fire until morning. 16 It was always like this: the cloud covered it and at night it looked like fire. 17 Whenever the cloud lifted from the tent, the Israelites would set out, and wherever the cloud settled, the Israelites would set up camp. 18 At Yahweh's command the Israelites set out and at Yahweh's command they set up camp.[106] They stayed camped while the cloud dwelled over the Dwelling Place. 19 When the cloud remained over the Dwelling Place for many days, the Israelites obeyed Yahweh's directive and did not set out.

[105] According to the instructions for the passover sacrifice in Exodus 12 and Leviticus 23, anyone who fails to bring the passover offering at its appointed time is subject to being cut off from their people. These Israelites are looking for a way around that penalty.

[106] This section is reminiscent of the passage at the beginning of the eight-day inauguration of Yahweh's Dwelling place (Exod 40:36–38), in which the narrator describes the behavior of the cloud and its relationship to the Meeting Tent. This serves as a kind of envelope structure, marking the beginning and end of this scene in the broader story of the priestly narrative.

[20] Sometimes the cloud remained for a few days over the Dwelling Place; they set up camp at Yahweh's instruction and they set out at Yahweh's instruction. [21] Sometimes the cloud remained only from evening until morning, and they would set out when the cloud lifted in the morning. Day or night, whenever the cloud lifted, they would set out. [22] Whether for two days or a month or a year, however long the cloud remained over the Dwelling Place, dwelling over it, the Israelites remained in camp and did not set out. When it lifted, then they set out. [23] They set up camp at Yahweh's command, and they set out at Yahweh's command. They obeyed Yahweh's directive, as Yahweh commanded through Moses.

[10:1] Yahweh spoke to Moses: [2] "Make 2 silver trumpets; you should make them of hammered work. They should be used to summon the community, and to signal when the camp should set out. [3] When they are both blown, the entire community should meet you at the entrance to the Meeting Tent. [4] If only one is blown, then the leaders, the heads of the Israelite regiments,[107] should meet you. [5] If you blow with short blasts, those camped on the east side should set out. [6] When you blow with short blasts a second time, those camped on the south side should set out. A short blast should be blown whenever they need to set out. [7] When the community needs to be gathered, you should blow, but not with short blasts. [8] Aaron's sons, the priests, should blow the trumpets. This will be a perpetual law for you throughout your generations.

[10:9] "When you go to war in your land against an adversary who attacks you, you should sound short blasts with the trumpets, so that you can be remembered in front of Yahweh your God and be saved from your enemies. [10] When you have days of celebration, your appointed festivals, or the beginning of your months, you should blow the trumpets with your burnt offerings and with your sacrifices of well-being. They will be a reminder for you in front of your God. I am Yahweh your God."

---

[107] This subdivision should be understood as a slightly smaller military unit than the divisions mentioned in earlier chapters. Multiple regiments make up a single division.

7

Leaving Mount Sinai

Numbers 10:11 In the second year, on the twentieth day of the second month, the cloud lifted from the Dwelling Place of the *edut*, ¹² and the Israelites set out on their travels from the wilderness of Sinai. The cloud settled down in the wilderness of Paran. ¹³ They set out for the first time at Yahweh's command through Moses. ¹⁴ The first standard to set out was the Judahite camp, by their divisions. Nahshon son of Amminadav was in charge of its divisions. ¹⁵ Netanel son of Zuar was in charge of the division from the Issacharite tribe, ¹⁶ and Eli'av son of Helon was in charge of the division from the Zebulunite tribe.

¹⁰:¹⁷ Then the Dwelling Place was dismantled, and the Gershonites and Merarites, who carried the Dwelling Place, set out.

¹⁰:¹⁸ The next standard to set out was the Reubenite camp, by their divisions. Elizur son of Shedeur was in charge of its divisions. ¹⁹ Shelumiel son of Zurishaddai was in charge of the division from the Simeonite tribe. ²⁰ Eliasaph son of Deuel was in charge of the division from the Gadite tribe.

¹⁰:²¹ Then the Kehatites, who carried the sacred objects, set out. The Dwelling Place would be erected again before they arrived.

¹⁰:²² Then the standard from the Ephraimite camp set out, by their divisions. Elishama son of Ammihud was in charge of its divisions.

[23] Gamli'el son of Pedazur was in charge of the division from the Manassite tribe. [24] Avidan son of Gideoni was in charge of the division from the Benjaminite tribe.

[10:25] Then the standard of the Danite camp set out as the rear guard for all the camps, by their divisions. Ahi'ezer son of Ammishaddai was in charge of its divisions. [26] Pagi'el son of Ochran was in charge of the division from the Asherite tribe. [27] Ahira son of Enan was in charge of the division from the Naphtalite tribe.

[10:28] This was the order of the Israelites when they set out in their divisions.

[12:16] After the people set out from the [wilderness of Sinai],[1] they camped in the wilderness of Paran. [13:1] Yahweh said to Moses, [2] "Send out men to spy on the land of Canaan, which I am going to give to the Israelites. Send one man from each ancestral tribe, someone who is one of their leaders." [3] So Moses sent them at Yahweh's command from the wilderness of Paran, all the men were Israelite leaders. [4] These were their names: From the tribe of Reuben: Shammua son of Zakkur, [5] from the tribe of Simeon: Shapat son of Hori, [6] from the tribe of Judah: Caleb son of Yefunneh, [7] from the tribe of Issachar: Yigal son of Joseph, [8] from the tribe of Ephraim: Hoshea son of Nun, [9] from the tribe of Benjamin: Palti son of Rafu, [10] from the tribe of Zebulun: Gaddi'el son of Sodi, [11] from the tribe of Joseph—from the tribe of Manasseh: Gaddi son of Susi, [12] from the tribe of Dan: Ammiel son of Gemalli, [13] from the tribe of Asher: Setur son of Micha'el, [14] from the tribe of Naphtali: Nahbi son of Vofsi, [15] from the tribe of Gad: Ge'u'el son of Machi. [16] These are the names of the men Moses sent to spy on the land, though Moses called Hoshea son of Nun, Joshua.

[1] In the compiled text, this place name is "Hazerot." In the nonpriestly story, the events of Numbers 12 (Miriam and Aaron challenging Moses) happen in Hazerot. In the priestly narrative, the Israelites have not traveled anywhere else yet. When these two stories were combined, the place name in the priestly itinerary notice in this verse was changed from "the wilderness of Sinai" (see Num 10:12) to "Hazerot" to harmonize the two stories and to get the Israelites back to the wilderness of Paran. In the priestly narrative, this is simply a resumptive repetition designed to bring the reader back to this stage of the Israelites' travels after a lengthy list of the marching order.

^{13:17} Moses sent them to spy on the land of Canaan, ²¹ so they went up and spied on the land from the wilderness of Zin to Rehov, near Lebo-Hamat. ²⁵ They returned from spying on the land after 40 days, ²⁶ and they came to Moses, Aaron, and the entire Israelite community in the wilderness of Paran. ³² They brought back to the Israelites a disparaging report of the land on which they had spied. "The land that we traveled through to spy on is a land that consumes its inhabitants! All the people that we saw in it are extremely large men!"

^{14:1} The entire community raised their voices, ² and all the Israelites complained against Moses and Aaron. The whole community said to them: "If only we had died in the land of Egypt or that we had died in this wilderness! ³ Why is Yahweh bringing us to this land to be cut down by the sword? Our wives and our children will be abducted! Wouldn't it be better for us to return to Egypt?" ⁴ They said to each other, "Let's appoint a leader and go back to Egypt!" ⁵ Moses and Aaron fell to the ground in supplication in front of the entire gathered Israelite community. ⁶ But Joshua son of Nun and Caleb son of Yefunneh, who were part of the group who spied on the land, tore their garments ⁷ and said to the whole Israelite community, "the land that we traveled through to spy on is an exceptionally good land! ⁸ If Yahweh is satisfied with us, he will bring us to this land and give it to us—a land that is flowing with milk and honey! ⁹ But do not rebel against Yahweh! Don't be afraid of the people of the land; they are ours to consume.[2] Their protection has been removed from them and Yahweh is with us. Don't be afraid of them!" ¹⁰ The entire community wanted to stone them, but the presence of Yahweh appeared to all the Israelites at the Meeting Tent, ²⁶ and Yahweh spoke to Moses and Aaron: ²⁷ "How long will this evil community continue complaining against me? I have heard the Israelites' complaints that they are lodging against me. ²⁸ Say to them: 'As I live, says Yahweh, I will do for you exactly as I have heard with my ears! ²⁹ In this wilderness, your corpses will fall. Everyone who was mustered, all of you numbered from the age of twenty and up who has complained against me, ³⁰ not one of you will enter the land that I swore to settle you in, except for Caleb son of Yefunneh and Joshua son of Nun. ³¹ Your children, who you thought would be plundered—I will

[2] Literally: food for us.

bring them in so that they know the land that you have rejected. [32] But your corpses will fall in this wilderness [33] while your children wander in the wilderness for forty years, suffering for your infidelity, until every last one of your corpses falls in the wilderness. [34] You will bear your punishment for forty years, according to the number of days that you spied on the land—forty days, a year for each day—so that you will know my hostility. [35] I, Yahweh, have spoken. I will do this to this entire evil community, which has met together to go against me. In this wilderness they will die out completely!"

[14:36] But as for the men that Moses had sent to spy on the land, the ones who returned and incited the entire community to complain against him by disparaging the land, [37] the men who spread disparaging reports about the land—they died of a plague[3] in front of Yahweh. [38] Of the men who went to spy in the land, only Joshua son of Nun and Caleb son of Yefunneh survived.

[15:1] Yahweh said to Moses, [2] "Speak to the Israelites and say to them: 'When you enter the land of your settlement that I am giving you,[4] [3] and you want to sacrifice a food gift to Yahweh from the herd or from the flock, whether as is a burnt offering or a sacrifice to fulfill a vow or a freewill offering or one during one of your appointed festivals, sacrificing it to create a pleasing smell for Yahweh, [4] the person bringing his gift to Yahweh as a grain offering should also bring a tenth of a measure of fine flour mixed with a quarter *hin* of oil. [5] With a burnt offering or a sacrifice of well-being, you should also sacrifice a quarter *hin* of wine as a libation for each lamb. [6] Or, if it is a ram, you should sacrifice a grain offering: two-tenths of a measure of fine flour mixed with a third of a *hin* of oil. [7] You should bring a third of a *hin* of wine as a libation for a pleasing smell for Yahweh. [8] If you sacrifice a herd animal

[3] It is worth underscoring here that the only people who die of plague are the 10 other men (listed in Num 13:4–15) who went to spy on the land with Caleb and Joshua, while Yahweh's curse covers the entire population of Israelite men from the age of 20 and older. The spies die immediately whereas the rest of that generation takes 40 years to die out in the wilderness.

[4] Barely a breath after his condemnation of the current generation, Yahweh launches into a new set of laws, meant for the next generation of Israelites to implement when they arrive in the land, those who are under 20 years old.

to Yahweh, either as a burnt offering or as a sacrifice to fulfill a vow or as a well-being offering, [9] there should be a grain offering with the herd animal: three-tenths of a measure of fine flour mixed with a half *hin* of oil. [10] You should bring a half *hin* of wine as a libation, for a food gift with a pleasing smell for Yahweh. [11] The same should be done with an ox or a ram or any sheep or goat. [12] Whatever number of them that you sacrifice, you should do the same with each one, however many there are. [13] Every citizen should sacrifice these things in this way when bringing a food gift with a pleasing smell for Yahweh.

[15:14] 'When a foreigner who is staying with you, or someone who settles down in your midst throughout your generations, wants to sacrifice a food gift with a pleasing smell for Yahweh, the assembly[5] should sacrifice as you sacrifice. [15] There should be one law for you and for foreigners who live among you. This is a perpetual law throughout your generations: both you and the foreigner are the same in front of Yahweh. [16] There should be one instruction and one rule for you and for the foreigner living with you.'"

[15:17] Yahweh said to Moses, [18] "Speak to the Israelites and say to them: 'When you enter the land that I am bringing you to [19] and you eat some of the bread from the land, you should set some aside as a gift for Yahweh. [20] You should set aside a portion from the first batch of your dough as a gift. You should set it aside like a gift from the threshing floor. [21] You should give Yahweh some of the first batch of your dough as a gift throughout your generations.

[15:22] 'If you unintentionally fail to enact any of these commandments that Yahweh has declared to Moses, [23] anything that Yahweh commanded you through Moses from the time that Yahweh commanded it and after, throughout your generations[24]—if it was done unintentionally without

[5] Here, the assembly (*qahal*) literally refers to those people who are assembled in the land Yahweh has given the Israelites (i.e., Canaan). It does not necessarily refer only to Israelite citizens. When the term *qahal* is meant to refer to Israelites alone, it is often used in construct with the phrase "Israelite community" (*adat yisrael*). The absence of this specifier here suggests that the law applies to anyone assembled in the land, and thus that non-Israelites living among the Israelites are also subject to Yahweh's rules, at least to some extent.

recognition by the community, then the entire community should sacrifice a bull from the herd as a burnt offering, for a pleasing smell for Yahweh, along with its grain offering and its libation according to the rule, and one male goat as a decontamination offering. [25] The priest should effect purification on behalf of the entire Israelite community and then they will be forgiven because it was unintentional. For their unintentional error they brought their gift of a food offering for Yahweh and their decontamination offering in front of Yahweh. [26] The entire Israelite community, including the foreigners living among them, will be forgiven because the entire community unintentionally acted in error.

[15:27] 'If it is an individual person who unintentionally commits an error, they should bring a year-old female goat as a decontamination offering. [28] The priest should effect purification on behalf of the person who erred unintentionally—because they erred unintentionally in front of Yahweh—effecting purification on their behalf so that they are then forgiven. [29] There is one instruction for both the Israelite citizen and the foreigner who is living among you who errs unintentionally.

[15:30] 'But the person who errs intentionally, whether it is a citizen or a foreigner, he offends Yahweh. That person should be cut off from their people. [31] He has disdained Yahweh's word and broken his command. That person should be completely cut off. He has brought his guilt on himself.'"

[15:32] When the Israelites were in the wilderness, they discovered a man gathering sticks on the sabbath day. [33] The ones who found him brought the stick gatherer to Moses, Aaron, and the entire community. [34] They detained him because it was not clear what should be done with him. [35] Yahweh said to Moses, "The man should be put to death; the entire community should stone him outside the camp." [36] So the entire community brought him outside the camp, and they stoned him to death just as Yahweh commanded Moses.

[15:37] Yahweh said to Moses, [38] "Speak to the Israelites and tell them that they should make fringes on the corners of their garments throughout their generations, and that they should put a blue thread with the fringe on the corner. [39] That should be your fringe so that you can look at it and remember all Yahweh's commandments and follow them, and so that you do not stray[6] after either your heart or eyes that you might desire to follow. [40] This is so that you remember and follow all my commandments so that you can be holy to your God. [41] I am Yahweh your God who brought you out of the land of Egypt to be your God. I am Yahweh your God."

Exodus 16:2 The entire Israelite community complained against Moses and Aaron in the wilderness.[7] [3] The Israelites said to them, "If only we had died by Yahweh's hand in the land of Egypt, when we sat with pots filled with meat and when we ate bread until we were full! But you have brought us out to this wilderness to make this entire assembly die of hunger!" [6] Moses and Aaron said to all the Israelites, "By the evening you will know that it was Yahweh who brought you out of the land of Egypt, [7] and by morning you will see Yahweh's presence. He has heard your complaints against Yahweh, for who are we that you would complain against us?" [8] Moses continued: "Yahweh is going to give you meat to eat in the evening and enough bread in the morning to fill you because Yahweh has heard the complaints that you've lodged against him. What about us? Your complaints are not against us, but against Yahweh."

[16:9] Then Moses said to Aaron, "Say to the entire community of Israelites: 'Come in front of Yahweh because he has heard your complaints!'" [10] So Aaron spoke to the entire Israelite community and they turned toward the [Meeting Tent].[8] There the presence of Yahweh appeared in

[6] The term used here in Hebrew is the same one used earlier in the story to describe the actions of the men who were sent to spy on the land of Canaan, and whose forgetfulness of Yahweh's commands and promise led to their demise in the wilderness.

[7] This episode is one of four episodes in the priestly narrative that are located in a different place in the compiled version of the Pentateuch. These episodes were relocated from their original locations by the editor(s) who combined the priestly and nonpriestly materials into the Pentateuch; they have been moved back to their most plausible original positions here. For a more detailed discussion of this phenomenon, see the discussion in the introduction to this volume.

[8] In the compiled texts, it reads "wilderness" here, which is clearly a later redactional change. When the priestly manna story was relocated from its original place in the story (here) to match the nonpriestly manna story immediately after the Israelites' departure from Egypt, the Meeting Tent was not yet constructed and so a redactor would have had to change the location the Israelites turn toward.

a cloud. [11] Yahweh spoke to Moses: [12] "I have heard the Israelites' complaints. Tell them: 'In the evening you will eat meat, and, in the morning you will have your fill of bread so that you know that I am Yahweh your God.'"

[16:13] In the evening quails came and covered the camp, and in the morning there was a layer of dew all over the camp. [14] When the layer of dew lifted, there was a thin and flaky substance on the surface of the wilderness, like frost on the ground. [15] When the Israelites saw this, they said to each other, "What is it?"[9] because they didn't know what it was. Moses said to them, "It is the bread that Yahweh gave you to eat. [16] This is what Yahweh commanded about it: 'gather as much of it as each person needs to eat, an *omer* per person for all of you; each person should gather enough for their own tent.'"

[16:17] So the Israelites did this: some gathered a lot and others only a little. [18] When they measured it by the *omer*, the one who had gathered a lot did not have any extra and the one who gathered a little did not lack; each gathered as much as they needed to eat. [19] Moses said to them: "Let no one keep any leftovers until tomorrow morning." [20] But they did not listen to Moses and the men kept some of it until the next morning. It became infested with worms and smelled horrible, and Moses became angry with them.

[16:21] In this way they gathered it every morning, each person as much as they needed to eat. When the sun became warm, it melted. [22] On the sixth day, they would gather twice as much bread: 2 *omers* per person. When all the leaders of the community came and told Moses this, [23] he said to them: "This is what Yahweh said! Tomorrow is a day of complete cessation, a sacred sabbath for Yahweh. Bake what you want to bake and boil what you want to boil. Everything that is leftover can be kept until morning." [24] So they kept it until morning as Moses commanded and it did not stink horribly and there were no worms in it. [25] Then Moses said, "Eat it today because it is a sacred sabbath for Yahweh; you will not find any in the field."

---

[9] In Hebrew, this is *"man-hu,"* which is where the name of the substance comes from, *man* (in English, usually "manna").

16:31 The Israelites named it manna. It was like coriander seed—white and tasting like wafers with honey. 32 Moses said, "This is what Yahweh commanded: 'Let one full *omer* of it be kept for all your generations so that they see the bread that I fed you in the wilderness when I brought you out from the land of Egypt.'" 33 Moses said to Aaron, "Take one jar and put an *omer* of manna in it. Set it in front of Yahweh to be kept for all your generations." 34 As Yahweh commanded Moses, Aaron put it in front of the *edut* to be kept. 35 The Israelites ate the manna for 40 years, until they entered a settled land; they ate the manna until they came to the border of the land of Canaan. 36 (An *omer* is a tenth of an *ephah*.)

Numbers 16:1 Now, Korah son of Yitzhar son of Kehat son of Levi[10] took 2 250 Israelite men, leaders of the community, reputable men who were chosen from the assembly, 3 and they gathered against Moses and Aaron and said to them, "Enough of you! The entire community—all of them!—are holy. Yahweh is in their midst. Why are you elevating yourselves above Yahweh's assembly?" 4 When Moses heard this, he fell to his face.[11] 5 He said to Korah and the entire community, "In the morning Yahweh will make known who he is, who is holy, and who can approach him. Whomever he chooses can approach him. 6 Do this: take your fire pans, Korah and his community, 7 and put fire on them and set incense on them in front of Yahweh tomorrow. The man Yahweh chooses is the holy one. Enough of you, Levites!"

16:8 Then Moses said to Korah, "Listen to me, Levites! 9 Is it not enough for you that the god of Israel set you apart from the Israelite community, letting you approach him to do your work in Yahweh's Dwelling Place and to stand in front of the community to serve them? 10 He has brought you forward, along with all your fellow Levites. Are you also angling for the priesthood? 11 Is it for this that you and your

[10] The extended genealogy for the character of Korah offers some important information: not only is Korah a Levite, but he is also one of the Kehatite Levites—that is, those responsible for caring for and transporting the most holy objects related to Yahweh's Dwelling Place.

[11] Moses falling to his face in reaction to this accusation parallels his reaction earlier in the story when the Israelites turned against him with the return of the spies.

community have gathered against Yahweh? What is Aaron that you complain against him?"[12]

16:16 Moses said to Korah, "You and your community should come in front of Yahweh tomorrow, you and them along with Aaron. 17 Each of you should take his firepan and put incense on it. Then each of you should bring his firepan in front of Yahweh, 250 firepans, along with you and Aaron with your firepans."

16:18 So each of them took his firepan and put fire on it and then set incense on that. They stood at the entrance to the Meeting Tent with Moses and Aaron. 19 Then Korah gathered the entire community with them at the entrance to the Meeting Tent, and the presence of Yahweh appeared to the whole community. 20 Yahweh said to Moses and Aaron, 21 "Separate yourself from this community so that I can consume them in a flash." 22 But they fell on their faces in supplication and said, "God, the god of the spirits of all flesh, if one man commits an error, will you rage against the entire community?" 23 Yahweh said to Moses, 24 "Say to the community: 'Move away from around the Dwelling Place.'" 26 So he told the community 27 and they moved away from around the Dwelling Place. 35 Then fire burst out from Yahweh and consumed the 250 men who were offering the incense.[13]

17:1 Yahweh said to Moses, 2 "Tell Eleazar son of Aaron the priest to remove the firepans from the charred remains and scatter[14] the coals far away. 3 The firepans of those who have overstepped (thus costing them their lives) have become holy. Make them into a hammered sheet of metal to use as a covering for the altar. Because they presented them in front of Yahweh, they became holy, and now they will become

[12] This phrase echoes Moses's response to the Israelites' complaints in the previous chapter, when they were upset about lack of food.

[13] This scene parallels the one narrating the deaths of Aaron's two eldest sons (Nadav and Avihu).

[14] The verb used in the Hebrew here is *zerah,* which sounds similar to the adjective used to describe the offering Nadav and Avihu attempted to make: *eish zarah.* This is almost certainly intentional on the part of the authors of this story in order to tie it more closely to the deaths of Aaron's two sons in their attempt to step beyond their prescribed roles.

a sign for the Israelites." [4] Eleazar the priest took the bronze firepans used by the ones who burned to death, and he hammered them into a covering for the altar [5] as a reminder for the Israelites so that no ordinary person, no one who was not one of Aaron's descendants, would come near to offer incense in front of Yahweh, and so that no one would become like Korah and his community, just as Yahweh told him through Moses.

[17:6] But the next day, the entire Israelite community complained against Moses and Aaron. "You have killed Yahweh's people!" [7] As the community gathered against Moses and Aaron, they turned toward the Meeting Tent;[15] a cloud had covered it and the presence of Yahweh had appeared. [8] When Moses and Aaron reached the Meeting Tent, [9] Yahweh said to Moses, [10] "Remove yourselves from this community because I am going to consume them in a flash!"[16] But they fell on their faces [11] and Moses said to Aaron, "take a firepan and put coals on it from the altar and then put incense on it and quickly take it to the community to effect a purification[17] for them because a fury has burst forth from Yahweh and a plague is beginning!"[18] [12] So Aaron took it, as Moses said, and ran into the midst of the community as the plague was beginning among the people. He put on the incense and effected a purification for the people. [13] He stood between the dead and the living until the plague was stopped, [14] but 14,700 people died of the plague, not counting those who died in the Korah debacle. [15] When the plague was stopped, Aaron returned to Moses at the entrance of the Meeting Tent.

[15] Compare with the parallel event in Exodus 16:10.

[16] Compare with the parallel event in Numbers 16:21. This scene is taking elements from two of the previous scenes of Israelite complaints and weaving them together.

[17] This is the same phrase that typically means to "effect purification" of the altar or some part of the sanctuary, but here it is being applied to the Israelites themselves. The context in this case is still one of purifying, but in this case of purifying the people from the plague that is going to break out among them.

[18] The mention of the plague here recalls the plague that killed the ten men who spied out the land in Numbers 14:37, thus linking it to yet another instance of the Israelites being punished for their complaints against Yahweh.

17:16 Yahweh said to Moses, 17 "Speak to the Israelites and take 12 staffs from them, a staff from each of the ancestral houses from the leaders of those ancestral houses. Write each man's name on his staff. 18 Write Aaron's name on the staff for Levi. There should be one staff for the head of each ancestral house. 19 Put them in the Meeting Tent in front of the *edut* where I meet you. 20 The man whom I will choose, his staff will sprout. Then I will put an end to the Israelites' endless complaints against you." 21 Moses told the Israelites this and all the leaders of the tribes gave him a staff, one staff for each leader of an ancestral house, 12 staffs total plus Aaron's staff with them. 22 Moses put the staffs in front of Yahweh in the Tent of the *edut*. 23 The next day, Moses entered the Tent of the *edut* and Aaron's staff for the house of Levi had sprouted. Not only had it sprouted; it had produced blossoms and created almonds! 24 Moses brought all the staffs out from in front of Yahweh to the Israelites. Each man identified and took his own staff. 25 Yahweh said to Moses, "Return Aaron's staff in front of the *edut*, to be kept as a sign for these rebellious people so that their complaints against me might cease and so that they do not die." 26 Moses did what Yahweh commanded him; so he did. 27 The Israelites said to Moses, "Ah! We are going to die. We are doomed. All of us are doomed. 28 Anyone who comes near to Yahweh's Dwelling Place will die. Are we all going to die?"

18:1 Yahweh said to Aaron, "You and your sons and your ancestral house will bear responsibility for wrongs done to the sanctuary; you and your sons will bear responsibility for the wrongs committed in your priesthood. 2 Furthermore, you should bring your brothers, the Levites (your ancestral tribe) with you. They should be linked[19] to you and serve you and your sons when you are in front of the Tent of the *edut*. 3 They should perform their duties for you and for the entire Tent. However, they must not approach the sacred furniture or the altar, or else both they and you will die. 4 They should be linked to you in order that they perform the duties of the Meeting Tent, all the labor for the Tent, but no ordinary person can approach you 5 when you perform the duties of the sanctuary or the altar so that fury never again descends on the Israelites.

---

[19] In the Hebrew, the verb here sounds similar to the name "Levi."

[18:6] "Therefore, I take your brothers, the Levites, for you from among the Israelites as a gift. They are dedicated to Yahweh to perform the work of the Meeting Tent, [7] while you and your sons should perform your priestly duties for everything concerning the altar and the area inside the curtain. You should perform your duties, and I will endow your priesthood with a gift.[20] Though an ordinary person who encroaches must be put to death."

[18:8] Yahweh said to Aaron. "I am now giving you responsibility for my gifts, all the sacred offerings of the Israelites. I am giving them to you as a consecrated portion, to your sons as a perpetual due. [9] These things will be yours from the holiest of the food offerings: all their gifts—from their grain offerings to their decontamination offerings to their guilt offerings that they return to me—all the holiest offerings belong to you and your sons. [10] You must consume them according to their highest level of holiness: only males can eat them; you must treat them as sacred.

[18:11] "These things are also yours: their gift offerings—that is, all the Israelites' elevation offerings, I am giving to you, your sons, and your daughters as a perpetual due. Anyone in your household who is pure can eat them. [12] All the best oil and the best new wine and grain, their best products that they give to Yahweh: I am giving them to you. [13] The first fruits of everything in their land that they bring to Yahweh will be yours. Anyone in your household who is pure may eat them. [14] Anything that is dedicated[21] in Israel will be yours. [15] The firstborn of

[20] The Hebrew here is very unclear, and perhaps somewhat corrupted. Typically, the term *abodah* is not used to describe the work of the priests, but in this case it could be referring to the priestly labor that parallels the Levitical labor: namely, the responsibility for the areas off-limits to the Levites enumerated in the previous clause. The term "gift" is left hanging, however. The sense seems to be that the priests must do the Levitical labor for the areas off-limits to the Levites, but in return Yahweh will give them a gift. The identity of this gift is twofold, and the use of the term in this verse points both backward to the Levites as a gift for the priests, and forward to Yahweh's coming enumeration of parts of the Israelites' sacrificial offerings that will become the priests' gifts. The fact that this term is ill defined in this verse is likely in part because it can refer to either (or perhaps even both) of these gifts for the priesthood.

[21] This is a specific category of objects (*herem* in Hebrew) that are dedicated to Yahweh either during the process of a vow or sometimes in the context of war.

every womb for all living creatures, whether human or animal, that are given to Yahweh will be yours. However, firstborn human beings and the firstborn of impure animals must be redeemed. [16] Their redemption price should be calculated from the age of one month and up: their monetary value is 5 shekels by the sanctuary shekel (this is twenty *gerahs*). [17] But the firstborn ox, or firstborn sheep, or firstborn goat you do not have to redeem. They are sacred. You should toss their blood on the altar and turn their fat to smoke as a food offering for a pleasing smell for Yahweh. [18] But their meat will be yours; like the breast of the elevation offering or like the right thigh, it will be yours. [19] All the sacred gifts that the Israelites set apart for Yahweh, I am giving to you, your sons, and your daughters as a perpetual due. It is a perpetual covenant of salt[22] in front of Yahweh for you and your descendants."

[18:20] Yahweh said to Aaron, "You will not inherit anything in their land. You will not have your own portion among them. I am your portion and your inheritance among the Israelites.

[18:21] "Now for the Levites, I am giving all the tithes in Israel as their inheritance in exchange for the work that they do, the work in the Meeting Tent. [22] The Israelites should never again[23] encroach on the Meeting Tent, thus incurring guilt and dying. [23] The Levites will do the work of the Meeting Tent, and they will bear responsibility for it. This is a perpetual law for all your generations. But they will not inherit a share of land among the Israelites [24] because I am giving the tithes that the Israelites bring to Yahweh as a gift to the Levites as their portion. This is why I have told them that they will not inherit a share of land among the Israelites."

[18:25] Yahweh said to Moses, [26] "Speak to the Levites and say to them: 'When you take the tithe from the Israelites, the one that I am giving you as your inheritance, you should set apart some of it as a gift for Yahweh, as a tithe from the tithe. [27] It will be granted to you as your gift,

[22] Like the "salt of god's promise" earlier in the story (Lev 2:13), this theme returns here as a way of emphasizing the staying power of Yahweh's gift to the priests.

[23] This "never again" almost certainly refers back to the 250 men who died attempting to offer incense in Numbers 16.

like the grain from the threshing floor and the fullness of the wine vat. ²⁸ In this way you should set apart a gift for Yahweh from all the tithes that you take from the Israelites. Then you should give Yahweh's gift to Aaron the priest from them. ²⁹ From all your gifts, you should set apart every gift for Yahweh: the best part of everything is the part that should be consecrated.' ³⁰ Also say to them: 'When you have removed its best part from it, then it is granted to the Levites like the produce of the threshing floor or the produce of the wine vat. ³¹ You and your household can eat it anywhere. It is your wage in exchange for your work in the Meeting Tent. ³² You will not incur guilt from it once you have set apart its best portion, but you must not defile the Israelites' sacred gifts, or you will die.'"

¹⁹:¹ Yahweh spoke to Moses and Aaron: ² "This is the decree of instruction that Yahweh commanded. Tell the Israelites to bring you an unblemished red cow with no defect on it and which hasn't had a yoke laid on it.[24] ³ You should give it to Eleazar the priest, and he should take it outside the camp. It should be slaughtered in his presence. ⁴ Then Eleazar the priest should take some of its blood with his finger and sprinkle it seven times toward the front of the Meeting Tent. ⁵ Then the cow should be burned with him watching; its skin, its meat, and its blood, along with its dung,[25] should be burned. ⁶ The priest should take cedar wood, hyssop, and crimson yarn and throw them into the fire with the cow. ⁷ Then the priest should wash his garments and bathe his body in water. After that he may reenter the camp, but the priest will be impure until evening. ⁸ The person who has done the burning must also wash his garments and bathe his body in water. He will be impure until evening. ⁹ A man who is pure should gather the ashes of the cow and put them outside the camp in a pure place. They will be kept for the Israelite community as purificatory water. It is a decontamination offering. ¹⁰ The person who gathers the cow's ashes must also wash his garments. He will be impure until evening. This is a perpetual law for the Israelites and the foreigners who live among them.

[24] This final clause has a patterned repetitive sound in the Hebrew: *lo alah aleha ol*.
[25] This is the only time in this story that the animal's dung is burned along with the rest of it.

19:11 A person who touches a human corpse will be impure for seven days. 12 He should decontaminate himself on the third and seventh days. Then he will be pure. If he does not decontaminate himself on the third and seventh days, he will not become pure. 13 Anyone who touches a corpse, the body of a human being who has died, and does not decontaminate himself, has made Yahweh's Dwelling Place impure. That person will be cut off from Israel because the purificatory water was not tossed on him and he remained impure; his impurity is still on him.

19:14 This is the instruction: When a human being dies in a tent, anyone who enters the tent and anyone who is in the tent will be impure for seven days. 15 Every open vessel whose lid wasn't closed is impure. 16 In an open field, anyone who touches someone who had died by a sword, someone who has died of natural causes, a human bone, or a grave will be impure for seven days. 17 They should take some of the ashes from the burnt decontamination offering for the impure person and put fresh water with them in a vessel. 18 Then a person who is pure should take hyssop and dip it in the water and sprinkle it around the tent, on all the vessels, on the people who were there, or on the person who touched a bone, the person who was killed, or died naturally, or a grave. 19 The pure person should sprinkle it on the impure person on the third and the seventh days, decontaminating them by the seventh day. He should then wash his garments and bathe in water. He will be pure in the evening. 20 Anyone who becomes impure but does not decontaminate himself will be cut off from the assembly because he has made Yahweh's sanctuary impure. The purificatory waters were not tossed on him; he is impure. 21 This will be a perpetual law for them. The person who sprinkled the purificatory waters should wash their garments; anyone who touched the purificatory waters will be impure until the evening. 22 Anything that the impure person touches will become impure; a person who touches him will be impure until the evening."

20:1 Now, the entire Israelite community arrived in the wilderness of Zin in the first month.[26] 2 But there was no water for the community,

[26] The last location given for the community in this story was at the time of the spies debacle, when they were in the wilderness of Paran in the second month of the second year. The spies themselves went to the wilderness of Zin (among other places) in

so they gathered against Moses and Aaron. [3] They said, "If only we had died when our relatives died in front of Yahweh![27] [4] Why have you brought Yahweh's assembly to this wilderness for us and our animals to die here?" [6] Moses and Aaron left the assembly and went to the entrance of the Meeting Tent where they fell on their faces and the presence of Yahweh appeared to them. [7] Yahweh spoke to Moses: [8] "You and your brother Aaron—take the staff[28] and assemble the community. Command the rock in their presence to give its water. You will bring out water for them from the rock and you will quench the thirst of the community and their animals." [9] So Moses took the staff from in front of Yahweh as he commanded him, [10] and Moses and Aaron gathered the community in front of the rock. He said to them, "Listen, rebels! Can we get water from this rock for you?" [11] Moses raised his hand and struck the rock with his staff twice. Gushing water burst forth, and the community and their animals drank.

20:12 Yahweh said to Moses and Aaron, "Because you did not trust me to display my holiness in the presence of the Israelites you will not bring this assembly into the land that I am giving them."[29] [13] These are the waters of Meribah, where the Israelites challenged Yahweh, and through which Yahweh displayed his holiness.

---

their trip to spy on the land of Canaan. Now, in the first month of an unnamed year, the Israelite community itself reaches the extreme southern border of Canaan in the wilderness of Zin. Given the events that follow in this chapter, it is likely that this is either the 40th year of their wanderings, or else very near it.

[27] This is either an allusion to the death of the 250 men who brought firepans in front of Yahweh in Numbers 16, or, more likely, the death of more than 14,000 by plague after the Israelites' revolt in Numbers 17.

[28] Presumably, this is Aaron's staff that flowered from the story in Numbers 17. Not only does it serve a specific purpose in this story, but it is also meant to be a reminder to the Israelites not to rebel lest they also be killed.

[29] The exact offense committed by Moses and Aaron is a bit unclear, though it becomes more apparent when Moses's actions here are compared to those in the other complaint stories. In the previous stories, Moses defers the complaint from himself, telling the people that they complain against Yahweh, and that Yahweh will answer them. When the complaint is addressed, Moses tells the people that their complaint has been answered so that they know that Yahweh is their god. In this case, Moses says nothing about Yahweh, and instead performs the miraculous act himself, thus perhaps implying that he himself has the power to make water appear from a rock without the assistance of Yahweh.

²⁰:²² The Israelites set out and the entire community arrived at Mount Hor. ²³ Yahweh spoke to Moses and Aaron at Mount Hor, at the boundary of the land of Edom: ²⁴ "Let Aaron be gathered to his ancestors because he cannot enter the land that I am giving to the Israelites because you rebelled against me with the waters of Meribah. ²⁵ Take Aaron and his son Eleazar and bring them up Mount Hor. ²⁶ Strip Aaron of his garments and put them on his son Eleazar. Then Aaron will be gathered [to his ancestors]; he will die there." ²⁷ So Moses did as Yahweh commanded: they went up Mount Hor in view of the entire community. ²⁸ Moses stripped Aaron of his garments and put them on his son Eleazar. Then Aaron died on the summit of the mountain, and Moses and Eleazar descended the mountain. ²⁹ The entire community saw that Aaron had died, and the entire house of Israel mourned Aaron for thirty days.

²⁵:⁶ Then one of the Israelite men came and brought a Midianite woman into his family[30] in plain sight of Moses and the entire Israelite community while they were weeping at the entrance to the Meeting Tent. ⁷ When Phineas, son of Eleazar son of Aaron the priest saw this, he got up from the community, taking a spear in his hand. ⁸ He followed the Israelite into the tent[31] and he stabbed them both, the Israelite man and the woman in the stomach. The plague against the Israelites was then stopped.[32] ⁹ Those who died in the plague: 24,000.

²⁵:¹⁰ Yahweh said to Moses, ¹¹ "Phineas, the son of Eleazar son of Aaron the priest has stayed my fury against the Israelites by demonstrating his zeal for me among them so that I did not obliterate the people with my jealousy. ¹² Therefore declare: 'I am granting him my covenant of accord. ¹³ It will belong to him and to his descendants after him; a covenant of perpetual priesthood because he acted zealously for his god and effected purification on behalf of the Israelites.'"[33]

[30] Literally: his brothers.

[31] The word for tent here is a highly unusual one: *kubbah*. It is almost certainly used to create assonance with the word used for stomach later in the sentence: *kebah*.

[32] In this case, the narrator does not report that Yahweh sees this infraction and sends a plague, but the reader is left to fill in those gaps according to the pattern they've seen in earlier episodes in this story.

[33] Phineas's means of effecting purification in this case was shedding the blood of human beings who broke Yahweh's commands. This is highly unusual in the priestly narrative.

^{25:14} The name of the Israelite who was killed, the one killed with the Midianite woman was Zimri son of Salu, head of the Simeonite ancestral house. ¹⁵ The name of the Midianite woman who was killed was Kozbi daughter of Zur; he was the head of an ancestral house in Midian.

^{21:4[34]} The Israelites set out from Mount Hor ¹⁰ and set up camp at Obot. ¹¹ Then they set out from Obot and set up camp at Iyye-Avarim, in the wilderness bordering Moab to the east. ^{22:1} Again the Israelites set out and they set up camp in the steppes of Moab, across the Jordan from Jericho.

^{25:16} Yahweh then said to Moses, ¹⁷ "Prepare to attack the Midianites and defeat them! ¹⁸ They attacked you with the trickery they used to deceive you in the matter of Kozbi daughter of the Midianite leader who was killed on the day of the plague."

^{25:19} After the plague, ^{26:1} Yahweh said to Moses and to Eleazar son of Aaron the priest, ² "Take a census of the entire Israelite community from the age of twenty and up, according to their ancestral houses—all Israelites who are able to go to war." ³ So, on the steppes of Moab on the Jordan opposite Jericho, Moses and Eleazar the priest said to them, ⁴ "Take a census of the whole community of Israelites,[35] from the age of twenty and up, as Yahweh commanded Moses."

The Israelites who came out of the land of Egypt were:

^{26:5} Reuben, Israel's firstborn. The descendants of Reuben: of Enoch, the Enochite family; of Pallu, the Palluite family; ⁶ of Hezron, the Hezronite family; of Karmi, the Karmite family. ⁷ These are the Reubenite families. Their total muster: 43,730.

[34] These itinerary notices are also among the four episodes that have been relocated in the compiled Pentateuch. They have been returned to what is likely their original location in this edition. For further discussion of this, see the introduction to this volume.

[35] This first clause is missing in the Hebrew, likely as the result of a scribal error while copying the text; it otherwise mimics Yahweh's command in verse 2 almost exactly.

26:12 The descendants of Simeon, according to their families: of Nemu'el, the Nemu'elite family; of Yamin, the Yaminite family; of Yachin, the Yachinite family; 13 of Zerah, The Zerahite family; of Sha'ul, the Sha'ulite family. 14 These are the Simeonite families: 22,200.

26:15 The descendants of Gad, according to their families: of Zafon, the Zafonite family; of Haggi, the Haggite family; of Shuni, the Shunite family; 16 of Ozni, the Oznite family; of Eri, the Erite family; 17 of Arod, the Arodite family; of Areli, the Arelite family. 18 These are the Gadite families. Their total muster: 40,500.

26:20 The descendants of Judah according to their families: of Shelah, the Shelahite family; of Perez, the Perezite family; of Zerah, the Zerahite family. 21 These are the descendants of Perez: of Hezron, the Hezronite family; of Hamul the Hamulite family. 22 These are the Judahite families. Their total muster: 76,500.

26:23 The decendants of Issachar according to their families: of Tolah, the Tolahite family; of Puvah, the Punite family; 24 of Yashuv, the Yashuvite family; of Shimron, the Shimronite family. 25 These are the Issacharite families. Their total muster: 64,300.

26:26 The descendants of Zebulun according to their families: of Sered, the Seredite family; of Elon, the Elonite family; of Yahle'el, the Yahle'elite family. 27 These are the Zebulunite families. Their total muster: 60,500.

26:28 The descendants of Joseph according to their families: Manasseh and Ephraim. 29 The descendants of Manasseh: of Machir, the Machirite family; Machir fathered Gilad. Of Gilad, the Giladite family. 30 These are the descendants of Gilad: of Iyezer, the Iyezerite family; of Helek, the Helekite family; 31 of Asri'el, the Asri'elite family; of Shechem, the Shechemite family; 32 of Shemidah, the Shemidaite family; of Hefer, the Heferite family; 33 but Zelofhad son of Hefer had no sons, only daughters. The names of Zelofhad's daughters were: Mahlah, Noa, Hoglah, Milkah, and Tirzah. 34 These are the Manassite families. Their total muster: 52,700. 35 These are the descendants of Ephraim according to their families: of Shutelah, the Shutelahite family; of Becher, the

Becherite family; or Tachan, the Tachanite family. [36] These are the descendants of Shutelah: of Eran, the Eranite family. [37] These are the Ephramite families. Their total muster: 32,500. These are the Josephites according to their families.

[26:38] The descendants of Benjamin according to their families: of Bela, the Belaite family; of Ashbel, the Ashbelite family; of Ahiram, the Ahiramite family; [39] of Shefufam, the Shefufamite family; of Hufam, the Hufamite family. [40] These were the descendants of Bela: Ard and Na'aman. [Of Ard], the Ardite family, and of Na'aman, the Na'amanite family. [41] These are the descendants of Benjamin according to their families. Their total muster: 45,600.

[26:42] These are the descendants of Dan according to their families: of Shuham, the Shuhamite family. These are Danite families according to their families. [43] All the Shuhamite families, by their muster: 64,400.

[26:44] The descendants of Asher according to their families: of Yimnah, the Yimnite family; of Yishvi, the Yishvite family; of Beriah, the Beri'ite family; [45] the descendants of Beriah: of Hever, the Heverite family; of Malki'el, the Malki'elite family; [46] (the name of Asher's daughter was Serah). [47] These are the families of Asher's descendants. Their total muster: 53,400.

[26:48] The descendants of Naphtali according to their families: of Yahze'el, the Yahze'elite family; of Guni, the Gunite family; [49] of Yezer, the Yezerite family; of Shillem, the Shillemite family. [50] These are the families of the Naphtalites according to their families. Their total muster: 45,400.

[26:51] This is the muster of the Israelites: 601,730.

[26:52] Yahweh said to Moses, [53] "The land should be apportioned to these groups as an inheritance according to the number of names. [54] For the larger family, you will grant a larger inheritance; for the smaller family, you will grant a smaller inheritance. Each inheritance should be assigned according to the muster. [55] However, the land should be apportioned by lot; they will inherit according to the names in their ancestral tribes. [56] Each portion will be assigned by a lot, whether for a larger or smaller family."

[26:57] This is the muster of the Levites according to their families: of Gerson, the Gershonite family; of Kehat, the Kehatite family; of Merari, the Merarite family. [58] These are the families of Levi: the Livnite family, the Hevronite family, the Mahlite family, the Mushite family, the Korahite family—Kehat fathered Amram. [59] The name of Amram's wife was Yocheved daughter of Levi, who was born to Levi in Egypt. She gave birth to Aaron and Moses for Amram. [60] Nadav, Avihu, Eleazar, and Ithamar were born to Aaron, [61] but Nadav and Avihu died when they brought an unauthorized offering in front of Yahweh. [62] Their total muster was 23,000, each male from the age of one month and older. They were not included in the muster with the Israelites because they were not assigned an inheritance alongside the Israelites. [63] These are those mustered by Moses and Eleazar the priest when they mustered the Israelites on the steppes of Moab at the Jordan near Jericho. [64] Among these, there was no one who was mustered by Moses and Aaron the priest when they mustered the Israelites in the wilderness of Sinai.[36] [65] Yahweh said of them, "they will die in the wilderness!" And not one of them remained except for Caleb son of Yefunneh and Joshua son of Nun.

[27:1] Then the daughters of Zelofhad came forward. (Zelofhad was the son of Hefer son of Gilad son of Machir son of Manasseh from the Manassite family, a descendant of Joseph.) These are the names of his daughters: Mahlah, Noa, Hoglah, Milkah, and Tirzah. [2] They stood in front of Moses, Eleazar the priest, the leaders, and the entire community at the entrance to the Meeting Tent. [3] "Our father has died in the wilderness. He was not a part of the community that gathered against Yahweh with Korah, but rather he died for his own sin. He left no sons. [4] Why should our father's name be removed from his family simply because he had no sons? Give us his allotted portion among our uncles." [5] So Moses brought their case before Yahweh, [6] and Yahweh

[36] This reference to the previous muster (Num 1–3) confirms that 40 years have passed and the generation that was supposed to die out in the wilderness has in fact died out.

said to Moses, [7] "Zelofhad's daughters are right in their petition. Give them an allotted portion for an inheritance among their uncles. Transfer their father's inheritance to them. [8] Then, say to the Israelites: 'If a man dies without a son, then his inheritance should transfer to his daughter. [9] If he has no daughter, then you should assign his inheritance to his brothers. [10] And if he has no brothers, you should assign his inheritance to his paternal uncles. [11] If he has no paternal uncles, then you should assign his inheritance to his closest relative from his family, and he will inherit it. This will be a procedural law for the Israelites, just as Yahweh commanded Moses.'"

[27:12] Yahweh said to Moses, "Ascend this mountain of Avarim to see the land that I have given to the Israelites. [13] Once you see it, you will be gathered to your ancestors just as your brother Aaron was [14] because you rebelled against me in the wilderness of Zin when the community was rebellious, and you did not display my holiness for them with the water." (These are the waters of Meribah, in the wilderness of Zin.)

[27:15] Moses said to Yahweh, [16] "Let Yahweh, the god of the spirits of all flesh[37] put someone in charge of the community [17] who can go out before them and who can come in before them, who can take them out and bring them in, so that Yahweh's community will not become like sheep who have no shepherd." [18] Yahweh said to Moses, "Take Joshua son of Nun, a man with wisdom,[38] and lay your hand on him. [19] Stand him in front of Eleazar the priest and in front of the entire community and commission him in their presence. [20] Then give some of your authority to him so that the entire Israelite community will obey him. [21] But he must stand before Eleazar the priest, who will inquire on his behalf for the decision rendered by the *urim* in front of Yahweh. Only by its instruction will he go out with all the Israelites, the whole community." [22] Moses did as Yahweh commanded him: he took Joshua and stood him before Eleazar the priest and before the entire

[37] This is the same invocation Moses used in the story of the rebellion of Korah (Num 16:22) in a successful attempt to prevent Yahweh from destroying the entirety of the Israelite community along with Korah and his followers.

[38] Literally: a man with a spirit in him.

community [23] and he laid his hands on his head and commissioned him, just as Yahweh said through Moses.

[28:1] Yahweh spoke to Moses: [2] "Command the Israelites and say to them: 'You must be sure to offer my offerings—my food, my food offerings with a pleasing smell—to me at their appointed times.' [3] Say to them: 'These are the food offerings you should offer to Yahweh: 2 unblemished one-year-old male lambs each day as a regular burnt offering. [4] You should sacrifice the first lamb in the morning and the second lamb in the evening, [5] with a tenth of an *ephah* of fine flour mixed with a quarter *hin* of beaten oil as a grain offering. [6] It is the regular burnt offering that was instituted at Mount Sinai for a pleasing smell, a food gift for Yahweh. [7] Its libation: a quarter of a *hin* per lamb, poured out in the sanctuary as a strong drink offering for Yahweh. [8] The second lamb you should sacrifice at twilight; you should sacrifice it with the same grain offering and libation as in the morning. It is a food offering with a pleasing smell for Yahweh.

[28:9] 'On the sabbath day: 2 unblemished year-old male lambs with two-tenths of a measure of fine flour mixed with oil as a grain offering and its libation. [10] It is the sabbath burnt offering for each sabbath, in addition to the regular burnt offering and is libation.

[28:11] 'In the beginning of your months, you should bring a burnt offering to Yahweh: 2 bulls from the herd, 1 ram, and 7 one-year-old male sheep, all unblemished, [12] along with three-tenths of a measure of fine flour mixed with oil as a grain offering for each bull, and two-tenths of a measure of fine flour mixed with oil as a grain offering for each ram, [13] and one-tenth of a measure of fine flour mixed with oil as a grain offering for each lamb. It is a burnt offering with a pleasing smell, a food gift for Yahweh. [14] Their libations should be: a half of a *hin* of wine per bull, a third of a *hin* of wine per ram, and a quarter of a *hin* of wine per lamb. This is the monthly burnt offering for each new month of the year. [15] Also: 1 male goat should be sacrificed as a decontamination offering for Yahweh, along with the regular burnt offering and its libation.

[28:16] 'In the first month, on the fourteenth of the month, it is the passover for Yahweh. [17] On the fifteenth day of the first month, it is a festival. For seven days, unleavened bread must be eaten. [18] The first day should be a declared holy day. No work of any kind can be done. [19] You should bring a food gift of a burnt offering to Yahweh: 2 bulls from the herd, 1 ram, and 7 one-year-old male lambs—be sure they are unblemished—[20] along with their grain offerings of fine flour mixed with oil: you should offer three-tenths per bull, two-tenths per ram, [21] and one-tenth per sheep for all seven sheep. [22] Also: 1 male goat to effect purification on your behalf. [23] You should sacrifice these in addition to the morning burnt offering (that is, the regular burnt offering). [24] You should sacrifice the same things daily for seven days as food, a food gift with a pleasing smell for Yahweh. They should be offered in addition to the regular burnt offering with its libation. [25] The seventh day will be a declared holy day for you. No work of any kind can be done.

[28:26] 'On the day of the first fruits, when you bring your new grain offering to Yahweh on your feast of weeks, it should be a declared holy day. No work of any kind can be done. [27] You should bring a burnt offering as a pleasing smell for Yahweh: 2 bulls of the herd, 1 ram, and 7 one-year-old male lambs [28] along with their grain offerings of fine flour mixed with oil: three-tenths per bull, two-tenths per ram, [29] and one-tenth per lamb for all 7 lambs. [30] Also: 1 male goat to effect purification on your behalf, [31] in addition to the regular burnt offering, its grain offering, and its libation that you sacrifice. Be sure that they are unblemished.

[29:1] 'In the seventh month, on the first of the month, it will be a declared holy day for you. No work of any kind should be done. It is a day for you to blow horns. [2] You should sacrifice a burnt offering as a pleasing smell for Yahweh: 1 bull from the herd, 1 ram, and 7 one-year-old male lambs, all unblemished, [3] with their grain offerings of fine flour mixed with oil: three-tenths per bull, two-tenths per ram, [4] and one-tenth per lamb for all 7 lambs. [5] Also: 1 male goat, a decontamination offering to effect purification on your behalf, [6] in addition to the monthly burnt offering with its grain offering, and the regular burnt offering with its grain offering, and their libations according to their specifications, as a pleasing smell, a food gift for Yahweh.

[29:7] On the tenth day of the seventh month: this is a declared holy day for you. You should humble yourselves and no work should be done. [8] You should bring a burnt offering for Yahweh as a pleasing smell:

1 bull from the herd, 1 ram, and 7 one-year-old male lambs—be sure they are unblemished—[9] with their grain offerings of fine flour mixed with oil: three-tenths per bull, two-tenths per ram, [10] and one-tenth per lamb for all 7 lambs. [11] Also: 1 male goat as a decontamination offering. This is in addition to the decontamination offering for purification and the regular burnt offering with its grain offering, and their libations.

[29:12] 'On the fifteenth day of the seventh month, it will be a declared holy day for you. No work of any kind can be done. You should celebrate a festival for Yahweh for seven days. [13] You should bring a burnt offering as a food gift with a pleasing smell for Yahweh: 13 bulls from the herd, 2 rams, and 14 one-year-old male lambs—they should all be unblemished—[14] with their grain offerings of fine flour mixed with oil: three-tenths per bull for all 13 bulls, two-tenths per ram for both rams, [15] and one-tenth per lamb for all 14 lambs. [16] Also: 1 male goat as a decontamination offering, in addition to the regular daily offering with its grain offering and its libation.

[29:17] 'On the second day: 12 bulls from the herd, 2 rams, and 14 one-year-old male lambs, all unblemished, [18] along with their grain offerings and libations, in the right amounts as prescribed for the bulls, rams, and lambs. [19] Also: 1 male goat as a decontamination offering in addition to the regular daily offering with its grain offering and their libations.

[29:20] 'On the third day: 11 bulls, 2 rams, and 14 one-year-old male lambs, all unblemished, [21] along with their grain offerings and libations, in the right amounts as prescribed for the bulls, rams, and lambs. [22] Also: 1 male goat as a decontamination offering in addition to the regular daily offering with its grain offering and libation.

[29:23] 'On the fourth day: 10 bulls, 2 rams, and 14 one-year-old male lambs, all unblemished, [24] along with their grain offerings and libations, in the right amounts as prescribed for the bulls, rams, and lambs. [25] Also: 1 male goat as a decontamination offering in addition to the regular daily offering with its grain offering and its libation.

[29:26] 'On the fifth day: 9 bulls, 2 rams, and 14 one-year-old male lambs, all unblemished, [27] along with their grain offerings and libations, in the right amounts as prescribed for the bulls, rams, and lambs. [28] Also: 1 male goat as a decontamination offering in addition to the regular daily offering with its grain offering and its libation.

[29:29] 'On the sixth day: 8 bulls, 2 rams, and 14 one-year-old male lambs, all unblemished, [30] along with their grain offerings and libations, in the right amounts as prescribed for the bulls, rams, and lambs. [31] Also: 1 male goat as a decontamination offering in addition to the regular daily offering with its grain offering and its libations.

[29:32] 'On the seventh day: 7 bulls, 2 rams, and 14 one-year-old male lambs, all unblemished, [33] along with their grain offerings and libations, in the right amounts as prescribed for the bulls, rams, and lambs. [34] Also: 1 male goat as a decontamination offering in addition to the regular daily offering with its grain offering and libation.

[29:35] 'On the eighth day it will be an assembly for you. No work of any kind can be done. [36] You should bring a burnt offering as a food gift with a pleasing smell to Yahweh: 1 bull, 1 ram, and 7 one-year-old male lambs, all unblemished, [37] with their grain offerings and their libations, in the right amounts as prescribed for the bull, ram, and lambs. [38] Also: 1 male goat as a decontamination offering in addition to the regular daily offering with its grain offering and libation.

[29:39] 'These are the things that you should sacrifice to Yahweh at your appointed times, in addition to your vow offerings, freewill offerings, burnt offerings, grain offerings, libation offerings, and well-being offerings.'"

[30:1] So Moses told the Israelites everything that Yahweh commanded Moses. [2] Moses then spoke to the heads of the Israelite tribes: "This is what Yahweh commanded: [3] If a man makes a vow to Yahweh or swears an oath binding himself with an obligation, he cannot break his word. He must do whatever came out of his mouth. [4] If a woman makes a vow to Yahweh or is bound with an obligation while she is unmarried in her father's house, [5] and her father hears of her vow or of her self-imposed obligation and he did not silence her, then all her vows and all her obligations that she imposed on herself will stand.

[6] But if her father forbids her when he hears of it, then no vow or self-imposed obligation of hers will stand. Yahweh will forgive her because her father forbids her. [7] If she gets married while her vow or the statement she spoke to obligate herself are in force, [8] when her husband hears of it and he does not silence her, then her vows and her self-imposed obligations will stand. [9] But if, when her husband hears, he forbids her vow or her self-imposed obligation, he will break her vow or her self-imposed obligation, and Yahweh will forgive her.

[30:10] "But, in the case of a widow or divorced woman's vow, any obligation she imposes on herself will stand. [11] If she was in her husband's house when she makes the vow or imposes an obligation on herself by oath, [12] and her husband heard of it and he did not silence her, then any of her vows or self-imposed obligations will stand. [13] But if her husband did break them when he heard of them, whatever she said, whether a vow or a self-imposed obligation, will not stand; her husband broke them, and Yahweh will forgive her. [14] Every vow and every oath that she imposes on herself her husband can allow to stand or her husband can break. [15] If her husband does not silence her from day to day, then he upholds her vows or her self-imposed obligations; he upholds them because he did not silence her when he heard it. [16] But if he breaks them sometime after he hears it, he will incur her guilt."

[30:17] These are the laws that Yahweh commanded Moses between a man and his wife, and between a father and his unmarried daughter who is in his household.

[31:1] Yahweh said to Moses, [2] "Get vengeance on the Midianites for the Israelites.[39] Then you will be gathered to your ancestors." [3] So Moses

---

[39] One major question that this chapter raises is of timing. Yahweh gave nearly the same command to Moses at the end of Numbers 25 after the episode with Phineas. Why is it being carried out only now, many chapters later, and only after the Israelites have left the area of the Midianites and gone to Moabite territory? The answer is rather simple: when it comes to warfare in the priestly narrative, there is a continual concern for the protection of women and children. If the Israelites had gone to war immediately in Numbers 25, their women and children would have been in danger. By progressing several stages on their journey before launching this attack, Moses has ensured that they are safe while the soldiers carry out their campaign.

spoke to the people: "Prepare some of your men to go to war so that they can bring Yahweh's vengeance against Midian. [4] Raise 1,000 men from each of the Israelite tribes to send to war."

[31:5] So, out of the regiments of Israel, 1,000 per tribe were raised: 12,000 men armed for battle. [6] Moses sent them to war, 1,000 from each tribe, along with Phineas son of Eleazar the priest, who had the sacred vessels and the trumpets for blowing in his hand. [7] They waged war against Midian just as Yahweh commanded Moses, and they killed every male. [8] They killed the kings of Midian along with everyone else they cut down: Evi, Rekem, Zur, Hur, and Reva, the 5 Midianite kings.

[31:9] The Israelites took the Midianite women and their children captive; they plundered all their animals and their herds and all their wealth; [10] and they burned all their settled towns and their encampments. [11] They took all the spoil and plunder, both human and animal, [12] and they brought the captives and the spoils to Moses, Eleazar the priest, and the entire Israelite community at the camp in the steppes of Moab along the Jordan, across from Jericho.

[31:13] Moses, Eleazar the priest, and all the leaders of the community came out to meet them outside the camp. [14] But Moses became angry with the leaders of the army, the commanders of regiments, and the commanders of battalions[40] who came from battle. [15] Moses said to them, "Have you let every female live? [16] Even when it was them who made the Israelites act against Yahweh so that a plague came against Yahweh's community? [17] Now, kill every male child, and every woman who has had sex with a man! [18] But let any woman who had not had sex with a man live. [19] As for you—you should set up camp outside the camp for seven days—every one of you or your captives who has killed someone or who has touched a corpse must decontaminate themselves on the third and the seventh days. [20] All your garments, anything of leather or goats' hair, and anything made of wood must be decontaminated."

[40] A battalion is a smaller military unit than a regiment, typically made up of several hundred soldiers as opposed to regiments, which have several thousand.

[31:21] Eleazar the priest said to the soldiers who had returned from battle, "This is the decree of instruction that Yahweh commanded Moses: [22] gold, silver, copper, iron, tin, and lead—[23]anything that can withstand fire—must be passed through the fire so that it becomes pure. However, they must also be decontaminated with the waters of purification. Anything that cannot withstand fire must pass through water. [24] You must wash your garments on the seventh day and you will be pure. After that you can enter the camp."

[31:25] Yahweh said to Moses, [26] "You, Eleazar the priest, and the heads of the ancestral houses of the community should take an inventory of the spoils that were captured, both human and animal. [27] Divide the spoils between the soldiers who went to battle and the rest of the community. [28] You should also remove a portion for Yahweh: for the soldiers who returned from war: 1 out of every 500 things, be it human, cattle, donkeys, or sheep. [29] Take it from their half and give it to Eleazar the priest as a gift for Yahweh. [30] From the Israelites' half, take one out of every 50 of human beings, cattle, donkeys, or sheep (all the animals) and give it to the Levites who perform the duties of Yahweh's Dwelling Place."

[31:31] Moses and Eleazar the priest did as Yahweh commanded Moses: [32] The spoil remaining from what the soldiers had plundered was 675,000 sheep, [33] 72,000 cattle, [34] 61,000 donkeys, [35] and 32,000 human beings (that is, the women who had not had sex with a man). [36] The half share of those who had gone to war was 337,500 sheep [37] (Yahweh's portion of the sheep: 675), [38] 36,000 cattle (Yahweh's portion: 72), [39] 30,500 donkeys (Yahweh's portion: 61),[40] 16,000 human beings (Yahweh's portion: 32). [41] Moses gave the portions for Yahweh's gift to Eleazar the priest, just as Yahweh had commanded Moses.

[31:42] From the Israelites' half share that Moses took from the soldiers, [43] the community's half share, was 337,5000 sheep, [44] 36,000 cattle, [45] 30,500 donkeys, [46] and 16,000 human beings. [47] Moses took one out of every 50 animals and humans from the Israelites' half share and he gave them to the Levites, who performed their duties in Yahweh's Dwelling Place, just as Yahweh commanded Moses.

[31:48] Then the leaders of the troops (the leaders of regiments and battalions) approached Moses. [49] They said to Moses, "Your servants have counted the soldiers in our command. None of us are missing. [50] We have brought an offering for Yahweh, what each of us found: items of gold, bracelets, signet rings, earrings, and pendants, to effect purification on our behalf in front of Yahweh." [51] Moses and Eleazar the priest accepted the gold from them, all kinds of finery. [52] All the gold gifts that were given to Yahweh by the leaders of regiments and battalions: 16,750 shekels. [53] (The soldiers, however, kept their plunder for themselves.) [54] Moses and Eleazar the priest accepted the gold from the leaders of regiments and battalions, and they brought it to the Meeting Tent as a reminder for the Israelites in front of Yahweh.

[32:2] Then the Gadites and the Reubenites came and spoke to Moses, Eleazar the priest, and the leaders of the community: [5] "Let this land be granted to your servants as an allotted portion." [6] Moses said to the Gadites and the Reubenites, "Will your relatives go to war while you stay here?" [16] They stepped forward and said, "we will build enclosures for our sheep and cattle and towns for our children here, [17] and our children can remain in the fortified cities because of the inhabitants of the land."[41]

[32:20] Moses said to them, "If you station yourselves in front of Yahweh,[42] ready for battle, [21] and each of your soldiers crosses over the Jordan in front of Yahweh until his enemies have been expelled before him [22] and the land has been subdued in front of Yahweh—only after that may you return. Then this land will become your allotted portion from Yahweh. [24] Build towns for your children and enclosures for your flocks."

[41] This rationale is a callback to the story of the spies in Numbers 13–14 and their original reason for not wanting to conquer the land of Canaan. This fear is clearly still present in the Israelite community, even among this second generation.

[42] According to the order of the march described in Numbers 2, the Gadites and the Reubenites are in the second division, the one that precedes the Levites with the disassembled Meeting Tent, and thus they are literally "in front of Yahweh" in the battle marching order.

[32:25] The Gadites and the Reubenites said to Moses, "your servants will do as my lord commands. [26] Our children, wives, flocks, and cattle will remain here in the towns of Gilad [27] while your servants, each one prepared for war, will cross over in front of Yahweh for battle, just as my lord ordered."

[32:28] Then Moses instructed Eleazar the priest, Joshua son of Nun, and the leaders of the Israelites' ancestral tribes about them, [29] and he said to them, "If the Gadites and the Reubenites cross over the Jordan with you in front of Yahweh, each one prepared for war, and the land is subdued in front of you, then you can give them the land of Gilad as an allotted portion. [30] But if they do not cross over as soldiers with you, then they will receive their allotted portions with you in the land of Canaan." [31] The Gadites and the Reubenites answered: "Whatever Yahweh has instructed your servants, so we will do! [32] We will cross over into the land of Canaan as soldiers in front of Yahweh so that we can inherit our allotted portion across the Jordan!"

[32:34] So the Gadites built Divon, Atarot, Aro'er, [35] Atrot-Shofan, Yazer, Yogbehah, [36] Beit-Nimrah and Beit Haran as fortified towns and enclosures for flocks. [37] The Reubenites built Heshbon, Ele'ale, Kiryat-aim, [38] Nevo, Ba'al Meon (some names were changed), and Sivmah; they named the cities they built.

[33:50] Yahweh spoke to Moses in the steppes of Moab, at the Jordan across from Jericho: [51] "Speak to the Israelites and say to them: 'When you cross over the Jordan into the land of Canaan, [52] and you evict all those living in the land, you should destroy their statues, you should destroy their casted images, and you should demolish their cultic sites. [53] Then you can take possession of the land and live in it because I have granted you the land to live in. [54] You should then apportion the land by lot among your families: you should increase the share for the larger groups and decrease it for the smaller groups. The inheritance should go to the person that the lot falls on; you should apportion according to your ancestral tribes. [55] But if you do not evict those living in the land, the people you permit to remain will be barbs in your eyes and thorns in your sides. They will attack you across the land that you are trying to live in, [56] and I will do to you the things I had planned to do to them!'"

34:1 Yahweh said to Moses, 2 "Command the Israelites and say to them: 'When you enter the land of Canaan—this is the land that will fall to you as an inheritance—the land of Canaan according to its borders: 3 your southern region will extend from the wilderness of Zin along the side of Edom, and your southern border on the east will be at the end of the Salt[43] Sea. 4 Your border will go south around the ascent of Akrabbim and continue to Zin. Its limits will be south of Kadesh Barnea, and it will go out to Hazar-Addar and cross over to Azmon. 5 Then the border will turn from Azmon toward the wadi of Egypt, and its end will be at the sea.

34:6 'The western border will be the coast of the Great Sea; this will be your western boundary.

34:7 'This will be your northern border: from the Great Sea mark a line to Mount Hor, 8 and from Mount Hor mark a line to Levo-Hamat; the limit of the border will be Zedad. 9 The border will then continue to Zifron, and its limit will be at Hazar-Enan. This will be your northern border.

34:10 'You should mark a line for your eastern border from Hazer-Enan to Shefam. 11 The border should go down from Shefam to Rivlah on the eastern side of Ain and continue down to reach the eastern slope of the Sea of Kinneret. 12 Then the border should continue along the Jordan and its limit is at the Salt Sea. This will be your land according to its borders on all sides.'"

34:16 Yahweh said to Moses: 17 "These are the names of the men who will apportion the land for you: Eleazar the priest and Joshua son of Nun. 18 You should also take one leader from each tribe to apportion the land. 19 These are the names of those men: from the Judahites, Caleb son of Yefunneh; 20 from the Simeonites, Shmuel son of Ammihud; 21from the Benjaminites, Elidad son of Kislon; 22 from the Danites, a leader, Bukki son of Yogli; 23 from the descendants of Joseph—from the Manassites, a leader, Hanni'el son of Efod; 24 from the Ephraimites, a leader, Kemuel son of Shiftan; 25 from the Zebulunites, a leader,

[43] Known today as the Dead Sea.

Elizafan son of Parnak; [26] from the Issacharites, a leader, Palti'el son of Azzan; [27] from the Asherites, a leader, Ahihud son of Shelomi; [28] from the Naphtalites, a leader, Pedahel son of Ammihud. [29] These are the people whom Yahweh designated to apportion the land of Canaan to the Israelites.'"

[35:1] Yahweh said to Moses on the steppes of Moab, along the Jordan across from Jericho, [2] "Command the Israelites to give a portion of their allotted inheritance to the Levites as towns for them to live in; you should also give them open fields around their towns. [3] The towns will be theirs to live in, and their open fields will be for their cattle, their livestock, and all their other animals. [4] The open fields around the towns that you give the Levites should extend 1,000 cubits outward from the walls of the town on all sides. [5] You should measure 2,000 cubits outside the town on the eastern side, 2,000 on the southern side, 2,000 on the western side, and 2,000 on the northern side. The town should be in the center, and it will be the open fields for their towns.

[35:6] "The towns that you designate for the Levites should include 6 cities of refuge, where you can allow someone who commits manslaughter to flee. In addition to these, you should designate 42 towns. [7] The total number of towns that you designate for the Levites is 48, each with their open fields. [8] As for the towns that you designate from the Israelites' allotted portions, you should take more from the larger tribes and less from the smaller tribes; each should give their towns to the Levites in proportion to what they inherited."

[35:9] Yahweh said to Moses, [10] "Speak to the Israelites and say to them: 'When you cross the Jordan into the land of Canaan, [11] you should create cities to be your cities of refuge so that someone who unintentionally kills a person can flee there. [12] The cities should be a refuge from the person seeking vengeance so that the person who has killed someone will not himself be killed until there is a trial before the community. [13] You should designate 6 cities of refuge for yourselves: [14] three cities should be designated across the Jordan, and 3 should be designated in the land of Canaan; these are your cities of refuge. [15] These 6 cities are for the Israelites and the foreigners who live among them for refuge, so that someone who unintentionally kills a person can flee there.

35:16 'However, someone who strikes another person with an iron object and kills them is a murderer; the murderer should be put to death. 17 If he strikes someone with a stone in his hand and that person dies then he is a murderer; the murderer should be put to death. 18 Or, if he strikes someone with a wooden weapon and that person dies, then he is a murderer; the murderer should be put to death. 19 The one designated to take revenge for bloodshed[44] should put the murderer to death; when he encounters him, he should put him to death. 20 Similarly, if he pushed him with malice or threw something at him on purpose and the person died, 21 or if he struck him with his hand in a hostile manner and that person died, the person who struck the blow should be put to death—he is a murderer. The one designated to take revenge for bloodshed should put the murderer to death when he encounters him.

35:22 'But if he pushed the person impulsively without any malice, or he threw an object at him without planning to do so, 23 or he dropped a deadly stone object without looking and someone died, and they were not enemies and he did not intend to harm him, 24 then the community should judge between the person who killed someone and the one designated to take revenge for that bloodshed, according to these laws. 25 The community should protect the person who killed someone from the one designated to take revenge; the community should send him back to the city of refuge, and he should live there until the death of the high priest who was anointed with the sacred oil. 26 But if the person who killed someone ever leaves the borders of the city of refuge to which he fled, 27 and the person designated to take revenge for the bloodshed finds him outside the borders of the city of refuge, then the person designated to take revenge can kill him and he will not incur responsibility for that bloodshed. 28 He must remain inside the city of refuge until the death of the high priest; after the death of the high priest, the person who killed someone can return to his allotted portion of land. 29 This will be your procedural law for all your generations in all your settlements.

35:30 'If someone kills a person, the murderer can be killed only with evidence given by witnesses; the testimony of one witness is not

[44] Sometimes translated as "blood avenger."

sufficient to put a person to death. [31] You must not take a ransom payment for the life of a murderer who is subject to the death penalty; he must be put to death. [32] You must not take a ransom payment instead of fleeing to a city of refuge, thus permitting someone to return to live on his land before the death of the priest. [33] You must not pollute the land that you live on—blood pollutes the land, and the land cannot be purified from blood that is spilled on it except with the blood of the one who spilled it. [34] You must not render impure the land you are living in, the land where I live with you, because I, Yahweh, live among the Israelites.

[36:1] 'The heads of the ancestral families of Gilad son of Machir son of Manasseh, one of the Josephites, came and petitioned Moses and the leaders of the Israelite ancestral houses. [2] They said, "Yahweh commanded my lord to apportion the land to the Israelites as an inheritance by lot. My lord was also commanded by Yahweh to give our relative Zelofhad's inheritance to his daughters. [3] But if one of them marries someone from another Israelite tribe, their inheritance will be taken away from our ancestral inheritance and added to the inheritance of the tribe they marry into, and so our allotted inheritance will be reduced. [4] Indeed, even when the Israelites have the jubilee, their inheritance will be added to the inheritance of the tribe they marry into, and their inheritance will be removed from that of our ancestral tribe.'"

[36:5] Moses commanded the Israelites at Yahweh's order: "The petition of the Josephite tribe is valid. [6] This is what Yahweh has commanded concerning the daughters of Zelofhad: they can marry anyone they want as long as they marry into a family within their father's tribe. [7] No inheritance of the Israelites should pass from tribe to tribe; the Israelites should remain attached to the inherited portion of their ancestral tribe. [8] Every daughter from the Israelite tribes who inherits a portion must marry someone from a family within her father's tribe so that every Israelite can keep their ancestral inheritance. [9] No inherited portion should pass from tribe to tribe; each of the Israelite tribes should remain attached to their inherited portion."

[36:10] The daughters of Zelofhad did what Yahweh commanded Moses: [11] Mahlah, Tirzah, Hoglah, Milkah, and Noa, the daughters of Zelofhad, married sons of their uncles, [12] thus marrying into families of the descendants of Manasseh son of Joseph. Their inheritance stayed within their father's tribe.

[36:13] These are the commandments and the procedures that Yahweh commanded the Israelites through Moses in the steppes of Moab at the Jordan near Jericho.

Deuteronomy 1:3 In the fortieth year, on the first day of the eleventh month, Moses told the Israelites everything that Yahweh commanded for them. [32:48] Then, on that same day, Yahweh said to Moses, [49] "Ascend this mountain of Avarim to the mountain that is in the land of Moab across from Jericho. Look at the land of Canaan that I am giving to the Israelites as their allotted portion. [50] You will die on the mountain that you are about to climb, and then be gathered to your ancestors just as your brother Aaron died on Mount Hor and was gathered to his ancestors [51] because you rebelled against me in the midst of the Israelites at the waters of Meribah in the wilderness of Zin when you did not demonstrate my holiness among the Israelites. [52] You can look at the land from a distance, but you cannot enter the land that I am giving to the Israelites."

[34:1] So Moses went up from the steppes of Moab to the mountain that was across from Jericho, and he looked at the whole land. [5] Then Moses died, as Yahweh said. [7] Moses was 120 years old when he died, but his eyesight was not impaired, and his energy had not flagged. [8] The Israelites wept for Moses in the steppes of Moab for 30 days. Then the days of mourning for Moses came to an end, [9] and Joshua son of Nun was filled with a spirit of wisdom because Moses had laid his hands on him. The Israelites obeyed him; they did exactly as Yahweh had commanded Moses.

Appendix

Possible materials from the Priestly Narrative in the Book of Joshua

Joshua 3:1 Early the next morning, Joshua and all the Israelites set out from the [steppes of Moab] and came to the Jordan.[1] 4:13 About 40,000 soldiers crossed over for battle in front of Yahweh to the steppes of Jericho.[2] 19 The people came up from the Jordan on the tenth day of the first month and set up camp at Gilgal on the eastern border of Jericho. 5:10 While the Israelites were encamped at Gilgal, they offered the passover in the evening of the fourteenth day of the month, in the plains of Jericho. 11 On the day after the passover, they ate some of the produce of the land—unleavened bread and parched grain on that very day. 12 The next day, when they ate the produce of the land, the manna ceased to appear.[3] The Israelites never again had manna; they ate from the produce of the land of Canaan that year.

[1] In the compiled text, "Moab" reads "Shittim," which is where the Israelites are described as being in the nonpriestly story in Numbers 25.

[2] The city of Jericho is only mentioned in the priestly narrative in the Pentateuch; no other source ever refers to Jericho. The majority of the final scenes from the priestly narrative in the Pentateuch take place in the steppes of Moab across from Jericho. The story has set up the Israelites immediately on the other side of the Jordan River from this city, and now they are crossing the river to enter it.

[3] This is exactly as Yahweh said would happen in Exodus 16:35: "The Israelites ate the manna for 40 years, until they entered a settled land; they ate the manna until they came to the border of the land of Canaan."

^{6:1} Now Jericho had closed up completely because of the Israelites; no one could leave and no one could enter. ² But Yahweh said to Joshua, "Look, I am going to deliver Jericho and its king and soldiers into your hands. ³ Have all your soldiers march around the city, circling the city one time. Do this for six days. ⁴ Then, with seven priests carrying seven rams' horns in front of the ark, on the seventh day you should march around the city seven times with the priests blowing the horns. ⁵ When they sound a long blast on the ram's horn, when you hear the sound of the horn, all the people should let out a loud shout. Then the walls of the city will collapse and the people can advance straight ahead."

^{6:6} So Joshua son of Nun summoned the priests and said to them, "Lift up the ark of the covenant, and have seven priests carrying seven rams' horns in front of Yahweh's ark."[4] ⁷ Then he said to the people, "Go forward and march around the city. The soldiers should pass in front of Yahweh's ark."

^{6:8} As Joshua was speaking to the people, the seven priests carrying their seven rams' horns in front of Yahweh went forward, blowing their horns with the ark of Yahweh's covenant following them. ⁹ Then the frontline soldiers went in front of the priests who were blowing the horns, and the rear guard went behind the ark,[5] with the horns sounding the whole time. ¹⁰ But Joshua commanded the people: "Do not shout! Don't allow your voices to be heard! Don't even let a sound come past your lips until I tell you to shout—then you can shout." ¹¹ Yahweh's ark circled the city once, and then they returned to camp and spent the night in the camp. ¹² Early the next morning, Joshua arose and the priests again lifted up Yahweh's ark. ¹³ The seven priests carrying the seven rams' horns marched in front of Yahweh's ark while continually blowing the horns. The frontline soldiers marched in front of them and the rear guard followed after Yahweh's ark, with the horns

[4] The presence of the phrase "ark of the covenant" here differs some from what the Priestly Narrative called the ark earlier in the story—the ark of the *edut*. Nonpriestly texts refer to the ark of the covenant, and the redactional processes of the book of Joshua differ from those of the Pentateuch. It is quite possible that this is an editorial change to bring this priestly story more into line with nonpriestly stories in the book.

[5] This is precisely the order of the military march described in Numbers 2, with the ark at the center of the march.

sounding the whole time. [14] They circled the city once on the second day and then returned to camp. They did this for six days.

[6:15] Then, on the seventh day, they woke up early in the morning—at dawn—and they circled the city in the same way seven times. Only on that day did they circle the city seven times. [16] On the seventh circuit, the priests blew their horns, and Joshua said to the people, "Shout because Yahweh has designated this city as yours! [17] The city and everything in it should be dedicated to Yahweh[6]—[19] all the silver and gold, objects made of copper and iron are sacred for Yahweh; they must go to Yahweh's treasury." [20] So the people shouted when the horns were sounded; when the people heard the sound of the horns, they let out a loud shout and the walls of the city collapsed. Then the people went straight ahead into the city and they captured the city. [21] They dedicated everything in the city—whether man or woman, from young to old, ox, sheep, and donkey—by killing them with swords, [24] and they burned the city and everything in it down, except for the silver and gold, and the copper and iron objects. They were given to the treasury of Yahweh's house.

[8:1] Yahweh said to Joshua, "Don't be afraid or dismayed. Take all the soldiers with you and go up to Ai. Look, I am delivering it, along with its king, people, city, and land, into your hands. [2] You should do to Ai and its king as you did to Jericho and its king, except you can keep the spoils and the cattle for yourselves. Now, set up an ambush behind the city!"

[8:3] Joshua and all the soldiers arose and went to Ai. Joshua chose 30,000 men—the top soldiers—and sent them forward at night. [4] He commanded them: "Look, you should set up an ambush behind the city. Do not set up too far from the city! You should all remain alert. [5] I, along with all the rest of the soldiers, will approach the city, and when they come out against us, we will retreat. [6] They will follow us until we have lured them away from the city. They will be thinking, 'They're fleeing from us!' But while we are fleeing from them, [7] you will get up

[6] This particular notion of *herem*, or dedication (as I have translated here), is consistent with the presentation of the same idea in the story of the war with the Midianites in Numbers 31.

from your ambush and seize the city. Yahweh has given this city into your hands! [8] When you seize the city, burn it to the ground, as Yahweh told us to do. There—I have given you your orders."[7]

8:9 Joshua sent them out and they went to the location of the ambush. They settled down between Beit-El and Ai, just to the west of Ai. But Joshua spent the night with the rest of the people. [10] Early the next morning, Joshua mustered the people, and he and the elders marched to Ai in front of the people. [11] All the soldiers who were with him advanced and came near the city. They set up camp to the north of Ai, with a valley between them and Ai.[8] [12] Then he took around 5,000 men and stationed them in an ambush between Beit-El and Ai, west of the city. [13] They stationed the people—the main contingent of soldiers to the north of the city, and its rear guard[9] to the west of the city. Joshua spent the night in the valley. [14] When the king of Ai saw this, he and all his people (the city's inhabitants) rushed out early in the morning to meet Israel in battle in front of Aravah. But he did not know about the ambush that was behind the city. [15] Joshua and all Israel feigned defeat before them and fled toward the wilderness. [16] All the people who were in the city were summoned to pursue them. They pursued Joshua and they were lured away from the city. [17] There was not a single man left in Ai or Beit-El who did not go after Israel. They left the city wide open while they pursued Israel.

8:18 Yahweh said to Joshua, "Stretch out the spear that is in your hand toward Ai, because I will deliver it into your hands."[10] So Joshua stretched out his hand with the spear in it toward the city; [19] and when he stretched out his hand, the contingent of the ambush quickly got up from their location and rushed into the city and captured it. They

---

[7] The episode of this second major battle mirrors the structure of the story of the battle of Jericho (in Josh 6:1–5), with Joshua first telling the soldiers what the plan is, followed by the narrator's account of its fulfillment.

[8] Just as in the battle of Jericho, the Israelite army sets up on the outskirts of the city and allows itself to be seen by the enemy. In this case, there is a twist to the story in that that the Israelites use this strategy to trick the inhabitants of Ai.

[9] Literally: its heel.

[10] There is an unmistakable allusion here to Aaron stretching out his hand with the rod to bring the plagues upon the Egyptians. (See, for example, Exod 7:19.)

quickly set the city on fire. [20] The people of Ai who had been in pursuit looked behind them and saw smoke rising to the heavens from the city. They could not flee in any direction because the people who had fled toward the wilderness had turned around toward their pursuers. [21] (When Joshua and all Israel saw that the ambush had captured the city and that smoke was rising up from the city, they turned around and attacked the people from Ai.) [22] Then the others then came out of the city toward them, and they were surrounded by Israelites on both sides who struck them down until no one remained, either surviving or escaping.

8:24 When Israel had finished slaughtering the inhabitants of Ai who had pursued them into the open wilderness, striking them down with the sword until none remained, all Israel returned to Ai and put it to the sword.[11] [25] The total fallen on that day, both men and women—the entire population of Ai—was 12,000.

8:26 Joshua did not lower his hand with the spear until all the inhabitants of Ai had been destroyed.[12] [27] Only the cattle and the spoils of that city were plundered by Israel, according to the instructions Yahweh had given Joshua.

10:28 Joshua captured Makkedah on that same day, and put it to the sword, along with its king, entirely destroying every person in it. There were no remaining survivors. [29] Then Joshua and all Israel continued from Makkedah to Livnah, and they attacked Livnah. [30] Yahweh also delivered it into Israel's hands, along with its king, and they put it and everyone inside to the sword. There were no remaining survivors.

10:31 From Livnah, Joshua and all Israel continued on to Lachish. They set up camp and attacked it. [32] Yahweh delivered Lachish into Israel's

[11] Presumably, this means that they killed any noncombatants (women and children) who remained and had survived the fire.

[12] Joshua's raised arm through the entirety of the destruction of Ai mirrors an earlier scene in the priestly narrative when Moses raised his arm to split the waters of the Red Sea to permit the Israelites to pass through on dry land. In that episode, when Moses lowers his hand, the waters come rushing back and destroy the Egyptians.

hands, and they captured it on the second day. They put all the people in it to the sword, just as they did with Livnah. [34] Then Joshua and all Israel continued from Lachish to Eglon. They set up camp and attacked it. [35] They captured it the same day, and they put it to the sword, destroying all the people in it, as they did with Lachish.

[10:36] Joshua and all Israel ascended from Eglon to Hevron and attacked it. [37] They captured it and put it to the sword along with its king and all its towns and people in it. There were no remaining survivors. Just as he did with Eglon, he destroyed it and everyone in it.

[10:38] Then Joshua and all Israel turned to Devir and attacked it. [39] He captured it, along with its king and all its towns. They put them to the sword and destroyed all the people in it. There were no remaining survivors, just as he did with Hevron, just as he did with Devir and its king, and just as he did with Livnah and its king.

[10:40] Joshua struck down the whole land: from the hill country to the Negev, the lowlands and the slopes, along with all their kings. There were no remaining survivors. He entirely destroyed everything that breathed, just as Yahweh, the god of Israel, had commanded. [41] Joshua conquered from Kadesh Barnea to Azzah, the whole land of Goshen up to Giveon. [42] Joshua conquered all those kings and their lands in one campaign, because Yahweh, the god of Israel, was fighting for Israel. [43] Then Joshua and all Israel returned to the camp at Gilgal.

[11:23] Joshua took the whole land, just as Yahweh had said to Moses, and Joshua distributed it as an inheritance for Israel according to their tribal portions. The land was quiet from the war.

[14:1] This is what the Israelites inherited in the land of Canaan, what Eleazar the priest, Joshua son of Nun, and the leaders of the Israelite tribes distributed to them: [2] their inheritance was decided by lot, just as Yahweh had commanded through Moses.[13] [4] But they did not designate a portion for the Levites in the land, but rather towns to live in

---

[13] As commanded by Yahweh in Numbers 33:50–56.

along with open fields for their flocks and herds.[14] 5 Just as Yahweh had commanded Moses, thus the Israelites did: they apportioned the land.

15:1 The lot for the tribe of Judah, according to their families, was the farthest south: from Edom to the wilderness of Zin. 2 Their southern border ran from the edge of the Salt Sea, from the south-facing bay 3 and went out to the south to the ascent of Akrabbim and continued to Zin and went up to Kadesh Barnea, then continued to Hezron and went up to Addar, and turned at Karka, 4 then continuing to Azmon and going out to the Wadi of Egypt, the boundary that ran along the sea. This will be your southern border. 5 The eastern border was the Salt Sea until the edge of the Jordan. The northern boundary was from the bay of the sea to the mouth of the Jordan. 6 The border then went up to Bet-Hoglah and continued north of Bet-Aravah, then the border went up to the Stone of Bohan son of Reuben. 7 Then the border went to Devir from the valley of Achor, and turned north toward Gilgal, opposite the ascent of Adummim, which is south of the wadi. Then the border continued to the waters of Ein-Shemesh and ended at Ein-Rogel. 8 Then the border went up to the valley of Ben-Hinnom, along the southern slope of the Jebusites (this is Jerusalem), and the border continued to the top of the mountain that is to the west of the valley of Hinnom and to the northern edge of the valley of Refa'im. 9 The border then curved from the top of the mountain to the spring of the waters of Neftoah. Then it went out to the towns of Mount Efron and the border curved to Ba'alah (this is Kiryat Ye'arim). 10 Then the border turned to the west from Ba'alah toward Mount Se'ir and continued past the northern slope of Mount Ye'arim (this is Kesalon), and descended to Bet-Shemesh and continued to Timnah. 11 The border then went out to the northern slope of Ekron and the border turned to Shikkeron and continued to Mount Ba'alah, going out to Yavneel, with the border continuing out to the sea. 12 The western border was the coast of the Great Sea. These are the borders of the Judahites, according to their families.

[14] Yahweh already said in Numbers 18:24 that the Levites would not have their own designated share of land like the rest of the tribes. The command to designate towns and open fields for them instead came in Numbers 35:1–5.

15:20 This is the allotted portion of the tribe of Judah, according to their families: 21 the towns at the end of the tribe of Judah, near the border of Edom in the south were: Kavzeel, Eder, Yagur, 22 Kinah, Dimonah, Adadah, 23 Kedesh, Hazor, Yitnan, 24 Zif, Telem, Be'alot, 25 Hazor-Hadattah, Kiryat-Hezron (this is Hazor), 26 Amam, Shema, Moladah, 27 Hazar-Gaddah, Heshmon, Bet-Pelet, 28 Hazar-Shu'al, Be'er-Sheva, Bizyoteyah, 29 Ba'alah, Iyyim, Ezem, 30 Eltolad, Kesil, Hormah, 31 Ziklag, Madmannah, Sansannah, 32 Leva'ot, Shilhim, Ayin, and Rimmon. Total towns: 29 with their villages. 33 In the lowlands: Eshta'ol, Zorah, Ashnah, 34 Zano'ah, Ein-Gannim, Tappu'ah, Einam, 35 Yarmut, Adullam, Socoh, Azekah, 36 Sha'arayim, Aditaim, Gederah, Gederotayim—14 towns with their villages. 37 Zenan, Hadashah, Migdal-Gad, 38 Dilan, Mizpeh, Yokte'el, 39 Lachish, Bozkat, Eglon, 40 Kabbon, Lahmas, Kitlish, 41 Gederot, Bet-Dagon, Na'amah, Makkedah—16 towns with their villages. 42 Livnah, Eter, Ashan, 43 Yiftah, Ashnah, Neziv, 44 Ke'iylah, Akziv, Mareshah—9 towns with their villages. 45 Ekron, with its region and villages: 46 From Ekron to the sea: everything near Ashdod along with its villages. 47 Ashdod with its region and villages, and Azzah with its region and villages, all the way to the Wadi of Egypt and the shore of the Great Sea. 48 In the hill country: Shamir, Yattir, Socoh, 49 Dannah, Kiryat-Sannah (this is Devir), 50 Anav, Eshtemoh, Anim, 51 Goshen, Holon, Giloh—11 towns and their villages. 52 Arav, Dumah, Eshan, 53 Yanim, Bet- Tappu'ah, Afekah, 54 Humtah, Kiryat-Arba (this is Hevron), Ziyor—9 towns with their villages. 55 Ma'on, Karmel, Zif, Yuttah, 56 Yizre'el, Yokde'am, Zano'ah, 57 Kayin, Givah, Timnah—10 towns and their villages. 58 Halhul, Bet-Zur, Gedor, 59 Ma'arat, Bet-Anot, Eltekon—6 towns with their villages. 60 Kiryat-Ba'al (this is Kiryat Ye'arim) and Rabbah—2 towns and their villages. 61 In the wilderness: Bet-Aravah, Middin, Sekakah, 62 Nivshan, Ir-Melah, Ein-Gedi—6 towns with their villages.

16:1 The lot for the Josephites ran from the Jordan near Jericho, each of the waters of Jericho, into the wilderness: from Jericho going up to the hills of Beit-El, 2 and going out from Beit-El to Luz, continuing to the border of the Arkites at Atarot, 3 then going out to the west to the border of the Yafletites as far as Lower Bet-Horon and Gezer. It ended at the sea.

16:4 The Josephites received their inheritance, Manasseh and Ephraim:

16:5 This was the lot[15] of the Ephraimites, according to their families: the border of their inheritance went in the east from Atarot-Addar to Upper Bet-Horon, 6 then the border continued to the sea. On the north was Mikmetah, and then the border turned to the east toward Ta'anat-Shiloh, and continued beyond it on the east to Yano'ah. 7 From Yano'ah, it went down to Atarot and Na'arah, brushed Jericho, and ended at the Jordan. 8 From Tappu'ah the border continued on the west to Wadi Kanah, and it ended at the sea. This was the inheritance of the tribe of Ephraimites, according to their families.

17:1 This is the lot for the tribe of Manasseh, as the firstborn of Joseph. To Machir, the firstborn of Manasseh, the father of Gilad: the Gilead and Bashan. 2 To the remaining Manassites, according to their families: the descendants of Avi'ezer, the descendants of Helek, the descendants of Asri'el, the descendants of Shechem, the descendants of Hefer, and the descendants of Shemidah. These are the male descendants of Manasseh son of Joseph, according to their families. 3 But Zelofhad son of Hefer son of Gilad son of Machir son of Manasseh did not have any sons, but only daughters. The names of his daughters were: Mahlah, Noa, Hoglah, Milkah, and Tirzah. 4 They came in front of Eleazar the priest and Joshua son of Nun and the leaders, saying, "Yahweh commanded Moses to give us an inheritance among our relatives."[16] So he gave them an inheritance among their father's brothers, in accordance with what Yahweh said. 5 Ten portions fell to Manasseh, apart from the areas of Gilead and Bashan which are on the other side of the Jordan. 6 (Manasseh's daughters inherited a portion along with his sons, and the land of Gilead belonged to the other Manassites.)

17:7 The border of Manasseh went from Asher to Mikmetah, which is near Shechem. Then the boundary continued south toward the inhabitants of Ein-Tappu'ah. 8 The area of Tappu'ah belonged to Manasseh, but

[15] The compiled text here reads "border," though the consonantal Hebrew words for border and lot are extraordinarily close: g-r-l vs. g-b-l, and it is entirely possible that a scribe inadvertently wrote "border" (which appears numerous times in this passage) instead of "lot."

[16] This recounts the episode in Numbers 27:1–11.

Tappu'ah itself, on the border of Manasseh, belonged to the Ephraim-ites. [9] The border then went down to Wadi Kanah, though the towns south of the wadi belonged to Ephraim, as a settlement within the ter-ritory of Manasseh. The border of Manasseh went from the north of the wadi and ended at the sea. [10] To the south belonged to Ephraim, and to the north belonged to Manasseh; the sea was its border.

[18:1] Then the entire Israelite community assembled at Shiloh and they brought the Meeting Tent to reside there because the land had been subdued[17] by them. [2] There were seven tribes among the Israelites who had not yet received their allotted portion. [10] So Joshua cast lots for them at Shiloh, in front of Yahweh, and Joshua apportioned the land to the Israelites, to each a portion.

[18:11] The lot for the tribe of Benjamin, according to their families, came up. The borders that came for their lot were between the Judahites and the Josephites. [12] The boundary on the northern side started from the Jordan and continued up the northern side of Jericho and ascended to the west into the hill country and ended in the wilderness of Bet-Even. [13] From there the border continued to Luz, to the slope of Luz (this is Beit-El), and then the border went down to Atarot-Addar, on the mountain south of Lower Bet-Horon. [14] Then the border turned and curved to the western edge and went to the south from the mountain on the south side of Bet-Horon and ended at Kiryat-Ba'al (this is Kir-yat Ye'arim), a Judahite town. That was the western edge. [15] The south-ern edge began at the end of Kiryat Ye'arim and the border went out to the west and continued to the spring of the waters of Neftoah. [16] Then the border went down to the edge of the mountain that was next to the valley of Ben-Hinnom, which is at the northern end of the valley of Refa'im, and continued down the valley of Hinnom, and further down to Ein-Rogel. [17] It turned to the north and went out to Ein-Shemesh, and continued out to Gelilot, which is opposite the ascent of Adum-mim, then it went down to the Stone of Bohan son of Reuben. [18] It continued along the northern edge of the Aravah and then descended into Aravah. [19] Then the border continued to northern slop of Bet-

[17] This language of subduing the land hearkens back to the negotiations between Yahweh and the tribes of Reuben and Gad in Numbers 32:29.

Hoglah, and the border ended at the northern bay of the Salt Sea, at the southern end of the Jordan. [20] The Jordan was the boundary on the eastern side. This is the allotted portion of the Benjaminites, by its boundaries on all sides, according to their families.

[18:21] The towns belonging to the Benjaminites, according to their families, were Jericho, Bet-Hoglah, Emek-Keziz, [22] Bet-Aravah, Zemaraim, Beit-El, [23] Avvim, Parah, Ofrah, [24] Kefar-Ammoni, Ofni, and Geva—12 towns along with their open fields. [25] Giveon, Ramah, Be'erot, [26] Mizpeh, Kefirah, Mozah, [27] Rekem, Yirpe'el, Taralah, [28] Zela, Ha'eleph, Yevusi (this is Jerusalem), Givah, and Kiryat—14 towns with their open fields. This is the allotted portion of the Benjaminites according to their families.

[19:1] The second lot came out for Simeon, for the Simeonites according to their families. Their allotted portion was inside the allotted portion of the Judahites. [2] Their allotted portion was: Be'er-Sheva, Sheva, Moladah, [3] Hazar-Shu'al, Balah, Ezem, [4] Eltolad, Betul, Hormah, [5] Ziklag, Bet-Markabot, Hazar-Susah, [6] Bet-Leva'ot, Sharuhen—13 towns with their villages. [7] Ayin, Rimmon, Eter, and Ashan—4 towns with their villages, [8] along with all the villages that were around these towns, up to Ba'alat-Be'er and Ramat-Negev. This is the allotted portion for the tribe of Simeon according to their families. [9] The allotted portion of the Simeonites came from the Judahite portion because the Judahite portion was too big for them, so the Simeonites received their portion from it.

[19:10] The third lot came up for the Zebulunites according to their families. The border of their portion went as far as Sarid, [11] then its border went to the west and to Maralah, brushing Dabbeshet and the wadi that is alongside Yokne'am. [12] It continued from Sarid to the east, toward the sunrise, along the border of Kislot-Tavor; then it continued to Davrat and up to Yafia. [13] From there it continued east to Gat-Hefer and Et-Kazin, and went out to Rimmon, where it turned to Ne'ah. [14] Then the border turned to the north to Hannaton. Its end was at the valley of Yiftah-El, [15] Kattat, Nahalal, Shimron, Yidalah, and Bet-Lehem—12 towns with their villages. [16] This was the allotted portion of the Zebulunites according to their families, these towns with their villages.

¹⁹:¹⁷ The fourth lot went out for the Issacharites, the Issacharites according to their families. ¹⁸ Their borders were: Yizre'el, Kesulot, Shunem, ¹⁹ Hafarayim, Shiyon, Anaharat, ²⁰ Rabit, Kishyon, Evez, ²¹ Remet, Ein-Gannim, Ein-Haddah, Bet-Pazzez. ²² The border brushed Tavor, Shahazumah, and Bet-Shemesh. Their borders ended at the Jordan—16 towns and their villages. ²³ This was the allotted portion of the tribe of Issachar according to their families, the towns and their villages.

¹⁹:²⁴ The fifth lot went out for the Asherites according to their families. ²⁵ Their border went from Helkat, Hali, Beten, Akshaf, ²⁶ Alammelek, Amad, Mishal, and brushed Karmel on the west and Shihor-Livnat. ²⁷ It went to the east to Bet-Dagon, and brushed Zebulun and the valley of Yiftah-El on the north, and also Bet-Emek and Nei'el. It continued to the north to Kavul, ²⁸ Evron, Rehov, Hammon, and Kanah, all the way to Zidon-Rabbah. ²⁹ Then the border turned to Ramah, and to the fortified city of Tyre. Then the border turned to Hosah and it ended at the sea, with Mehevel, Akziv, ³⁰ Umah, Afek, and Rehov—22 towns and their villages. ³¹ This was the allotted portion for the tribe of Asher according to their families, these cities and their villages.

¹⁹:³² The sixth lot came out for Naphtali, for the Naphtalites according to their families. ³³ Their borders ran from Helef, Elon-Beza'ananim, Adami-Nekev, and Yavne'el to Lakkum. Its end was at the Jordan. ³⁴ Then the border went to the west to Aznot-Tavor, and continued out from there to Hukok, and brushed Zebulun on the south and Asher on the west and Judah at the Jordan on the east. ³⁵ Its fortified towns were Ziddim, Zer, Hammat, Rakkat, Kinneret, ³⁶ Adamah, Ramah, Hazor, ³⁷ Kedesh, Edre'i, Ein-Hazor, ³⁸ Yir'on, Migdal-El, Horem, Bet-Anat, Bet-Shemesh—19 towns and their villages. ³⁹ This was the allotted portion for the tribe of Naphtali according to their families, the towns and their villages.

¹⁹:⁴⁰ The seventh lot went to the Danites, according to their families. ⁴¹ Their allotted inheritance was: Zorah, Eshta'ol, Ir-Shemesh, ⁴² Sha'alabbin, Ayyalon, Yitlah, ⁴³ Eylon, Timnah, Ekron, ⁴⁴ Eltekeh, Gibbeton, Ba'alat, ⁴⁵ Yehud, Benei-Berak, Gat-Rimmon, ⁴⁶ Mei-Yarkon, and Rakkon (near the border of Yafo). ⁴⁸ This was the allotted portion of the tribe of Dan according to their families, these towns and their villages.

^{19:51} These are the allotted inheritances that Eleazar the priest, Joshua son of Nun, and the heads of the Israelites' ancestral houses assigned by lot in Shiloh in front of Yahweh at the entrance to the Meeting Tent. When they finished dividing the land, ^{20:1} Yahweh said to Joshua, ² "Say to the Israelites: 'Designate cities of refuge for yourselves, which I commanded you about through Moses, ³ so that a person who kills someone unintentionally may flee there. They will be a refuge for you from the person who would seek vengeance for bloodshed. ⁴ One should flee to one of these cities and stand at the entrance to the gate of the city to tell his case to the elders of that city. They will admit him into the city and give him a place to live with them. ⁵ If the person seeking vengeance pursues him, they will not hand over the person who killed someone because he struck someone without intending harm and was not a previous enemy of his. ⁶ He should live in that city until he can stand in front of the court for judgment, or until the death of the high priest at that time. Then the person who killed someone can return to his town and his house, to the town he fled from.'"[18]

^{20:7} So they set apart Kedesh in Galilee, in the hill country of Naphtali, and Shechem in the hill country of Ephraim, and Kiryat-Arba (this is Hevron) in the hill country of Judah. ⁸ On the other side of the Jordan, east of Jericho, they designated Bezer in the wilderness on the plain from the tribe of Reuben, and Ramot in Gilad from the tribe of Gad, and Golan in Bashan from the tribe of Manasseh.[19] ⁹ These are the towns that were designated for all the Israelites and the foreigners living with them for anyone who accidentally killed someone to flee to, so that he did not die at the hand of the one seeking vengeance for bloodshed, until he could appear before the court.

^{21:1} The heads of the Levite families approached Eleazar the priest, Joshua son of Nun, and the heads of the Israelites' ancestral tribes

[18] This is a repetition of the instruction given by Yahweh in Numbers 35:6–15. Verses 4–6 are not in the Septuagint version of this text, and it is possible that they are a much later addition to this story.

[19] In the compiled text, this reads the "half tribe of Manasseh," which is a non-priestly concept from the book of Numbers that has most likely been conflated by an editor here with the priestly full tribe of Manasseh that is one of two Josephite tribes.

[2] and said to them at Shiloh, in the land of Canaan, "Yahweh has commanded, through Moses, that we be given cities to live in along with their open fields for our cattle."[20] [3] So the Israelites designated portions of their own allotted inheritances, from their towns and villages, for the Levites, in accordance with Yahweh's command.

[21:4] The first lot went out for the Kehatite family. The Levites who were descendants of Aaron the priest received 13 cities from the tribes of Judah, Simeon, and Benjamin. [5] The remaining Kehatites received 10 cities from the families of the tribes of Ephraim, Dan, and Manasseh. [6] The Gershonites received by lot 13 cities from the families of the tribes of Issachar, Asher, Naphtali, and Manasseh in Bashan. [7] The Merarites received 12 cities from the families of the tribes of Reuben, Gad, and Zebulun. [8] The Israelites assigned the Levites these cities along with their open fields by lot, just as Yahweh had commanded Moses.

[21:9] From the tribes of Judah and Simeon, they designated these cities, listed by name: [10] They belonged to the descendants of Aaron, the Levitical family of Kehatites because the first lot was theirs. [11] They gave them Kiryat-Arba (this is Hevron) in the hill country of Judah, and the open fields around it. [12] They gave the fields of the town and its villages to Caleb son of Yefunneh as his allotted portion. [13] To the decendants of Aaron the priest, they gave Hevron—a city of refuge for people who have killed someone—along with its open fields, Livnah with its open fields, [14] Yattir with its open fields, Eshtemoa with its open fields, [15] Holon with its open fields, Divir with its open fields, [16] Ayin with its open fields, Yuttah with its open fields, Bet-Shemesh with its open fields—9 cities from these two tribes. [17] From the tribe of Benjamin: Giveon with its open fields, Geva with its open fields, [18] Anatot with its open fields, Almon with its open fields—4 cities. [19] The total number of cities for the descendants of Aaron the priests: 13 cities with their open fields.

[21:20] For the remaining Kehatite families among the Levites, the cities in their lot were from the tribe of Ephraim. [21] They gave them a city of refuge for someone who has killed a person—Shechem and its open

[20] As commanded by Yahweh in Numbers 35:1–5.

fields in the hill country of Ephraim, Gezer with its open fields, [22] Kivzayim and its open fields, Bet-Horon and its open fields—4 cities. [23] From the tribe of Dan: Eltekei with its open fields, Gibbeton with its open fields, [24] Ayyalon with its open fields, Gat-Rimmon with its open fields—4 cities. [25] From the tribe of Manasseh: Tanak with its open fields, Gat-Rimmon with its open fields—2 cities. [26] The total number of cities and their open fields for the remaining Kehatites: 10.

21:27 To the Gershonites among the Levites: from the tribe of Manasseh: a city of refuge for someone who has killed a person—Golan in Bashan with its open fields, and Be'eshterah with its open fields—2 cities. [28] From the tribe of Issachar: Kishyon with its open fields, Davrat with its open fields, [29] Yarmut with its open fields, Ein-Gannim with its open fields—4 cities. [30] From the tribe of Asher: Mishal with its open fields, Avdon with its open fields, [31] Helkat with its open fields, Rehov with its open fields—4 cities. [32] From the tribe of Naphtali: a city of refuge for someone who has killed a person—Kedesh in Galilee with its open fields, Hamot-Dor with its open fields, Kartan with its open fields—3 cities. [33] The total number of cities and their open fields for the Gershonite families: 13.[21]

21:34 To the remaining Levites, the families of the Merarites: from the tribe of Zebulun: Yokne'am with its open fields, Kartah with its open fields, [35] Dimnah with its open fields, Nahalal with its open fields—4 cities. [36] From the tribe of Reuben: Bezer with its open fields, Yahzah with its open fields, [37] Kedemot with its open fields, Meypa'at with its open fields—4 cities. [38] And from the tribe of Gad: a city of refuge for someone who has killed a person—Ramot in Gilad with its open fields, Mahanayim with its open fields, [39] Heshbon with its open fields, Yazer with its open fields—total cities, 4. [40] The total number of cities for the remaining Levites from the Merarite families, granted by lot: 12 cities. [41] The total number of Levitical cities from the allotted portions of the Israelites: 48 cities with their open fields.[22] [42] These cities were assigned, each city with its open field around it; so it was with all these cities.

[21] It is worth noting here that each tribe contributes cities in proportion to their size, precisely as Yahweh commanded in Numbers 35:8.

[22] As commanded in Numbers 35:8.

[21:43] Yahweh gave the entire land that he had sworn to their ancestors to Israel and they took possession of it and lived on it. [44] Yahweh gave them rest on all sides, just as he swore to their ancestors. Not a single one of their enemies had been left standing; Yahweh delivered all their enemies into their hands [45] and not one of the good things that Yahweh had promised to the house of Israel was absent; everything was fulfilled.[23]

[22:1] So then Joshua summoned the Reubenites and the Gadites [2] and said to them, "You have done everything that Moses, servant of Yahweh, commanded you, and you obeyed me in everything that I commanded you. [3] You have not abandoned your brothers this whole time up until now, but you have obeyed the instruction of Yahweh your god. [4] And now Yahweh your god has given rest to your brothers, just as he promised them. Therefore—turn back and go to your tents, to your allotted portions of land that Moses, servant of Yahweh, assigned to you on the other side of the Jordan." [6] Joshua blessed them and sent them out, and they returned to their tents.

[23] This seems as though it would be a fitting ending for the priestly narrative, a story that is so concerned with each and every one of Yahweh's commands being fulfilled. And indeed, at this point in the story, each and every one of Yahweh's commands has been fulfilled—save one. In the story of the Reubenites and the Gadites in the Transjordan in Numbers 32, a special deal is struck between the two tribes and Moses. If, and only if, these two tribes go to war with the rest of the Israelites, see the land entirely subdued and apportioned to the remaining tribes, then—and only then—will they be allowed to return to the Transjordan and take possession of the portions of land they requested to be their allotted inheritance. These are the same cities that they build in Numbers 32:34–38, and in which they have left their wives, children, and livestock. At this point in the story, the condition specified by Moses in Numbers 32:29 has finally been fulfilled. The last act of Joshua in this story, then, is to carry out Moses's command—to permit the Reubenites and Gadites to return to those cities in the Transjordan.

SELECTED BIBLIOGRAPHY

Alter, Robert. *The Art of Biblical Narrative.* New York: Basic Books, 2011.

Amit, Yairah. *Reading Biblical Narratives: Literary Criticism and the Hebrew Bible.* Minneapolis: Fortress Press, 2001.

Auerbach, Erich. "Odysseus' Scar." In *Mimesis: The Representation of Reality in Western Literature,* 3–23. Princeton, NJ: Princeton University Press, 2003.

Baden, Joel S. *The Composition of the Pentateuch: Renewing the Documentary Hypothesis.* Anchor Yale Bible Reference Library. New Haven, CT: Yale University Press, 2012.

———. "The Original Place of the Priestly Manna Story in Exodus 16." *Zeitschrift für die Alttestamentliche Wissenschaft* 122 (2010): 491–504.

———. "The Structure and Substance of Numbers 15." *Vetus Testamentum* 63, no. 3 (2013): 351–67.

Bakhtin, M. M. *The Dialogic Imagination: Four Essays.* Translated by Caryl Emerson and Michael Holquist. Austin: University of Texas Press, 1981.

Blenkinsopp, Joseph. "The Structure of P." *Catholic Biblical Quarterly* 38 (1976): 275–92.

Blum, Erhard. *Die Komposition der Vätergeschichte.* Wissenschaftliche Monographien zum Alten und Neuen Testament 57. Neukirchen-Vluyn: Neukirchener Verlag, 1984.

———. "Issues and Problems in the Contemporary Debate Regarding the Priestly Writings." In *The Strata of the Priestly Writings: Contemporary Debate and Future Directions,* edited by Sarah Shectman and Joel S. Baden, 31–44. Zürich: Theologischer Verlag Zürich, 2009.

———. *Studien zur Komposition des Pentateuch*. Beiheft zur Zeitschrift für die alttestamentliche Wissenschaft 189. Berlin: Walter de Gruyter, 1990.

Boorer, Suzanne. *The Vision of the Priestly Narrative: Its Genre and Hermeneutics of Time*. Atlanta: Society of Biblical Literature Press, 2016.

Boyd, Samuel. *Language Contact, Colonial Administration, and the Construction of Identity in Ancient Israel*. Harvard Semitic Monographs 66. Leiden: E. J. Brill, 2021.

Campbell, Antony F. "The Priestly Text: Redaction or Source?" In *Biblische Theologie und gesellschaftlicher Wandel: Für Norbert Lohfink SJ*, edited by Georg Braulik, Walter Groß, and Sean McEvenue, 32–47. Freiburg: Herder, 2013.

Campbell, Antony F., and Mark A. O'Brien. *Sources of the Pentateuch: Texts, Introductions, Annotations*. Minneapolis: Fortress Press, 1993.

Carpenter, J. Estlin, and G. Harford-Battersby. *The Hexateuch, According to the Revised Version*. Vol. 2. London: Longmans, Green, 1900.

Carr, David M. *The Formation of the Hebrew Bible: A New Reconstruction*. Oxford: Oxford University Press, 2011.

———. *Writing on the Tablet of the Heart: Origins of Scripture and Literature*. Oxford: Oxford University Press, 2005.

Chatman, Seymour Benjamin. *Story and Discourse: Narrative Structure in Fiction and Film*. Ithaca, NY: Cornell University Press, 1978.

Chavel, Simeon. *Oracular Law and Priestly Historiography in the Torah*. Forschungen zum Alten Testament 2. Series 71. Tübingen: Mohr Siebeck, 2014.

Cross, Frank Moore. *Canaanite Myth and Hebrew Epic: Essays in the History of the Religion of Israel*. Cambridge, MA: Harvard University Press, 1973.

Edelman, Diana V., Philip R. Davies, Christophe Nihan, and Thomas Römer, eds. *Opening the Books of Moses*. London: Routledge, 2014.

Feldman, Liane M. "The Idea and Study of Sacrifice in Ancient Israel." *Religion Compass* 14, no. 12 (2020): 1–14.

———. *The Story of Sacrifice: Ritual and Narrative in the Priestly Source*. Forschungen zum Alten Testament 141. Tübingen: Mohr Siebeck, 2020.

Fleming, Daniel. "Mari's Large Public Tent and the Priestly Tent Sanctuary." *Vetus Testamentum* 50 (2000): 484–98.

Fox, Michael. "The Sign of the Covenant: Circumcision in Light of the Priestly Aetiologies." *Revue Biblique* 4 (1974): 557–96.

Friedman, Richard E. *The Bible with Sources Revealed: A New View into the Five Books of Moses*. New York: HarperOne, 2005.

Frymer-Kensky, Tikvah. "The Strange Case of the Suspected Sotah." Vetus Testamentum 34, no. 1 (1984): 11–26.

Gaines, Jason M. H. *The Poetic Priestly Source*. Minneapolis: Fortress Press, 2015.

Gane, Roy E. *Cult and Character: Purification Offerings, Day of Atonement, and Theodicy*. Winona Lake, IN: Eisenbrauns, 2005.

Geller, Stephen A. "Blood Cult: Toward a Literary Theology of the Priestly Work of the Pentateuch." *Prooftexts* 12 (1992): 97–124.

Gorman Jr., Frank H. *The Ideology of Ritual: Space, Time and Status in the Priestly Theology*. Sheffield: JSOT Press, 1993.

Gruber, Mayer L. "Women in the Cult according to the Priestly Code." In *Judaic Perspectives on Ancient Israel*, edited by Jacob Neusner, Baruch A. Levine, and Ernest S. Frerichs, 35–48. Philadelphia: Fortress Press, 1987.

Guillaume, Philippe. *Land and Calendar: The Priestly Document from Genesis 1 to Joshua 18*. New York: T & T Clark, 2009.

Haran, Menahem. "Behind the Scenes of History: Determining the Date of the Priestly Source." *Journal of Biblical Literature* 100, no. 3 (1981): 333–21.

———. "Book-Scrolls at the Beginning of the Second Temple Period: The Transition from Papyrus to Skins." *Hebrew Union College Annual* 54 (1983): 111–22.

———. "Book-Size and the Device of Catch-Lines in the Biblical Canon." *Journal of Jewish Studies* 36, no. 1 (1985): 1–11.

———. "The Character of the Priestly Source: Utopian and Exclusive Features." *Proceedings of the World Congress of Jewish Studies* (1981): 131–38.

———. "The Priestly Image of the Tabernacle." *Hebrew Union College Annual* 36 (1965): 191–225.

———. "Shiloh and Jerusalem: The Origin of the Priestly Tradition in the Pentateuch." *Journal of Biblical Literature* 81 (1962): 14–24.

"Ezekiel, P, and the Priestly School." *Vetus Testamentum* 58, no. 2 (2008): 211–18.

Hurvitz, Avi. "The Language of the Priestly Source and Its Historical Setting—The Case for an Early Date." In *Proceedings of the Eighth World Congress of Jewish Studies: Panel Sessions—Bible Studies and Hebrew Language*, 83–94. Jerusalem: World Union of Jewish Studies, 1984.

———. *A Linguistic Study of the Relationship between the Priestly Source and the Book of Ezekiel*. Paris: Gabalda, 1982.

Jenson, Philip Peter. *Graded Holiness: A Key to the Priestly Conception of the World*. Sheffield: JSOT Press, 1992.

Knafl, Anne K. *Forming God: Divine Anthropomorphism in the Pentateuch*. Winona Lake, IN: Eisenbrauns, 2014.

Knohl, Israel. "The Priestly Torah versus the Holiness School: Sabbath and the Festivals." *Hebrew Union College Annual* 58 (1987): 65–117.

———. *The Sanctuary of Silence: The Priestly Torah and the Holiness School*. Winona Lake, IN: Eisenbrauns, 2007.

Kopilovitz, Ariel. "The Legislation of War: A Study of the Priestly War Legislation Reflected in the Story of the Israelite War against Midian (Numbers 31)." *Shnaton* 23 (2014): 17–53 [Hebrew].

Kratz, Reinhard G. "The Pentateuch in Current Research: Consensus and Debate." In *The Pentateuch: International Perspectives on Current Research*, edited by Thomas B. Dozeman, Konrad Schmid, and Baruch J. Schwartz, 31–62. Tübingen: Mohr Siebeck, 2011.

Levine, Baruch A., ed. *Numbers 21–36: A New Translation with Introduction and Commentary*. Anchor Yale Bible 4B. New Haven, CT: Yale University Press, 2000.

Lowth, Robert. *Lectures on the Sacred Poetry of the Hebrews*. London: Thomas Tegg, 1839.

Marquis, Liane M. "The Composition of Numbers 32: A New Proposal." *Vetus Testamentum* 63, no. 3 (2013): 408–32.

Mastnjak, Nathan. "Hebrew taḥaš and the West Semitic Tent Tradition." *Vetus Testamentum* 67 (2017): 204–12.

Meshel, Naphtali. "Food for Thought: Systems of Categorization in Leviticus 11." *Harvard Theological Review* 101, no. 2 (2008).

———. "The Form and Function of a Biblical Blood Ritual." *Vetus testamentum* 63, no. 2 (2013): 276–89.

———. *The "Grammar" of Sacrifice: A Generativist Study of the Israelite Sacrificial System in the Priestly Writings with The "Grammar" of *Σ*. Oxford: Oxford University Press, 2014.

———. "Hermeneutics and the Logic of Ritual." *Hebrew Bible and Ancient Israel* 7, no. 4 (2019).

———. "P1, P2, P3, and H: Purity, Prohibition, and the Puzzling History of Leviticus 11." *Hebrew Union College Annual* 81 (2010): 1–15.

———. "Toward a Grammar of Sacrifice: Hierarchic Patterns in the Israelite Sacrificial System." *Journal of Biblical Literature* 132 (2013): 543–67.

Milgrom, Jacob. "The Chieftains Gifts: Numbers, Chapter 7." *Hebrew Annual Review* 9 (1985): 221–25.

———. "The Dynamics of Purity in the Priestly System." In *Purity and Holiness: The Heritage of Leviticus*, edited by M. J. H. M. Poorthuis and Joshua Schwartz, 29–32. Leiden: E. J. Brill, 2000.

———. "Encroaching on the Sacred: Purity and Polity in Numbers 1–10." *Interpretation: A Journal of Bible and Theology* 51 (1997): 241–53.

———. "The Graduated Hatta't of Leviticus 5:1–13." *Journal of the American Oriental Society* 103, no. 1 (1983): 249–54.

———. "Israel's Sanctuary: The Priestly Picture of Dorian Gray." *Revue Biblique* 83 (1976): 390–99.

———. *Leviticus 1–16: A New Translation with Introduction and Commentary*. Anchor Bible 3. New Haven, CT: Yale University Press, 1991.

———. *Leviticus 17–22: A New Translation with Introduction and Commentary*. Anchor Bible 3A. New Haven, CT: Yale University Press, 2000.

——. *Leviticus 23–27: A New Translation with Introduction and Commentary* Anchor Bible 3B. New Haven, CT: Yale University Press, 2001.

——. "The Rationale for Biblical Impurity." *The Journal of the Ancient Near Eastern Society* 22 (1993): 107–11.

Nihan, Christophe. *From Priestly Torah to Pentateuch: A Study in the Composition of the Book of Leviticus.* Forschungen zum Alten Testament. Tübingen: Mohr Siebeck, 2007.

——. "The Holiness Code Between D and P: Some Comments on the Function and Significance of Leviticus 17–26 in the Composition of the Torah." In *Das Deuteronomius zwischen Pentateuch und Deuteronomistischem Geschichtswerk*, edited by Eckart Otto and Reinhard Achenbach, 81–122. Göttingen: Vandenhoeck & Ruprecht, 2004.

——. "The Torah between Samaria and Judah: Shechem and Gerizim in Deuteronomy and Joshua." In *The Pentateuch as Torah: New Models for Understanding Its Promulgation and Acceptance*, edited by Gary N. Knoppers and Bernard M. Levinson, 187–224. Winona Lake, IN: Eisenbrauns, 2007.

Noth, Martin. *A History of Pentateuchal Traditions.* Translated by Bernhard W. Anderson. Atlanta: Scholars Press, 1981.

Paran, Meir. *Forms of the Priestly Style in the Pentateuch: Patterns, Linguistic Usages, Syntactic Structures.* Jerusalem: Magnes Press, 1989.

Ridge, David B. "Numbers 16 and the Function of the Story of Dathan and Abiram in the E Document." Paper presented at the Chicago-Yale Pentateuch Colloquium, Yale Divinity School, New Haven, CT, March 1–3, 2020.

Roskop, Angela R. *The Wilderness Itineraries: Genre, Geography, and the Growth of Torah.* Winona Lake, IN: Eisenbrauns, 2011.

Ruwe, Andreas. "The Structure of the Book of Leviticus in the Narrative Outline of the Priestly Sinai Story (Exod 19:1–Num 10:10*)." In *The Book of Leviticus: Composition and Reception*, edited by Rolf Rendtorff and Robert A. Kugler, 55–78. Leiden: E. J. Brill, 2003.

Sanders, Seth L. *The Invention of Hebrew.* Urbana: University of Illinois Press, 2009.

Schaper, Joachim. "Priestly Purity and the Social Organisation in Persian Period Judah." *Biblische Notizen* 118 (2003): 51–57.

Schipper, Jeremy, and Jeffrey Stackert. "Blemishes, Camouflage, and Sanctuary Service: The Priestly Deity and His Attendants." *Hebrew Bible and Ancient Israel* 2 (2013): 458–78.

Schmid, Konrad. *The Old Testament: A Literary History.* Translated by Linda Maloney. Minneapolis: Fortress Press, 2012.

Schniedewind, William M. *How the Bible Became a Book.* Cambridge: Cambridge University Press, 2004.

Schwartz, Baruch J. "The Bearing of Sin in Priestly Literature." In *Pomegranates and Golden Bells: Studies in Biblical, Jewish, and Near Eastern Ritual, Law, and Literature in Honor of Jacob Milgrom*, edited by David P. Wright, David Noel Freedman, and Avi Hurvitz, 3–22. Winona Lake, IN: Eisenbrauns, 1995.

———. "Israel's Holiness: The Torah Traditions." In *Purity and Holiness: The Heritage of Leviticus*, edited by M. J. H. M. Poorthuis and Joshua Schwartz, 47–59. Leiden: E. J. Brill, 2000.

———. "Miqra' Qodesh and the Structure of Leviticus 23." In *Purity, Holiness, and Identity in Judaism and Christianity: Essays in Memory of Susan Haber*, edited by Carl S. Ehrlich, Anders Runesson, and Eileen Schuller, 11–24. Tübingen: Mohr Siebeck, 2013.

———. "'Profane' Slaughter and the Integrity of the Priestly Code." *Hebrew Union College Annual* 67 (1996): 15–42.

———. "The Prohibitions Concerning the 'Eating' of Blood." In *Priesthood and Cult in Ancient Israel*, edited by Gary Anderson and Saul Olyan, 34–66. JSOT Supplement Series 125. Sheffield: Sheffield Academic Press, 1991.

Shectman, Sarah. "The Priestly Language of Gender." *Hebrew Bible and Ancient Israel* 8 (2019): 416–30.

———. *Women in the Pentateuch: A Feminist and Source-Critical Analysis*. Hebrew Bible Monographs. Sheffield: Sheffield Phoenix Press, 2009.

———. "Women in the Priestly Narrative." In *The Strata of the Priestly Writings: Contemporary Debate and Future Directions*, edited by Sarah Shectman and Joel S. Baden, 175–86. Zürich: Theologischer Verlag, 2009.

Ska, Jean Louis. *"Our Fathers Have Told Us": Introduction to the Analysis of Hebrew Narratives*. Rome: Editrice Pontificio Istituto Biblico, 2000.

Smith, Mark E. "The Literary Arrangement of the Priestly Redaction of Exodus: A Preliminary Investigation." *Catholic Biblical Quarterly* 58, no. 1 (1996): 25–50.

Sommer, Benjamin D. "Dating Pentateuchal Texts and the Perils of Pseudo-Historicism." In *The Pentateuch: International Perspectives on Current Research*, edited by Thomas B. Dozeman, Konrad Schmid, and Baruch J. Schwartz, 87–108. Tübingen: Mohr Siebeck, 2011.

Spivak, Gayatri Chakravorty. "Can the Subaltern Speak?" In *Marxism and the Interpretation of Culture*, edited by Cary Nelson and Lawrence Grossberg, 271–316. London: Macmillan, 1988.

Stackert, Jeffrey. "Holiness Code and Writings." In *The Oxford Encyclopedia of The Bible and Law*, edited by Brent A. Strawn, 389–96. Oxford: Oxford University Press, 2015.

———. "How the Priestly Sabbaths Work: Innovation in Pentateuchal Priestly Ritual." In *Ritual Innovation in the Hebrew Bible and Ancient Judaism*, edited by Nathan MacDonald, 79–111. Beihefte zur Zeitschrift für die alttestamentliche Wissenschaft 468. Berlin: Walter De Gruyter, 2016.

———. "Political Allegory in the Priestly Source: The Destruction of Jerusalem, the Exile and their Alternatives." In *The Fall of Jerusalem and the Rise of the Torah*, edited by Peter Dubovsky, Dominik Markl, and Jean-Pierre Sonnet, 211–26. Tübingen: Mohr Siebeck, 2016.

———. *A Prophet Like Moses: Prophecy, Law, and Israelite Religion.* Oxford: Oxford University Press, 2014.

Stern, David. *The Jewish Bible: A Material History.* Seattle: University of Washington Press, 2017.

Tigay, Jeffrey. "The Priestly Reminder Stones and Ancient Near Eastern Votive Practices." In *Studies in the Bible, Its Exegesis, and Its Language*, edited by Moshe Bar-Asher, 339–55. Jerusalem: Bialik Institute, 2007.

Van Seters, John. *Abraham in History and Tradition.* New Haven, CT: Yale University Press, 1975.

Vayntrub, Jacqueline E. "Tyre's Glory and Demise: Totalizing Description in Ezekiel 27." *Catholic Biblical Quarterly* 82 (2020): 214–36.

von Contzen, Eva. "The Limits of Narration: Lists and Literary History." *Style* 3 (2016): 241–60.

von Soden, Wolfram. "Leistung und Grenze sumerischer und babylonischer Wissenschaft." *Die Welt als Geschichte* 2 (1936): 411–64, 509–57.

Watts, James W. *Leviticus 1–10.* Leuven: Peeters, 2013.

———. *Ritual and Rhetoric in Leviticus: From Sacrifice to Scripture.* Cambridge: Cambridge University Press, 2007.

Weinfeld, Moshe. "Social and Cultic Institutions in the Priestly Source Against Their Ancient Near Eastern Background." In *Proceedings of the Eighth World Congress of Jewish Studies*, 95–129. Jerusalem: World Union of Jewish Studies, 1983.

Wellhausen, Julius. *Die Composition des Hexateuchs und der historischen Bücher des alten Testaments.* Berlin: G. Reimer, 1899.

———. *Prolegomena to the History of Ancient Israel.* New York: Wipf & Stock, 2009.

Wells, Bruce. "Liability in the Priestly Texts of the Hebrew Bible." *Sapientia Logos* 5, no. 1 (2012): 1–31.

Wright, David P. "The Gesture of Hand Placement in the Hebrew Bible and in Hittite Literature." *Journal of the American Oriental Society* 106, no. 3 (1986): 433–46.

———. "Holiness in Leviticus and Beyond." *Interpretation: A Journal of Bible and Theology* 53, no. 4 (1999): 351–64.

————. "The Spectrum of Priestly Impurity." In *Priesthood and Cult in Ancient Israel*, edited by Gary Anderson and Saul Olyan, 150–81. Sheffield: Sheffield Academic Press, 1991.

Wright III, Benjamin G. "The Letter of Aristeas and the Question of Septuagint Origins Redux." *Journal of Ancient Judaism* 2 (2011): 303–25.

ABOUT THE AUTHOR

LIANE M. FELDMAN is Assistant Professor in the Skirball Department of Hebrew and Judaic Studies at New York University. Her research focuses on priestly writings in the Hebrew Bible and Second Temple-era Jewish literature, with an emphasis on literary representations of sacrifice and sacred space. She is author of the award-winning book *The Story of Sacrifice: Ritual and Narrative in the Priestly Source.*

Founded in 1893,
UNIVERSITY OF CALIFORNIA PRESS
publishes bold, progressive books and journals
on topics in the arts, humanities, social sciences,
and natural sciences—with a focus on social
justice issues—that inspire thought and action
among readers worldwide.

The UC PRESS FOUNDATION
raises funds to uphold the press's vital role
as an independent, nonprofit publisher, and
receives philanthropic support from a wide
range of individuals and institutions—and from
committed readers like you. To learn more, visit
ucpress.edu/supportus.